Theo-
logy
&
Life

# THEOLOGY AND LIFE SERIES

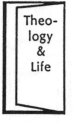

*Volume 27*

# Ethics:
# The Social Dimension

*Individualism and the
Catholic Tradition*

*by*

*Thomas F. Schindler, S.S.*

Michael Glazier
Wilmington Delaware

## ABOUT THE AUTHOR

Thomas F. Schindler, S.S., received his masters degree in theology from St. Paul's University in Ottawa, Ontario, and his doctorate in religious social ethics from the University of Chicago. He has taught at St. Patrick's Seminary in Menlo Park, Cal., St. Mary's Seminary and University in Baltimore, Md., and Aquinas College in Grand Rapids, Mich. Presently, he is Director of Ethics for Mercy Health Services in Detroit.

First published in 1989 by Michael Glazier, Inc., 1935 West Fourth Street, Wilmington, Delaware 19805.

Library of Congress Cataloging-in-Publication Data

Schindler, Thomas F.
    Morality in a social key: U.S. individualism and the Roman Catholic church/by Thomas F. Schindler.
      p.     cm.
    Bibliography: p.
    Includes index.
    ISBN 0-89453-741-5
    1. Christian ethics—Catholic authors. 2. Sociology, Christian (Catholic) 3. Individualism—Religious aspects—Catholic Church—Controversial literature. 4. Catholic Church—Doctrines. 5. United States—Moral conditions. I. Title.
BJ1249.S36    1989
241'.042—dc19                        88-82463
                                         CIP
    ISBN: Theology and Life Series 0-89453-295-2

Cover Design by Lillian Brulc
Typography by Angela Meades
Printed in the United States of America by Edwards Brothers, Ann Arbor, MI

*This book is dedicated to
my parents,
Adolph and Florence Wensink Schindler,
on their fiftieth wedding anniversary*

# Contents

# Preface

Social justice has been coming into its own in the U.S. religious sphere the last few years. It has been receiving a lot of positive press, due in no small part to the U.S. Roman Catholic bishops' pastorals on war and peace and on the economy. It is the subject of many homilies, and is included in many religious education projects. Those involved in social justice projects do not feel such a need to defend their activity. In fact, concern for and involvement in social justice no longer seems to be such a fringe activity.

This is not to say, of course, that social justice has been catapulted to the center of religious activity, much less that injustice is about to be vanquished. The atmosphere, however, is certainly different than it was a decade ago.

Still, even with all this new and renewed interest, social justice remains more than a bit of a puzzlement. Particularly is this the case when social justice is compared with personal morality. How one goes about making a moral decision in one's personal life seems fairly clear—even if not easily accomplished. But deciding about the morality of an economic system or a government program or a piece of legislation is something different. So different, in fact, that social justice appears to bear little connection with personal morality.

That is where the danger lies. The difference between personal and social morality too easily translates into a dichotomy; and this dichotomy too often leads to a depreciation of social morality. No matter how much social justice is raised in importance, when push comes to pull personal morality takes precedence.

But why does the dichotomy between personal and social morality exist? Undoubtedly many factors contribute to this. This book will explore and critique what I believe to be one of those factors: the individualism of U.S. culture. My thesis is that U.S. individualism, by emphasizing the separateness of the individual and by loosening the individual's ties to society, subordinates the social to the personal. I will further argue that, while the Roman Catholic tradition is an important and powerful resource for overcoming the problems caused by this individualism, it can serve as this resource only as the relation of the Roman Catholic church to U.S. culture is critically assessed. This assessment is necessary, in my judgment, because the Roman Catholic stance on morality, even though not itself individualistic, has at times been presented in ways that can easily be read as agreeing with U.S. individualism.

In looking at the implications of individualism for morality, I will concentrate on the basic elements of the moral life and moral decision-making—elements that are usually identified with personal morality. My goal is to show that there is a social dimension to these elements, and in that way to help bridge the gap between personal and social morality.

In sum, this book is fundamentally a discussion about culture, about the social dimensions and implications of everyday life. But this critique of U.S. culture and my suggestions about morality in turn raise a further question. If American Roman Catholic morality should take the form I propose, what type of political and economic structures are needed to support and promote it? I have decided not to answer the question at this time both because it would require much more space, and because it could easily shift the focus of discussion and argument away from what I am trying to do here.

A word of explanation is in order about the choice of individualism as the basis for my critique of U.S. culture. Why not use racism or sexism, especially since individualism is so much a middle-class problem? I have no easy answer to that question. I do not in the least doubt that racism and sexism are serious, fundamental problems in this country, nor do I challenge the identification of individualism with the middle class.

Individualism is, however, more than just a middle-class phenomenon. As the authors of *Habits of the Heart* point out, "the mobile middle classes define reality for most of us in the United States."[1] The reality thus defined has significant, at times devastating, effects on everyone in this country. The middle-class world of individualism is used to describe what it means to "make it"—to describe, that is to say, the goals held out to all members of society. Those from minority groups (defined in terms of power, not numbers) who "succeed" are held up as proof that the system "works" and as paradigms motivating their sisters and brothers to work harder within the status quo. The ideology of individualism, under the rubric of so-called "reverse discrimination," is used as an excuse for denying minorities the assistance they need to begin to participate significantly within society. This reached new highs—or is it new lows—in the Reagan administration. Finally, even though individualism trumpets the power of the individual, it leaves the individual isolated and prone to a deep sense of powerlessness. The resulting self-emptiness and self-anger easily get projected out on others, especially minorities: the blame-the-victim syndrome.

Thus, while individualism may indeed be a middle-class issue, its effects are in no way confined to those in that social rank. Any social analysis of the problems we face in the United States should, I believe, take individualism into account, as should any strategies to address those problems.

When I face honestly what is in this book, I have to confess that I feel more its scribe than its author. The ideas set forth here have been born, honed, and developed through interchanges with many different individuals and groups—in particular the students at St. Mary's Seminary and University in Baltimore, Maryland, and at Aquinas College in Grand Rapids, Michigan. More immediately, at various stages in the development of this book, the manuscript has been read and critiqued by Ann Agee, Gloria Albrecht, Jim Hug, S.J., Philip Keane, S.S., Dick Ullrich, Tom Ulshafer, S.S., and by some of my colleagues at the Sisters of Mercy Health Corporation: Diane Evangelista, John Knuerr, Ann Marie La Haie, RSM, and Bob Voglewede. To all I acknowledge my indebtedness and express my deep gratitude.

---

[1]Robert N. Bellah, et al., *Habits of the Heart* (Berkeley, CA: University of California Press, 1985), p. 306.

# PART ONE

## Setting the Problem

# Introduction

## The Problem is Individualism

Beginning a book on morality is similar to setting out for a new pair of shoes. By the time I actually begin to make the rounds of the shoe stores, a number of events have already occurred. It all started with a vague feeling that something was amiss. What the exact problem was, I could not be sure; I knew only that I was uncomfortable. Gradually I became aware that the difficulty had something to do with my legs. And, after checking out various possibilities, it became clear the heels of my shoes were worn down, thus straining my leg muscles in an unaccustomed fashion. After further consideration I decided the shoes do not warrant a reheeling; and so now I am off to the shoe store.

Just as the decision to shop for shoes does not appear out of the blue, so books do not suddenly materialize in the mind of an author like words on the display screen of a computer, merely waiting to be printed out. They begin in feelings of uneasiness, in a vague sense that something is not quite right. Only gradually is the source of this uneasiness pinpointed; and then the decision must be made whether the problem has been adequately addressed by others or whether it calls for a different approach. (This is not to say, of course, that the jump from pinpointing a problem to deciding that a new book is needed is always justified.)

This parallel between setting out to buy a new pair of shoes and the genesis of a book is important to bear in mind. It helps demystify books, keeping their subject matter rooted in human experience—a rooting especially important for any discussion of morality; and it helps the reader establish and maintain an active rather than a passive stance toward a book. Without an awareness of this parallel, the issues discussed in a book can seem distant from the wear and tear of everyday experience, existing only in the geography of the mind where all problems admit of tidy, if not easy, solutions. What is more, in the absence of such an awareness, the problems as well as the solutions discussed in the book can take on an aura of absoluteness: this is *the* problem that faces us, and this is *the* way of solving it.

Keeping in mind the parallel between buying shoes and writing a book, however, sets up a different dynamic. The book, having grown out of the author's initial feeling of uneasiness, is *a* way, not *the* way, of interpreting and understanding the times in which we live. And the solution the author offers is *a* way, not *the* way, of responding to the situation. As such, the book extends an invitation for the reader to enter into active dialogue.

Assuming that the reader will not read a book unless he or she has an interest in the area it covers prior to picking it up—an interest born out of some sense that all is not in perfect order, that all has not been adequately explained—the author invites the reader to try the book on for size. Does the analysis and interpretation of the problem fit the reader's uneasiness? Does it clarify and sharpen the contours of the problem? And what about the solution offered: does it "ring true"? Does it address the problem in a real way, presenting realistic options to a very real difficulty? In other words, just as the book, being more than merely an intellectual exercise for the author, represents an attempt to explore and make sense out of certain experiences, so it is an invitation to the reader to use it as a means to explore and interpret his or her own experience.

## *Relating Interpretation and Approach: Examples*

To concretize this point about the relationship of the awareness and interpretation of a problematic situation to the genesis and direction of a book, a couple of examples are in order. I will summarize briefly the arguments developed by two authors of books on morality to show how their initial analysis of the world led them to develop their presentations in different ways and to arrive at different conclusions. Since the subject matter of this book is the moral life and moral decision-making from a Roman Catholic point of view, the books I use as examples are also from that perspective.

In *Principles for a Catholic Morality*, Timothy O'Connell argues that the fundamental moral problem facing people today is the threat a deterministic and ideological understanding of human existence poses for the uniqueness of the person and our ability to know reality.

> It is true that during the past century human distinctiveness has come under attack from several quarters. It has been suggested that human persons are not really *free*. Rather they are determined by biological drives (psychoanalytic psychology) and cultural influences (behavioristic psychology). What is more, said some, the human ability to find and know the *truth* is largely self-deception (Marx). Persons do not see reality as it is, but as they would like it to be. Consequently, one should not speak of knowledge at all, but rather of self-serving ideology.[1]

Accordingly, O'Connell begins his discussion of morality with a consideration of the human act, that is, "an action done with at least a modicum of awareness and free choice."[2] His attention is focused primarily on the act of the individual person. While he states clearly that human beings are essentially social ("we are radically social beings"[3]), and that our "sociality, if it does not entirely constitute our particular human lives, nonetheless profoundly and extensively affects them,"[4] his main interest, because of his disapproval of deter-

---

[1]Timothy E. O'Connell, *Principles for a Catholic Morality* (New York: The Seabury Press, 1978), p. 45. Emphasis in original.

[2]Ibid., p. 46.

[3]Ibid., p. 110.

[4]Ibid.

minism, is in the uniqueness of individuals. "The fact of the matter is that I do 'gotta be me'. . . . Nothing takes precedence over the moral challenges of my own unique person and my own particular life."[5]

But, while O'Connell says that "I do 'gotta be me,'" he does not mean that we are free to do or be whatever we like. He holds, contrary to the ideologists, that we can achieve objective insight into the meaning of the human person through the use of our reason. This knowledge is "evaluative knowledge" concerned with "the goodness or beauty of a thing, with its value," rather than the "speculative knowledge" science obtains about facts; and, while our knowledge of morality based on insights into human nature may not be perfect, while it can change because of the openness of human nature, we can still achieve a real, trustworthy knowledge of the values essential to our humanity. On the basis of this knowledge, we are able to live out our freedom in a responsible manner by fulfilling our humanity and seeking to humanize our world. And so, even though not all the values we experience can be realized at once, "the virtuous person is the person who realizes those values as much as possible, while neglecting or attacking them as little as necessary."[6]

Because of the corrupting influence of determinism and ideologism, then, O'Connell stresses the uniqueness and freedom of the individual; and he argues that we can use our reason to get insight into our humanity which provides reliable moral guidance.

The other book I cite to exemplify the relationship between an author's interpretation of an initial problematic situation and the conclusions he or she reaches is Daniel Maguire's *The Moral Choice*. Maguire bases his approach on a different, although not unrelated, interpretation of present-day life than that which gives direction to O'Connell's thought. For Maguire, science is the problem, not because it threatens the distinctiveness of the human person, but because it is out of control, creating a Sorcerer's-Apprentice type world and threatening all of life. In such a world, the knowable is

[5]Ibid., p. 194.
[6]Ibid., p. 156.

limited to what can be measured; and as a result, morality, dealing with values which cannot be subjected to a scientific yardstick, is reduced to insignificance.

For Maguire, the world he criticizes is best symbolized by the Dadaist movement in art which has brought us such memorable artistic creations as the mustachioed Mona Lisa and the signed urinal. The absurdity of these pieces of art mirrors the absurdity of a world voided of the good and the beautiful, and placed under the control of technicians. This absurdity gives rise to fear and hopelessness. "The crisis of technological society, steeped as it is in impressive achievements, is that there is an ever-widening gap between vaulting technical intelligence on the one hand, and human fragility and precariousness on the other."[7]

Guided by this interpretation of the problematic, Maguire takes a different tack from O'Connell's in discussing the moral life and moral decision-making. While he by no means dismisses reason as an important element in morality, he does not give it the centrality that O'Connell does. For Maguire, "the foundation of morality is *the experience of the value of persons and their environment*."[8] It is an experience that does not admit of scientific analysis or proof: "This is an affective faith experience and is processual in form. It can increase or recede."[9]

Reason is not the source, but "an agent of that experience."[10] Its purpose is to reflect critically on the initial, affective experience, testing, challenging, harmonizing, correcting and reformulating the experience to guard against superficiality.[11] While reason is thus essential to morality in its full scope, it cannot claim exclusivity or primacy. If reason attempts to address morality apart from the foundational moral experience which is affective, it is blinded to the full

[7]Daniel Maguire, *The Moral Choice* (Garden City, New York: Doubleday and Company, Inc., 1978), p. 30.

[8]Ibid., p. 72. Emphasis in original.

[9]Ibid., p. 99.

[10]Ibid., p. 264.

[11]Ibid., 263.

range of morality and becomes heartless.[12] Thus, Maguire can write about creativity, surprise, the comic and the tragic as significant aspects of morality; and he can discuss "the feel of truth."[13]

The creativity in morality Maguire has in mind, however, is not divine in its scope—it is not creation out of nothing with no limit to the possibilities available to us. We are guided in our moral decisions by moral principles which "are the voice of history and the moral memory of the species."[14] Through these, we are alerted to the values in our world. As such, the social conditioning of our values and of our knowledge of those values is not only a fact, but a positive resource, in our existence. Still, individual creativity for Maguire has primacy of position. It is not surprising, therefore, to find him stressing "the pernicious possibilities of absorption into group consciousness,"[15] and the importance of each individual as "a unique font of ethical wisdom."[16]

In the actual process of moral decision-making, the principle of proportionality is a very important tool at a person's disposal.[17] "Since there are likely to be disvalues in the fore-

[12]Ibid., chapter 8.

[13]Ibid., title of chapter 9.

[14]Ibid., p. 220.

[15]Ibid., p. 323.

[16]Ibid., p. 310. On the other hand, in *A New American Justice* (Garden City, NY: Doubleday and Company, Inc., 1980), Maguire states the following: "The use of the term ['common good'] seems to import that individual good and community good cannot be conflated but must coexist in a perpetual bargaining posture. Just as the word 'rights' implies a challenge to what those rights claim, so the term 'common good' implies a reference to private, personal good as well as to the good of the social whole." (p. 86) "Although individual good is set within the common good, the two are not identical.... *May individual rights be sacrificed for the common good?* To rephrase the question: Does it make any sense to say that individuals who have done no wrong or who have assumed no contractual obligations should, at times, be required in a just society to sacrifice their privileges, rights, possessions, or career goals for broader social aims? The answer to this question is yes. And, more disconcertingly yet, these sacrifices will not be required equally of all but only of some, and even then often somewhat happenstantially. Furthermore, any society that survives does so by living with this enigmatic fact of life—however many monuments that society may build to individual rights" (p. 95). Emphasis in original.

[17]"In a sense, [proportionality] may be said to be the master principle in ethics." Maguire, *The Moral Choice*, p. 164.

seeable effects of all human choices, a judgment that value proportionally outweighs disvalue is implied in all moral choice...."[18] There is danger, however, that this principle can be used in a cold-hearted, mathematical way which looks to the net gain of the group and overlooks the loss to individuals. Only by searching for alternatives beyond those present in the immediate situation can the principle of proportionality be humanized and the resulting evils minimized. Viable alternatives, of course, depend upon the creative use of the imagination, or better, upon the imaginative person. In the end,

> the healthy moral self is in touch with its own depth. It reaches for the relief of originality; it tries to move as far as possible from the conditioning influences that would engulf and dominate, and it attempts to express its own unique contact with reality.[19]

These brief sketches of the arguments advanced by Timothy O'Connell and Daniel Maguire in no way do justice to the full range of their discussions. But such is not my intention here. They are examples showing that the direction taken by an author in discussing morality is in response to a particular problem and that the problem is itself an interpretation the author has made of an initial vague feeling of disquiet about the order of things.

Thus, O'Connell's emphasis on the freedom and knowledge of the individual in making moral decisions, which is a leitmotif running throughout his book, is understandable in light of his initial analysis of the present situation as one denying that such freedom and knowledge are possible. Likewise, there is a clear connection between Maguire's critique of an overly rationalized, overly scientific world with no room for values and his emphasis on the affective and creative dimensions of morality. In both instances, the authors in effect invite the reader to try out their analyses and their

---

[18]Ibid.
[19]Ibid., p. 377.

proposed responses on his or her own experience.

My own interpretation of the problematic and my own response to it through the approach I take to the moral life and to moral decision-making differs from those taken by O'Connell and Maguire. Of course they have to; otherwise, I would have difficulty explaining why I spent so much time writing this book and why I invite people to spend time reading it. Summarizing the approaches of O'Connell and Maguire, however, should serve to keep before you, the reader, the fact that what I offer is *a* way of looking at morality based on *a* way of looking at the difficulties besetting us in our world. The differences between their discussions and mine will also help place what I say in perspective.

## Individualism as the Problematic

Although the approach I take in this book is based on a different interpretation of the problematic from that offered by O'Connell and Maguire, I by no means find their analyses totally off the mark. The detrimental consequences of deterministic and ideological philosophies undermining human uniqueness, and of a technological culture voided of value and left at the mercy of a scientific mindset, are only too apparent.

The vague feeling of uneasiness and discomfort which originated this project surfaced when I was teaching various courses on social ethics while at the same time actively involving myself in some social justice projects. As I analyzed the U.S. situation to get at the more fundamental issues underlying the particular problems exercising myself and others whom I worked with, I became more and more convinced that the economic structures of this country are *a*, or possibly *the*, source of present difficulties. This led me to search for alternatives to U.S. capitalism; but it also forced me to consider how change might come about.

Since the problem is structural, it is not enough to convince individuals to change their personal lives. New economic frameworks have to be put in place; this requires organized, political efforts, not just individuals acting differently on their own. Now, structural change is difficult under the best of circumstances. I gradually began to see, however, there are factors present in U.S. culture that further complicate matters. Despite the great homage we in this country pay to the autonomy and power of the individual, individuals often have a deep sense of powerlessness that leads to passivity and resignation. Moreover, the uses of power connected with any group effort to change the political situation, and indeed political action itself, are viewed with suspicion and distaste.

The problem, it seemed, is as much cultural as economic. Attitudes present in the U.S. ethos stand in the way of structural change. As I inquired into this more, I kept bumping into the term "individualism" as a way to name this phenomenon. And unpacking this word "individualism" led me to see that it points to the same congeries of issues that I had identified as problematic in the U.S. economy.

This was good news and bad news. There are not two separate issues, only one. But how does one go about challenging the individualism of U.S. culture? How does one even get a handle on it? My own religious tradition seemed a good resource since Roman Catholicism has consistently opposed individualism, and Roman Catholicism's practices and way of enunciating faith present an alternative to it. Yet the Roman Catholic church in this country does not appear to stand in opposition to U.S. culture or even to represent a fundamental challenge to it. Roman Catholics are clearly not a marginal group in this country. In fact, they are at the center of things, not only having bought into the American dream but benefiting from it as a group more than almost any other religious denomination.[20] And no official state-

---

[20]"The income achievement of Catholics . . . provides little support for a theory of Catholic lack of industry or ambition. Catholics earn more money than any other Christian denomination—$1,421 above the national average and $1,211 above the northern metropolitan average. In both cases, Catholics have a firm grip on second place [behind the Jews] in the American family income sweepstakes. They are more than $300 ahead of Episcopalians nationally and almost $700 ahead of the third-place Methodists in northern cities. Furthermore, . . . on the mobility measure Catholics make more money than Jews when compared with those who have the same educational and occupational background. On the mobility measure

ments either from the U.S. bishops or from the Vatican ever seem to jar this nice fit.

Why is this? How can Roman Catholicism which is so opposed to individualism live so easily in the mainstream of a country considered by many the paragon of individualism?

Thus this study. My initial uneasiness has been interpreted as the problem of the individualism of U.S. culture and the way that it has co-opted Roman Catholicism. This has led me to search for some answers. How can Roman Catholicism enter into dialogue with U.S. culture without being taken in by it? How can Roman Catholicism critique the individualism of this country and use the anti-individualistic elements in its own tradition to highlight possible alternatives in U.S. society?

In the remainder of part one, I will flesh out this bare-bones summary of the problem, defining individualism, showing its destructive consequences, and pointing out how Roman Catholicism, despite its opposition to individualism, could be perceived as comfortable with U.S. culture. In the rest of the book I will discuss the basic elements in morality. I have become convinced that we should concentrate not so much on the specific moral decisions we make as on our underlying attitude toward morality in general. I will discuss the various dimensions of the moral life and moral decision-making in a way that draws upon the Roman Catholic tradition to critique U.S. individualism and to suggest possible alternatives.


## Some Preliminary Comments

Before doing so, however, I want to clarify some points. I am aware that the identification of individualism as the problem is itself problematic on a number of accounts. First, there is question whether it is possible to isolate any common elements in the United States, given all the diversity existing

nationally, Catholics are almost $200 ahead of Jews, and in the metropolitan regions of the North they are more than $700 ahead of Jews. . . ." Andrew Greeley, *The American Catholic: A Social Portrait* (New York: Basic Books, 1977), p. 57.

in our society, much less identify one particular factor as *the* fundamental problem.

While there are, to be sure, vast differences between the various individuals, the various subcultures, the various racial, ethnic and religious groupings in this country, there are some common factors that unite us in the U.S. and distinguish us from other societies. Arthur Mann writes about "the experience of native-born Americans who journey overseas in search of their origins."

> Usually, American blacks discover that they are not simply Gambian, American Irish that they are not merely Irish, American Japanese that they are not wholly Japanese, American Jews that they are not really Israeli, American Greeks that they are not just Greek. What is equally revealing, seldom do hosts regard visitors as being quite like themselves. The two differ in speech, values, behavior, attitudes, and manner. That they often feel mutual ties of kinship is also true. Yet the knowledge that they stem from a common source has the ironical but understandable effect of making them all the more conscious of the ways in which they have diverged.[21]

Despite the great variety in this country, there are certain underlying commonalities that distinguish the American Irish from their relatives living on the "Old Sod"—without, of course, so altering their heritage that they are not distinguishable from American Germans or Italians. In this book it is my contention that individualism is one such commonality, a primary one and a principal source of the major problems besetting us.

[21] Arthur Mann, *The One and the Many: Reflections on the American Identity* (Chicago: The University of Chicago Press, 1979), pp. 154-155. See also, E. Adamson Hoebel, "The Nature of Culture," in *Man, Culture, and Society*, ed. Harry L. Shapiro (New York: Oxford University Press, 1956), p. 173. James Sellers notes: "The United States is the 'oldest new nation,' we are often told by political scientists; and the national heritage, while it has certainly not turned out to be a 'melting pot,' has become a powerful background influence upon the identity of Americans, reshaping even the ways in which they express their ethnicity or their religion." James Sellers, "Membership in the American Community as a Component of Identity," *Journal of Religious Ethics* 6/2 (Fall 1978): 168.

Second, there is the difficulty of offering a definition, or at least a description, of individualism. Usually individualism is understood as referring to a social system in which the individual has primacy over society. That is included here. But, deeper than that, my concern here is to identify what we mean in U.S. culture when we speak of ourselves or of others as "individuals"—what that implies for the relation of the individual not only to society, but to self, to physical nature, and to God as well.

Moreover, individualism is often interpreted as placing the individual over against society and basically severing all connections between them. The individualism that characterizes U.S. culture, however, maintains a tie between the individual and society. The problem, as we shall see, is the nature of that linkage.

Third, it is difficult to take a critical stance toward individualism. Because individualism focuses attention on the individual and places our social rootedness so much in the background, we have somewhat the same difficulty discerning the social realities of individualism that a fish has identifying water. And, even once individualism has been recognized, it is difficult to treat seriously. We take individualism so for granted that other ways of approaching life can seem either impossible or unrealistic.

Finally, a friendly warning is in order. At times subjects are introduced in this book as examples that deserve much greater discussion. That discussion will have to wait for another time. My goal here is to show the difficulties caused by individualism; to indicate how Roman Catholicism can be drawn unawares into supporting something it claims to oppose; and to suggest what might be done to reorient our ways of thinking, valuing, and acting to emphasize our connection and interaction with our world rather than our separateness.

With these points in mind, let us get to the business of talking about individualism as a principal problem besetting this country and adversely affecting our moral enterprise.

# 1

# Individualism and U.S. Culture

Individualism is a slippery term and I probably have added more grease to it by broadening its reference. It obviously points to the relationship of the individual to society. But, as I have pointed out, it is my contention that the nature of that relationship includes as well and has implications for the way the individual relates with self, with the environment both human and nonhuman—and with God. Individualism, as I am using the word, concerns the totality of these relationships.

Presenting individualism, then, is more a matter of description than of definition. And because the reality that I seek to describe developed gradually in the history of the West, I will move briskly from the twelfth to the twentieth century, outlining its evolution. In doing so, I shall paint a broad-stroked picture. My purpose is not to present an in-depth study of individualism but to place the U.S. experience in historical perspective, to show the nature of the ties relating the individual to society in individualism, and to indicate primarily through examples what it means to speak of individualism as a culture reality.

## The Discovery of the Individual

This may sound very strange, especially to an American ear, but the individual is a relatively recent discovery. Now to be sure, we human beings have always appeared on the scene separately packaged. Physically we arrive and continue on through life as discrete units made up of blood, muscle, bone, etc., and bounded by a wrapping of skin that clearly demarcates us from other people and from our physical surroundings. But while physically we human beings exist only as individuals, the interpretation and evaluation of that individuality has differed over history.

> Every adult human being is aware of a distinction between himself and the people and things around him. Nevertheless, it is true that Western culture, and the Western type of education, has developed this sense of individuality [as people with frontiers, our personalities divided from each other as our bodies visibly are] to an extent exceptional among the civilizations of the world. In primitive societies the training of the child is usually directed to his learning the traditions of the tribe, so that he may find his identity, not in anything peculiar to himself, but in the common mind of his people.... Western individualism is therefore far from expressing the common experience of humanity. Taking a world view, one might almost regard it as an eccentricity among cultures.[1]

A couple of examples will concretize this eccentricity. As Colin Morris brings out in the above citation, in "primitive societies"—or, in less ethnocentrist terms, among peoples whose traditions differ substantially from those of the modern West—the individual has a distinctly different perception of himself or herself. There is always an awareness that one is separate from others; the fact that all languages contain the pronouns "I," "you," "he," and "she" indicates that.[2] But whereas we define ourselves in terms of those elements that distinguish us and set us *apart from* everyone else, others focus on the ties that make them *a part of* the lives of others and of the group.

---

[1]Colin Morris, *The Discovery of the Individual 1050-1200* (New York: Harper and Row, Publishers, 1972), pp. 1, 2.

[2]A. Irving Hollowell, *Culture and Experience* (n.p: University of Pennsylvania Press, 1966), p. 89.

Dorothy Lee, an anthropologist, finds an example of this in the language of the Wintu Indians of California. When speaking about the illness of his or her child, for instance, a Wintu parent never says, "My child is sick." Rather, the statement is, "I am sick my child." "My child is sick" presumes "a separate, bounded self acting upon another separate, bounded self." "I am sick my child" indicates "some kind of immediate participation in the experience of the other."[3] Among societies such as the Wintus,

> though the self and the other are differentiated, they are not mutually exclusive. The self contains some of the other, participates in the other, and is in part contained within the other. By this I do not mean what usually goes under the name of empathy. I mean rather that where such a concept of the self is operative, self-interest and other-interest are not clearly distinguished; so that what I do for my own good is necessarily also good for my unit, the surround, whether this is my family, my village, my tribe, my land, or even in general, the entire universe.[4]

Another example that contrasts with our way of understanding the individual is drawn from the ancient Greeks. In their love for perfection, the Greeks placed primary value on the self-sufficient and the perduring. Whatever possessed these attributes was termed an individual.

> In consequence, in view of the obvious instability of particular existences such as moderns usually term individuals, a species immutable in time and having form was the true individual. What moderns call individuals were particulars, transient, partial, and imperfect specimens of the true

---

[3]Dorothy Lee, "Culture and the Experience of Value," in *New Knowledge in Human Values*, ed. Abraham H. Maslow (Chicago: Henry Regnery Company, 1959), p. 173.

[4]Ibid., p. 174.

individual. Mankind as species is more truly an individual than this or that man.[5]

Where did this thinking originate according to which "we think of ourselves as people with frontiers, our personalities divided from each other as our bodies visibly are"?[6] While its beginning has generally been located in the Italian Renaissance of the 1400s, more and more scholars are tracing it back to the twelfth century. The shift in interpreting and valuing the individual that occurred at that time was not without its roots in previous ages, especially in the christian emphasis on interiority and the value of the individual soul, and in the humanism of ancient Greek and Roman literature; but its immediate catalysts were the many developments, shifts, and disruptions taking place in twelfth-century European society.

By the twelfth century, Europe was able to secure its boundaries against such groups as the Moslems and the Vikings. European society, which had broken up into small rural villages after the fall of the Roman Empire, began to reestablish itself in larger units in urban areas. Commerce increased and new economic structures were introduced. The gift economy, in which "goods and services are exchanged without having calculated values assigned to them,"[7] yielded to the profit economy. Monetary values were established for goods; and transactions were made on the basis of their profitability.

---

[5]John Dewey, *Experience and Nature* (New York: Dover Publications, Inc., 1958), p. 209. According to Raymond Williams in *The Long Revolution*, the word "individual" in the Middle Ages meant "inseparable." Its primary usage was in theological discussions about the Trinity or to indicate membership in some grouping. "The complexity of the term is at once apparent in this history, for it is the unit that is being defined, yet defined in terms of its membership of a class. The separable entity is being defined by a word that has meant 'inseparable,'" "...[T]o describe an individual was to give an example of the group of which he was a member, and so to offer a particular description of that group and of the relationship within it." Quoted in: *Man Alone*, eds. Eric and Mary Josephson (New York: Dell Publishing Co., Inc., 1975), p. 29.

[6]Morris, p. 1.

[7]Lester K. Little, *Religious Poverty and the Profit Economy in Medieval Europe* (Ithaca, New York: Cornell University Press, 1978), p. 4.

The development of these new economic structures gave rise to a middle class which was able to secure a degree of political autonomy in the midst of a mainly feudal society. The new society, indeed the new world, that was appearing offered people a much wider variety of options than had previously been available to them. This happened not only in secular society but within the church as well. New religious orders such as the Dominicans and Franciscans were founded at this time. With the broadening of options, individuals were forced to make choices; and this fostered a growth of self-consciousness, a sense of being distinct from others.

Also at this time emphasis on the orderliness of nature and on the goodness of matter as well as developments in mathematics through contributions from Arabic sources began to prepare the way for modern science. This promoted the ability of the intellect to alter the physical world, and gave a greater sense of importance and power to the individual who possessed this intellect.[8]

But at the same time, this new world was a more difficult and more complex one than had been known. It spawned problems that could not be solved by the inherited wisdom; and the conflict of values in a changing and more varied society made it difficult to establish a common search for new solutions. As a result, satire and pilgrimage—expressions of alienation[9]—also marked this new society. And this further deepened the sense of separateness.

This developing sense of the individual as a bounded and distinct self affected culture in many ways. The twelfth century, for example, "saw a marked move towards a more individual treatment of the portrait, which began increasingly to display details of appearance and personality."[10] Likewise, architectural and technological developments made possible

---

[8]See Lynn White, "Science and the Sense of Self: The Medieval Background of a Modern Confrontation," *Daedalus* 107/2 (Spring, 1978): 47-59.

[9]Morris, pp. 122 ff.

[10]Ibid., p. 95.

the moving of the fireplace from a central room in the house
to small rooms, thus permitting greater privacy.[11]

And, naturally enough, this discovery of the bounded and
separate individual led to the development of suitable forms
of religious piety. The Eucharist, rather than being the
primary expression of the oneness of the community as it
had been for the early church, became the object of private
devotion—the elevation of the host during the Mass as well
as the ritual of Benediction were first introduced at this time.
The corpus of the crucifix shifted from that of the risen
Christ to that of Jesus hanging dead on the cross, and
Christians were encouraged to identify inwardly with the
sufferings of Jesus' passion. And rather than focusing on the
general resurrection at the end of history with the Second
Coming of Christ, and on the corporate salvation of the
church, Christians stressed the judgment of the individual
immediately after death.[12]

But this emerging sense of self as separate and bounded by
no means left the individual isolated and totally unrelated to
other individuals or groups. As mentioned above, one of the
factors leading to this changed understanding of the self was
the widening range of options open to the individual in the
expanding world of the twelfth century. The resulting diversity was placed in a broader perspective that allowed the
individual to see the complementarity of the various roles
and the importance of each for the good of society as a
whole.

Thus for example, if a person chose to join the Franciscans
rather than the Dominicans, he or she did so both out of a
sense of having a real choice (since these orders underscored
their differences) and out of a sense that the choice made a
difference to oneself. This choice, however, was made in a
context that left the individual aware that in joining the
Franciscans rather than the Dominicans, he or she was also
acting for the good of the Order and of the church as a
whole.

[11]White, p. 55.

[12]Morris, chapter 7.

If twelfth-century authors were more aware of their motives for acting, of the process of making a choice, of interior change, it was not only because there were in fact a wider variety of social roles and a new diversity of religious groups which made choice necessary. It was also because people now had ways of talking about groups as groups, roles as roles, and about group formation. Therefore they could be conscious of choosing.[13]

This brief summary of the changes occurring in the twelfth century highlights some of the major elements composing the individualism I am speaking about in this book. The individual was perceived as a separate and bounded self. This impacted to a degree the economic and political configurations of the day. But it had a much greater influence on the culture, affecting the way people understood themselves and their relationship with others, with the environment, and with God. This sense of separateness, however, even though it included elements of alienation, did not lead to isolation. Rather it placed the individual in a different relationship with his or her environment. He or she was responding to and advancing the good of society as a whole.

## Individualism in the Modern West

While the modern Western notion of the self found its origin in twelfth-century Europe, the coming to age of this notion, marked by its becoming the organizing principle within society, was a gradual process. In the fifteenth century, the Protestant Reformation structured it into the religious dimension of life through emphasis on personal conversion and personal relationship with God. But as should be evident from the earlier discussion, the reformers did not create their stance out of whole cloth. They picked up on threads reaching back four centuries.

---

[13]Caroline Walker Bynum, "Did the Twelfth Century Discover the Individual?" *Journal of Ecclesiastical History* 31/1 (January, 1980): pp. 7-8.

In the seventeenth and eighteenth centuries there were dramatic changes in the political and economic spheres aiming at the empowerment of the individual. Not only were individuals to have a sense of self as bounded and separate, they also were to control their own destiny by enjoying a substantive influence on their society.

This meant the medieval political structures had to be changed. The hierarchy of kings and princes, popes and bishops which left the ordinary person at the bottom of the pyramid and at the mercy of what were perceived as arbitrary legislation and taxations was out of step with the sense of the importance of the self. Individuals had to be protected; and they had to be provided a voice in government.

Political structures which promoted and protected the individual as a distinct and bounded self were founded philosophically in the "contract theory" of Thomas Hobbes and John Locke. According to this theory, individuals existed prior to the development of society and government in some natural state. For reasons variously described, individuals agreed to bind themselves together in society through a mutually accepted contract.

This gives the individual precedence over society. And it reorients the axis of the individual's life; for, whereas previously the individual had been seen in relation to society, now primary emphasis is placed on the individual's prior existence in some state of nature. As a result, society has merely instrumental value, assisting the individual in obtaining from nature the fulfillment of his or her interests.

Government has a place within this society; but it too is merely ancillary to the self-authenticating activity of individuals. Government is important for the protection it affords against external threats, for its enforcement of contracts, and for whatever purposes individuals through their social contract decide it should act. At the same time, however, it remains an ever-present danger; for government can too easily overstep its bounds, taking control over individuals rather than serving them in their pursuit of self-interest.

Such a utilitarian attitude toward society ends up threatening the very individual it was meant to benefit. What is to prohibit one individual or a group of individuals from using others to further self-interest? To protect the individual, the liberal tradition set out a doctrine of natural human rights. These rights defend the individual from external coercion by governmental bodies or private entities. In the United States, these are spelled out in the Bill of Rights of the Constitution: civil and political rights such as freedom of assembly, freedom of speech, freedom of religion, all of which protect the individual against external intrusion.

In the economic sphere, mercantilism, which set the economic welfare of the nation above that of the individual or of any group within the nation, came under attack. According to Adam Smith, whose *Wealth of Nations*, published in 1776, was the gospel of the capitalist or the free enterprise system, the primary focus of the economy should be on individuals. There is in human nature "a certain propensity ... to truck, barter, and exchange one thing for another."[14] If individuals are allowed the necessary latitude to follow this propensity out, the nation will be the better off; for the true wealth of a nation lies not in its gold reserves but in its ability to produce goods.

In striving to harmonize the structures of politics and economics with the view of self as bounded and separate, the battle cry was "Freedom": freedom to follow one's conscience, freedom to express one's opinions and have them count, freedom to be about one's own business of producing, exchanging, and consuming. Because people were working mightily to break the hold of governmental and ecclesiastical structures, this freedom was defined negatively. The freedom demanded was *freedom from*: freedom from a church that maintained its power by placing itself as the indispensable mediator between the individual and God; freedom from a government that proclaimed and prosecuted decrees that were nothing more than the arbitrary will of the king; freedom from economic restraints that kept the individual a

---

[14]Adam Smith, *Inquiry into the Nature and Causes of the Wealth of Nations* (New York: The Modern Library, 1937), p. 13. For a discussion of the history of capitalism, see, for example, Robert L. Heilbroner, *The Worldly Philosophers* (New York: Simon and Schuster, 1969), chapters 3, 4, 7, and 9; Charles K. Wilber and Kenneth P. Jameson, *An Inquiry into the Poverty of Economics* (Notre Dame, Indiana: University of Notre Dame Press, 1983), pp. 23-35.

slave of the national treasury. The presumption was that, once liberated from these strictures, an individual's creativity would be released, and this could only be for the good.

The primary arena for the realization of this freedom was the marketplace. According to Adam Smith, as noted above, individuals have this "certain propensity . . . to truck, barter, and exchange one thing for another." Politics and governmental activities in general were seen as secondary and subsidiary to this. Government's principal responsibility is to provide internal and external protection, insuring that all live up to their contracts and that the nation as a whole is secure against outside threats.

The marketplace, then, because of its centrality in society, strongly influences the images by which we understand the self as bounded and separate. The self-interest the individual pursues tends to focus on the goods available through the marketplace. Relations with others are seen as contractual in nature, based on one's right to work to fulfill one's interests so long as this does not interfere with the right of others to do the same. But these relations are also competitive since the goods one wants are sought by others as well.

This provides the context for understanding the development of modern science. As the presence of kings and princes, popes and bishops stood in the way of the realization of new theories of society, so the presence of dogmas, customs, and traditions blocked the possibility of viewing and analyzing the world in ways different from the past. Science in its classical form served to support and continue the status quo of feudalism. For the classical scientist, the world was a hierarchically-ordered and unchanging world. True knowledge could only be of the fixed and immutable; and to obtain that, one made use of speculation and deduction to define the essences of species and to establish its proper placement in the cosmos.

Modern science furnished the means to break the hold of this eternal and hierarchical world. It attends to the changing rather than the immutable, to the ways that specific things interact with one another rather than to the essences of classes of things and their place in an unchanging order; to altering and mastering nature rather than contemplating it. And these tools are conceived in light of the individual's prominent place in the new society.

The philosopher René Descartes, a key figure in the development of modern science, believed that the new age coming to birth demanded a radical rethinking of all aspects of life. So he called everything into doubt, declaring "that only those things ought to be believed which are perfectly known and which cannot be doubted."[15] The one thing he could not doubt was his own existence; there can be no doubting without thinking and there can be no thinking without someone—some "I"—who thinks. And the subject matter about which this "I" thinks and has clear and distinct knowledge is the physical world—the world considered in its individual, physical components viewed quantitatively and mathematically, i.e., in terms of their length, breadth, weight, etc. The world that is the subject of our knowledge is the world of the physical scientist.

Not only is humankind provided the critical tools to break the hold of the past but these are posited in the intellect of the individual as well. In other words, the individual, understood as a separate and bounded self, became the locus for rational analysis and evaluation of the world. John Dewey sums it up this way:

> ...[P]hilosophical theories of knowledge were not content to conceive mind in the individual as the pivot upon which reconstruction of beliefs turned, thus maintaining the continuity of the individual with the world of nature and fellow men. They regarded the individual mind as a separate entity, complete in each person, and isolated from nature and hence from other minds. Thus a legitimate intellectual individualism, the attitude of critical revision of former beliefs which is indispensable to progress, was explicitly formulated as a moral and social individualism.[16]

---

[15]René Descartes, *Rules for the Direction of the Understanding*, in *From Descartes to Locke*, eds. T.V. Smith and Marjorie Greene (Chicago: The University of Chicago Press, 1957), p. 18.

[16]John Dewey, *Democracy and Education* (New York: The Macmillan Company, 1961), p. 297.

The purpose of this reason, naturally enough, is to assist the individual in his or her efforts to realize self-interest. Reason then is interpreted instrumentally and is not very helpful for addressing more substantive issues in human life. In other words, while reason is well suited to assist in satisfying individual wants, it offers little help in determining the overall orientation of an individual's or a society's existence. While it contributes greatly to the planning and production of hula hoops, Edsels, and aerosol dispensers, it offers no insight into whether or not they should in fact be produced. This is in line with Adam Smith's theory of the "invisible hand" which counsels the individual to attend to his or her own interests rather than to the good of society as a whole. Thus, Smith says of the merchant: "By pursuing his own interest he frequently promotes that of the society more effectually than when he really intends to promote it. I have never known much good done by those who affect to trade for the public good."[17]

Finally, religion also was tied into this new world of the individual as a separate and bounded self whose initiative and creativity were expressed primarily in the marketplace. Adam Smith recognized the importance of religion for the economic system he was propounding, particularly as a teacher of morality. According to him, the churches could present a looser or more liberal form of morality to the rich, since their position in society kept them in line. They would not want to lose face. The churches, however, should impose a much stricter morality upon the poor. Their anonymity in society provides few controls over their behavior, and "the vices of levity are always ruinous to the common people and a single week's thoughtlessness and dissipation is often sufficient to undo a poor workman for ever, and to drive him through despair upon committing the most enormous crimes."[18] More importantly, of course, such "vices of levity" could be even more ruinous for society than for the individual.

---

[17]Smith, p. 423.
[18]Ibid., 746.

Christianity was linked in still more subtle ways with this new form of society whose center was the separate self acting out of personal interest in the marketplace. Much has been made of the contribution that the Protestant work ethic made to the development of capitalism.[19] But Roman Catholics cannot self-righteously lay all credit for legitimating this new society at the door of Protestantism. As I showed earlier in this chapter, the origins of individualism predated the reformation. And as I shall argue shortly, Roman Catholicism, despite its condemnation of individualism, implicitly supports it through some of its stances and practices.

First, however, another element must be added, for this image of the individual as a separate and bounded self whose identity and relations are defined by his or her role in the free enterprise marketplace is not the total picture. Just as the individualism of the twelfth century was situated within a broader vision leading the individual to understand that concern for the good of self was related to the good of society, so too here.

Adam Smith's "invisible hand" is key in seeing the tie of the self to society. As I have already pointed out, Smith counseled people to work directly and explicitly for their own benefit and not for the good of society. But this does not mean he wanted people to be disinterested in what happened to society. His concern was strategic: how can society best be assisted?

His invisible hand gave the individual a basis for believing that by seeking personal success with all one's energies, he or she was benefiting more than just self. One may, to be sure, argue that in fact the invisible hand did not—and does not—work. That may well be the case. My point, however, is that the individualism which developed in the West concentrated the attention of a person on a certain notion of the self, viz., the bounded self apart from others; and this self precisely in its uniqueness was seen as related to the social whole, and

---

[19]See Max Weber, *The Protestant Ethic and the Spirit of Capitalism*, trans. Talcott Parsons (New York: Charles Scribner's Sons, 1958).

the fulfillment of this uniqueness was understood as contributing to the welfare of society.[20]

In addition, the religious, economic, and political developments I have described which structured society in light of the individual as a separate, bounded self took place within the context of a culture strongly bound by feudal ties. These webbed people together in various ways and at many different levels. As a result, individuals did not actually live as detached and isolated entities, nor did they have a sense of doing so.

To sum up the argument to this point, individualism as it has developed in the West has given primacy to the individual defined as a separate and bounded self freely pursuing one's own interests by right in the marketplace. In this pursuit, the self relates to others as possessors of similar rights and as competitors for the same goods. Society and government have instrumental value; the physical world provides the materials and science the means for meeting individuals' interests; religion legitimates and protects this worldview. But the individual remains related to society as a whole through informal ties and through the "invisible hand" which promises that society will benefit from the betterment of the individual.

Although the ideas, the social structures, and the controlling attitudes toward life we have been discussing reach back two hundred years, they are by no means museum pieces. There certainly have been changes: the development of the welfare state, for example, has brought with it a larger and more active government. But fundamentally the role of government remains the same—to be instrumental in assisting individuals to pursue their personal interests.

Over the years, the classical liberal philosophy has been challenged by those following a different philosophical tradition who have insisted that the individual be grounded in a web of social relations. This has had an impact. But as William M. Sullivan notes, "although contemporary thinkers may be compelled to accommodate the notion that values

---

[20]See Albert O. Hirschman, *The Passions and the Interests* (Princeton, New Jersey: Princeton University Press, 1977), p. 132.

arc essentially rooted in social life, liberals still assert that the justification of moral insight, if not its genealogy, requires holding fast to traditional liberal categories."[21]

Thus, while the classical liberal tradition has bowed and bent to changed times and new challenges from various quarters, the individualism I have described remains basically in place. It is still the coin of the realm in the West, securely deposited in the political philosophy and practice of nations and in the self-identity of their citizens.

### Individualism in the U.S.

I still have not made my point, however. My object here is not to talk about the effects that the individualism rooted in classical liberalism has had and continues to have on the West in general. I am arguing that these effects are seen particularly and distinctively in the U.S—to such an extent, in fact, that individualism is the defining characteristic of this culture.

Unlike other nations where the various elements that I have included in the description of individualism had to confront and accommodate themselves to customs of a previous era, the founders of the American experiment started, one could almost say, with a blank slate. The land was new for those who established this nation; no vestiges of a feudal tradition existed; there was no group memory of a common past experience, and what was remembered was precisely what people were seeking to escape. Within that context, the broad range of ideas comprising individualism could make themselves felt with special force.

In point of fact, unlike other nations which understood themselves in terms of bloodline or soil or social grouping, the citizens of this new nation found their self-definition in an idea—individualism. They used this idea to set themselves apart from, and to define themselves over against, others; and we, their heirs, continue to do the same.

[21]William M. Sullivan, *Reconstructing Public Philosophy* (Berkeley, CA: University of California Press, 1982), p. 106.

The historian Arthur Mann points this out well. He speaks of our national identity in terms of the Enlightenment; but as the context shows, Mann describes with the term "enlightenment" the same reality I do with "individualism."

> What, then, was an American? To the eighteenth-century founders, an American was a bundle of rights, freely chosen.... [They] expressed themselves in the language of the eighteenth-century Enlightenment, proclaiming that the American people had been born free and meant to stay free through institutions of their own making.... Unlike Europe, which the founders homogenized into a bundle of evil, America stood for liberty, opportunity, equality before the law, and a better tomorrow for everyone. Above all, this side of the Atlantic defied the conventional wisdom that no nation could survive without the historic props of king, aristocracy, and established clergy. A republican people were themselves a sufficient source of authority.... *Ideologically, in other words, the United States has been the land of the enduring Enlightenment.*[22]

This tradition informs our political and economic structures. And it is woven into the fabric of our manners and mores. It "lies at the very core of American culture,"[23] and gets celebrated in our myths about those who go it alone: the cowboy, the long-distance truck driver, the one who single-handedly takes on seemingly impossible odds and wins.

But, despite the flourish of the rhetoric and images connected with these myths, we in fact do not live as isolated individuals. There are forces that bind us to one another in U.S. culture. As individuals, we work not just for our own benefit but also for the well-being of our families—both immediate and extended—to which we are closely tied. Furthermore, we are "naturally" a society of belongers, joining neighborhood groups and various organizations, volunteering our time for numerous projects.

[22]Mann, pp. 56, 57, 58, 68. Emphasis added.

[23]Bellah et al., *Habits of the Heart* (Berkeley, CA: University of California Press, 1985), p. 142.

In addition, as the authors of *Habits of the Heart* have pointed out, we are heirs of both a religious and a republican individualism.[24] These are called individualisms because they strongly support "the dignity, indeed the sacredness of the individual."[25] But they place great emphasis on the connection of the individual to society. Religious individualism, which traces its roots back to the Puritans, set as its ideal "not material wealth but the creation of a community in which a genuinely ethical and spiritual life would be lived."[26] And republican individualism stressed the importance of the concerned citizen, holding up "the ideal of a self-governing society of relative equals in which all participate."[27]

Thus the uniqueness of U.S. individualism begins to take shape. We live in the "land of the enduring Enlightenment"; we refer easily to images of the individual standing apart from—even over against—society; but in our tradition and in the informalities of everyday life, we are linked to one another in many different ways.

Given that description of U.S. individualism, where is the cause for concern? The problem, in my judgment, is that the binding and bonding forces within our society are losing some of their power. According to the authors of *Habits of the Heart*, while religious and republican individualisms are indeed part of our cultural heritage, other forms of individualism (what they term "utilitarian" and "expressive" individualism) are much more dominant at the present time. Utilitarian individualism makes its presence felt in the public dimensions of our lives. It emphasizes the individual acting on one's own, getting ahead through one's own efforts, vigorously pursuing self-interest—"a life devoted to the calculating pursuit of one's own material interests."[28] Expressive individualism has developed in reaction against the cold, uncaring

---

[24]Ibid., pp. 28-31. See also, Sullivan, pp. 1-22; R. Jackson Wilson, *In Quest of Community* (New York: Oxford University Press, 1968), especially chapter 1.

[25]Bellah et al., p. 142.

[26]Ibid., p. 29.

[27]Ibid., p. 30.

[28]Ibid., p. 33.

world that utilitarian individualism seems to be creating. It shifts the spotlight from the public to the personal and private dimensions of the individual's life, but still focuses on the individual apart from society. The ideal now is not success in one's career or financial standing but "a life rich in experience, open to all kinds of people, luxuriating in the sensual as well as the intellectual, above all a life of strong feeling. . . . "[29] The image shifts from the hard-driving, success-minded young executive to the laid-back young Californian experiencing a sunset over the Pacific.

This change of emphasis from concerned citizen to individual seeking career success or fulfilling personal experience loosens the individual's connection with society; and this separation is not easily offset by the other factors I have mentioned. Religious and republican individualism have not totally disappeared from our culture; but they are now more a recessive part of our tradition that is strongly influenced and heavily impacted by utilitarian and expressive individualism. Individuals, to be sure, continue to work for their families and not just for themselves.[30] But the family can itself become an isolated entity and can function as a refuge from society, a haven of expressive individualism.[31] The habit of belonging continues to be a significant dimension of our culture. But the results are voluntary associations—aggregates of individuals who belong because they so choose, but who can also freely decide to disassociate themselves. While such associations are an important resource for carrying out particular projects, they are not an adequate means for rooting the individual in society as a whole,[32] particularly at a time when the forces of utilitarian and expressive individualism are so strong.

---

[29]Ibid., p. 34.

[30]Ehrenreich, however, notes that there has been a demise of the "breadwinner ethic" with men being less willing to assume the traditional financial responsibility for the family. See Barbara Ehrenreich, *The Hearts of Men: American Dreams and the Flight from Commitment* (Garden City, N.Y.: Doubleday, Anchor Books, 1984).

[31]See Christopher Lasch, *Haven in a Heartless Land: The Family Besieged* (New York: Basic Books, Inc., 1977); Bellah et al., chapter 4.

[32]This point will be discussed further in chapter 9, pp. 227-228.

Here we have, then, a further clarification of the uneasiness that originally led me to this project. The problem is indeed individualism. But the term refers to more than just the relation of the individual to society; it concerns as well the relation of the individual to self, to the physical environment, and to God. Moreover, the problem is not that the individual denies or is denied any link between the individual and society. Those ties exist at many different levels. At issue is the nature and quality of that linkage.

Not only is the problem becoming clearer, but so too is the solution. We have to find ways of stressing the social belonging of the individual. In doing so, however, we must be careful not to throw out our respect for the dignity of the individual and buy into some corporatism or tribalism that values only the group. We can accomplish this by recovering from our cultural tradition the basic ties that bind us as individuals to society, reinterpreting them in light of the present situation, and strengthening them.

First, though, we have to inquire further into what happens when the bonds between the individual and society are loosened. In particular we will look at the implications this has for the moral life and for moral decision-making.

# 2

# Individualism and Morality

The rhetoric and the reality of individualism in the U.S., as I have pointed out, are not always the same. In describing individualism we often invoke images of the cowboy, the loner, the outsider—people apart from, even over against, society. But in reality, the individualism of U.S. culture maintains definite ties between the individual and society.

The problem, as we have seen, is that these ties are presently strained. This situation is further exacerbated by the fact that the response made to it often is based more on the rhetoric than the reality of individualism. As the connection of the individual to society is relaxed, the individual (as I shall argue) feels more isolated and powerless. But, rather than seeking to strengthen the connection with society, we seem to resort instead to speeches about individual freedom and individual rights, to stories about individuals making it on their own, to images of the cowboy and the outsider—and lately of Rambo. This, of course, does not solve the problem; it only heightens it, straining further the ties of the individual to society.

In this chapter I will outline the issues raised by individualism for the moral life and moral decision-making when the individual-society relationship is weakened. In my judgment, this situation highlights the vulnerable points—the dark side—of U.S. individualism. And since individualism, as defined here, refers to the relation of the individual to society, to the physical environment, and to God as well, the problems are evident in the full range of our existence.

## Individualism and Alienation from Others

Alexis de Tocqueville, the French social theorist and states-man, traveled extensively through this country in 1831 to study the effects of democracy on the social structures and customs of a people. In *Democracy in America*, he warned that the situation he found in the United States could give rise to tyranny rather than freedom—a tyranny of public opinion. People in this country, he noted, are possessed of (or maybe better, possessed by) a powerful drive toward equality. Based on the rights due each person as an indi-vidual, everyone stands on equal footing within society, with equal right to vote and to speak, with equal opportunity to participate in the marketplace. But this equality, while seeming to give each individual a sense of self-sufficiency and power, has just the opposite effect.

> In times of equality men, being so like each other, have no confidence in others, but this same likeness leads them to place almost unlimited confidence in the judgment of the public. For they think it not unreasonable that, all having the same means of knowledge, truth will be found on the side of the majority.
>
> The citizen of a democracy comparing himself with others feels proud of his equality with each other. But when he compares himself with all his fellows, and mea-sures himself against this vast entity, he is *overwhelmed by a sense of his insignificance and weakness.*
>
> This same quality which makes him independent of each separate citizen *leaves him isolated and defenseless* in the face of the majority.
>
> So in democracies public opinion has a strange power of which aristocratic nations can form no conception. It uses no persuasion to forward its beliefs, but *by some mighty pressure of the mind of all upon the intelligence of each* it imposes its ideas and makes them penetrate men's very souls.[1]

[1] Alexis de Tocqueville, *Democracy in America*, trans. George Lawrence (Garden City, NY: Doubleday and Company, Inc., 1969), p. 435. Emphasis added.

In other words, contrary to what we normally expect, the separation of the individual from society does not lead to a greater feeling of power and self-sufficiency. It leaves us rather with a sense of inadequacy and powerlessness. And, even more unexpectedly, instead of distancing us from society, this separation enmeshes us more deeply in it. For we do not feel we have the power to take a stand against the current of public opinion; in fact, we feel compelled to follow it. As odd as it may seem, the more we press our independence, the more anxious we are to conform to generally accepted expectations.

In light of this, it is interesting to consider the freedom that is so central to individualism. This freedom, as I explained in the previous chapter, is a negative freedom—a freedom from. It protects us against external entities, especially government, overstepping their bounds. But it draws our attention away from the control that customs and opinions—in short, the generally accepted way of life within society—have over our minds and hearts. Consequently, even as we celebrate our freedom to think our own thoughts and to make them public, we can be a truly conformist people. "Refusal to accept established opinion and anxious conformity to the opinions of one's peers turn out to be two sides of the same coin."[2]

What impact does this conformity have on the moral enterprise?

Consider first of all its implications for moral decision-making. Here public opinion and culture in general can have a great influence, even a tyranny, over the individual. Adam Smith, the author of *The Wealth of Nations*, was not an economist by profession but a professor of moral philosophy. In addition to this book which served as the foundation for the free enterprise system, he wrote a volume on ethics entitled *The Theory of Moral Sentiments*. There he argued that the criterion for deciding morally what to do and for judging the morality of what has been done does not lie in the usefulness of actions for society. (This, of course, is not

[2]Bellah et al., p. 148.

surprising, given his theory of the "invisible hand.") Rather, he claimed that the judgment an "Impartial Spectator" would make on the action is the relevant criterion. How would some other person feel about it?

> We either approve or disapprove of the conduct of another man, according as we feel that, when we bring his case home to ourselves, we either can or cannot entirely sympathize with the sentiments and motives which directed it. And, in the same manner, we either approve or disapprove of our own conduct, according as we feel that, when we place ourselves in the situation of another man and view it, as it were, with his eyes and from his station, we either can or cannot entirely enter into and sympathize with the sentiments and motives which influenced it.[3]

Thus in the process of moral decision-making, I as an individual am closely circumscribed by the informal, but nonetheless authoritative and compelling, demands of commonly accepted behavioral patterns; for the judgments of the impartial spectator are based on the generally accepted opinions within society.[4] And, of couse, the more isolated and powerless I feel, the more my moral decisions will be based on a concern about what "they" will think if I act this way.[5]

I could, to be sure, just go my own way and do "my own thing," forgetting about what others will say. But the resulting isolation from others leaves me only more powerless and

[3]Adam Smith, *The Theory of Moral Sentiments* (New Rochelle, NY: Arlington House, 1969), p. 161.

[4]"But what was the source of the judgments rendered by the spectator? Smith's answer was that they came from the opinions of society. Our moral judgments, then, were in the nature of mirrored reflections; they relayed social values to the individual conscience. What distinguished social man from isolated man was that the former possessed a conscience sensitive to social influences, a 'mirror' of 'the countenance and behavior of those he lives with.'" Sheldon S. Wolin, *Politics and Vision* (Boston: Little, Brown and Company, 1960), p. 344.

[5]"Now the peculiar thing about Them is that They are created only by each one of us repudiating his own identity. When we have installed Them in our hearts, we are only a plurality of solitudes in which what each person has in common is his allocation to the other of the necessity for his own actions." R.D. Laing, *The Politics of Experience* (New York: Ballantine Books, 1977), pp. 83-84.

therefore more at the mercy of the "Impartial Spectator." And besides, while I trust myself with this type of freedom, I am not sure I want to trust others, particularly with all the crazy and destructive things going on today.

But even if I were to decide to challenge the generally accepted moral norms, I would be hard put to locate the necessary means of doing so. As the individual-society relation is weakened, the parameters of the moral life tend to narrow. The spotlight falls primarily on the individual's personal life: has the individual acted correctly in his or her own affairs? With the attention given primarily to the individual, society tends to disappear: only individuals and aggregates of individuals exist; society is merely an intellectual construct, a convenient way of referring to a collection of individuals. And so, moral judgments can be passed only on individuals. If there is something morally amiss, responsibility is traced to some individual, thus leaving little grounds for passing moral judgment on social structures or cultural values.

This, of course, only deepens the problem. With the present order of society effectively withdrawn from any moral scrutiny or judgment, we are further confronted by our powerlessness as individuals. What can freedom, the cornerstone of individualism, mean if our decisions are strongly conditioned by popular opinion and our lives are very much influenced by a system that cannot be challenged?

The problems in the moral enterprise are further exacerbated by the separation and alienation of the individual from the physical world. As noted earlier, the development of modern science was closely related to the social order inspired by individualism. For modern science, the real world is the world outside the mind, considered in its individual components as mathematically quantifiable and measurable. That world is distinct and separate from the individual, who is identified as the thinking self. Knowledge becomes the "dry, hard, cold"[6] achievement of a "lonely mind"[7] looking out on an alien world.

---

[6]John Dewey, *Reconstruction in Philosophy* (Boston: Beacon Press, 1957), p. 16.

[7]John Dewey, *A Common Faith* (New Haven, CT: Yale University Press, 1972), p. 86.

Consequently, the physical world is removed from the sphere of morality. Morality, after all, deals by its very nature with quality, not quantity, with matters as right or good, not as mathematically measurable. Therefore, it is unrelated and foreign to the world external to the thinking self. This, in turn, has the effect of extricating the methods of physical science and its manipulations of the material world from any moral judgment.

Limiting the scope of morality in this way is not confined to the natural sciences. With the prestige of modern science, political and economic structures are seen as part of the natural order which science explores. Thus the meaning and direction of society cease to be the result of meaningful political discourse and instead become the subject matter of a social *science*. The free enterprise economy may well carry with it some, even many, undesirable effects: poverty, ignorance, class division, and social unrest; but that should not cause us to look elsewhere. It is grounded in the laws of nature.[8] If it is as absurd to defy the laws of economics as to defy the laws of science, then both morality and the parameters of human endeavor are restricted.

In this mindset, morality, shut out of external reality, is likewise denied access to the individual's intellect. The intellect, as conceived by modern science, is analytical, reducing complex realities to their simple elements; it deals with what is, not what ought to be. The mind, then, is basically a technician which can tinker with particular parts of a system but cannot judge whether the system as a whole is good or bad, appropriate or inappropriate. If morality has no place

[8]"In short, positive economics is, or can be, an 'objective' science, in precisely the same sense as any of the physical sciences. Of course, the fact that economics deals with the interrelations of human beings, and that the investigator is himself part of the subject matter being investigated in a more intimate sense than in the physical sciences, raises special difficulties in achieving objectivity at the same time that it provides the social scientist with a class of data not available to the physical scientist. But neither the one nor the other is, in my view, a fundamental distinction between the two groups of sciences." Milton Friedman, *Essays in Positive Economics* (Chicago: The University of Chicago Press, 1953), pp. 4-5. See also: Peter Gay, *The Enlightenment*, vol. 2: *The Science of Freedom* (New York: W.W. Norton and Company, Inc., 1969), pp. 344-368.

in the rational, it must be part of the emotions. Saying that something is wrong, then, is merely an emotive reaction on our part, a statement of our feelings.

Yet while the external world, the "really real" world, is subject to the cold, matter-of-fact measurements and calculations of science, voided of value and morality, morality continues to be a part of people's lives and a subject of discussion. And since science is so highly valued, it is only natural that such discussions be influenced by the scientific way of thinking, even though morality is unscientific. Thus, if the physical world is treated piecemeal, the moral life is approached in this same fragmentary way.

Morality, then, attends to the particular acts of individuals, each looked at in isolation from others. The general orientation of a person's life or patterns of behavior are not considered. In decision-making or in examination of conscience, this morality focuses on an act in its immediacy rather than on its place and significance in the agent's biography.

Moreover, morality picks up on the centrality of calculation in the quantified world of science. Decision-making can easily become a matter of weighing consequences. The possible good results are measured against the potential evil effects, and from that the most appropriate action is calculated.

Thus, our highly valued freedom appears to evaporate even more, and we seem caught in a dilemma. We define our freedom in terms of separateness. Yet it is precisely the separation from others and from the physical world that is problematic. It all becomes a vicious circle. We believe strongly in the freedom and the self as defined by individualism. And so, not surprisingly, the more we feel empty or threatened, the more we struggle for our individual freedom. But this further isolates us.

## Individualism and Alienation from Self

Finally, we ask: who is this self celebrated by individualism? Why is it that, when the ties binding the individual to society are loosened, the individual is left so vulnerable?

Why cannot this individual stand alone, as our myths of the cowboy and the outsider seem to promise?

This self of individualism, first of all, is the possessor of civil rights: the right to free speech, to assembly, and so forth. But what content do these rights give to human life? In and of itself, the possession of rights is an empty thing. Rights take on meaning, positive or negative, as they are lived out. In the case of the freedom of speech, for instance, we can use this right to denounce poverty, to advocate the ERA, or to disseminate pornography. Each of these places us in a different relation with society and has a different effect on us personally. In speaking of the right of free speech, however, this differentiation is not made. It is simply stated that each one of us has this right. But on that basis, we can say nothing of who we are; we remain as empty as the right. To have substance, we as individuals must be more than just the possessors of rights.

Each one of us, secondly, has certain interests and wants that motivate our actions, especially in the marketplace. These are taken for granted. They are idiosyncratic, part of our givenness as individuals. The wants and interests of each of us are as good and as valuable as anyone else's; and we have a right to pursue their satisfaction so long as that pursuit does not interfere with the rights of another to do the same.

But what happens if those interests and wants are satisfied: does that satisfaction enter into the substance of the self; does it make us a different person? Or what if those interests and wants are not satisfied? Obviously, the individual is frustrated; but is the self less a self or a different self?

As a result, we can say that we have wants and interests and instincts just as we have rights. But that indicates little of who we are as persons; we still remain empty.

It is no wonder, then, that behaviorist psychology can talk about the manipulation of the individual, and that the advertising industry can make this manipulation an accepted part of everyday life. If reality is defined and dealt with in a mechanistic way by science, this same approach can easily be taken toward our person, especially when we stand alone, isolated, and vulnerable.

This ironic emptiness of the individual that can flow from

individualism is reflected in the conception of morality. A substantive self disappears and the notion of the moral life is emptied of any content. As mentioned above, with the attention of science focused on fragmentary aspects of reality, morality concentrates on our individual decisions. But our moral life, which is much more than the sum of the separate moral decisions we make, is then lost to sight.

Of course, we can speak about the moral decision-maker, and not just about moral decisions. But we are still left with a question about who we are as the person making such decisions. Do our decisions have any substantial effect on the person we are? Are we a different person because we acted in one way rather than another?

Further, the moral decisions themselves tend to be external in their orientation. As individuals we are deeply concerned to make sure the rights of others are not infringed. Now let me hasten to say that there is nothing wrong with respecting rights. But if that becomes the primary component of morality, what is the substance of the person concerned for such rights?

In his book on moral philosophy, Adam Smith writes:

> One individual must never prefer himself so much even to any other individual as to hurt or injure that other in order to benefit himself, though the benefit to the one should be much greater than the hurt or injury to the other. The poor man must neither defraud nor steal from the rich, though the acquisition might be much more beneficial to the one than the loss could be hurtful to the other. . . .
>
> . . . For one man to deprive another unjustly of any thing, or unjustly to promote his own advantage by the loss or disadvantage of another, is more contrary to nature than death, than poverty, than pain, than all the misfortunes which can affect him, either in his body, or in his external circumstances.[9]

---

[9]Smith, *The Theory of Moral Sentiments*, p. 195.

This shows clearly that, even though at times the self of individualism appears to be overly inner-directed and self-centered because of the great stress on individual freedom and individual rights, attention is actually focused on respect for the opinions and property of others.

And, even though the quote from Adam Smith was written over two centuries ago, this approach is not some quaint period piece. Consider the very influential theory of moral development propounded by Lawrence Kohlberg, a psychologist. While he betrays none of Adam Smith's disregard for the desperate condition of the poor, he continues this external, other-directed orientation. He describes stage six, the final stage of moral development, in this way:

> Stage 6: *The Universal-Ethical-Principle orientation.* Right is defined by the decision of conscience in accord with self-chosen *ethical principles* appealing to logical comprehensiveness, universality, and consistency. These principles are abstract and ethical (the Golden Rule, the categorical imperative); they are not concrete moral rules like the Ten Commandments. At heart, these are universal principles of *justice*, of the *reciprocity* and *equality* of human *rights*, and of *respect* for the dignity of human beings as *individual persons.*[10]

But again, what happens if we act justly and respect the dignity of others? Does it really make a difference in who we are? It is important, to be sure, that we not look out just for ourselves and walk on others in the process. But we cannot just look out for others either; we have to attend to the substance of ourselves, to who we are as individuals. If we fail to do so, we can end up as people who carefully observe the canons of justice but who personally are empty.

In saying that the main elements individualism attributes to the self leave the individuals empty, I do not mean that we actually live in a void. We all individually find various commitments and ways of life that make our existence meaning-

[10]Lawrence Kohlberg, "The Cognitive-Developmental Approach to Moral Education," *Phi Delta Kappan* 56/10 (June 1975): 671. Emphasis in original.

ful. We have to, otherwise we could make neither rhyme nor reason of anything.

My point is that what individualism claims as the main dimensions of the self are not adequate of themselves. They do not give us the substance and strength we need to stand up against the conformist forces within society and to help rebuild the connection between the individual and society. Nor is it enough simply that we be left on our own individually to make what we want to out of life. That only adds to our isolation as individuals. It leaves us more vulnerable to the pressures of society; it makes us more apt to buy into present social currents, such as utilitarian and expressive individualism.

We are faced, then, with the task of reinterpreting the self so as to preserve respect for the dignity of the person and allow the individual to participate fully in society.

This specifies more the problem of U.S. individualism, particularly as it affects the moral life and moral decision-making. As the connection between the individual and society is relaxed, we tend to fall back on popular images and specific aspects of individualism that further undermine the connection. The resulting isolation gives rise to a sense of powerlessness, leaving us as individuals more at the mercy of public opinion.

When we ask who the self of individualism is, we find that this individual—the bearer of freedom and rights, the possessor of interests that guide and motivate action—does not appear to have an adequate substance to respond to the difficulties at hand.

Our task, then, is becoming clearer. Not only must we strengthen the relationship of the individual to society, but we also have to determine what the appropriate substance—the appropriate character—of the self is so that the individual can participate in and contribute to society.

Before doing so, however, we will look at how the Roman Catholic church is implicated in this problem.

# 3

# U.S. Individualism and the Roman Catholic Church

A brief summary of the ground we have covered thus far will serve to introduce the final segment of this section of the book. In attempting to name the cause of my initial uneasiness, I have suggested that individualism is the source of the problem. The term individualism, I have argued, refers to a particular way of understanding the relation of the individual to society, and this understanding has implications as well for the way the individual relates to self, to the environment, and to God.

Within U.S. culture at the present, the individual-society connection has been loosened. This has tended to leave the individual with a sense of isolation and powerlessness. In addition, the self as defined by individualism is not adequate, in my judgment, to respond constructively to the issues at stake. This is raising serious issues in the moral enterprise.

To add the final touches to this picture of the problematic, we now consider the role of religion in U.S. individualism. And since I am approaching this discussion from an explicitly Roman Catholic perspective, I will focus here primarily on the way Roman Catholicism is implicated in the problems of U.S. individualism because of the manner in which the church interprets and addresses morality.

To head off some possible questions or objections to proceeding this way, I am not claiming that Roman Catholicism is at root individualistic or that it fosters a loosening of the individual-society connection. In fact, the Roman Catholic tradition clearly stands foursquare against any individualism which exalts the individual at the expense of society. In 1971, Pope Paul VI warned against adherence "to the liberal ideology which believes it exalts individual freedom by withdrawing it from every limitation, by stimulating it through exclusive seeking of interest and power, and by considering social solidarities as more or less automatic consequences of individual initiatives, not as an aim and a major criterion of the value of the social organization."[1] And the Roman Catholic tradition, in my judgment, challenges the way U.S. culture loosens the ties of the individual to society—as I shall show in the remainder of this book.

Nor am I implying that the Roman Catholic church is the sole, or even the principal, religious support of U.S. individualism. But it does not stand innocent. As noted earlier, the Protestant Reformers played a major role in structuring the idea of the individual as a separate and bounded self into Western society. But twelfth-century Catholicism was itself an important factor in the origins of this idea. And, in the development of U.S. social structures defined by individualism, Protestantism has been much more of a dominant factor than Roman Catholicism. Still, Roman Catholics, anxious to overcome doubts about their loyalty to the U.S., have gone out of their way to embrace U.S. culture,[2] emphasizing the congruences between the U.S. and the Roman Catholic traditions, while minimizing the differences.

Roman Catholicism's relationship to U.S. individualism and its present difficulties is similar, in my judgment, to what Max Weber saw as the relationship between the Protestant Reformation and capitalism. While founding or even assisting a new economic system was not at all what the Reformers were about, the new religious model they put forward was in fact an important factor in the development of the free enter-

---

[1] Pope Paul VI, "A Call to Action," *The Gospel of Peace and Justice*, ed. Joseph Gremillion (Maryknoll, NY: Orbis Books, 1976), para. 26, p. 498. See also, ibid., paras. 23, 35; Gremillion, pp. 496, 501.

[2] See Dorothy Dohen, *Nationalism and American Catholicism* (New York: Sheed and Ward, 1967). For an interesting discussion of the adaptation of Catholic symbols to U.S. culture, see Rev. Jerry. L. Chinnici, OFM, "The Church Is Being Challenged to Reshape," *The Catholic Voice*, October 18, 1982.

prise system. According to Weber,

> We shall . . . have to admit that the cultural consequences of the Reformation were to a great extent, perhaps in the particular aspects with which we are dealing predominantly, unforeseen and even unwished-for results of the labours of the reformers. They were often far removed from and even in contradiction to all that they themselves thought to attain.[3]

Similarly, while U.S. individualism—particularly in its problematic aspects—is "often far removed from and even in contradiction" to the Roman Catholic tradition, Roman Catholic support for it can be an "unforeseen and even unwished-for" result because of some of the ways in which the church establishes and presents its position on morality. I will argue that Roman Catholicism's approach to the moral life and to moral decision-making is of such a nature as to make it more likely for many Roman Catholics to adopt and accommodate themselves to individualism rather than to critique it and offer a constructive alternative.

Therefore, Roman Catholicism cannot absolve itself of all responsibility for the difficulties existing within the individualism of U.S. culture. One important way in which the church can exercise this responsibility is to examine critically how its approach to morality implicitly involves it in the individualism of U.S. culture and to determine how it might draw upon its tradition to present an alternative constructive vision. My purpose here is to offer some elements of that critical examination and constructive response.

More specifically, I will consider two aspects of the Roman Catholic tradition that, in my view, aid and abet some of the problems in the moral life and in moral decision-making caused by U.S. individualism. These are to be found (1) in the ways that a particular understanding of the sacrament of penance has influenced the Roman Catholic conception of morality, and (2) in the dichotomy that exists between Roman Catholic teaching on personal morality and its approach to social morality.

[3]Weber, p. 90. Emphasis added.

### The Sacrament of Penance and
### Roman Catholic Morality

Within the Roman Catholic community, the sacrament of penance or reconciliation holds great power over our understanding of morality. The parameters of morality are drawn by what we perceive to be the proper concerns of this sacrament. In other words, something is immoral because it is sinful; and it is sinful because, as an offense against God, it requires the absolution of the priest for forgiveness.

Not surprisingly, therefore, moral theology, the systematic reflection of the community on its experience of morality, has been greatly influenced by the sacrament. In fact, there was no separate study of moral theology prior to the Council of Trent in the sixteenth century. In response to the Protestant attack on the sacrament of penance, its place within the Roman Catholic Church was reaffirmed by the council. Moral theology then developed as a separate discipline to prepare priests better for hearing confessions and to offer them guidance in the administration of the sacrament. Reflection on confession or reconciliation, then, is a key element in understanding the Roman Catholic community's concept of morality.

But that immediately raises a problem. This sacrament is in a state of flux. Since the Second Vatican Council, it has been called reconciliation rather than penance or confession. Along with this shift in names, the celebration rituals have been altered and its theology has been reconceptualized. And perhaps most striking of all, Roman Catholics have not availed themselves of the sacrament in anywhere near the numbers and frequency they did prior to the council.

A strong case can be made, I believe, that we are in the midst of what Thomas S. Kuhn calls a paradigm shift. It is not just that this or that aspect of the sacrament is changing; the basic framework within which we have interpreted and celebrated it no longer appears adequate. But that shift has not been completed. We find ourselves in an "anomalous" situation.[4] Questions are being raised and contrary practices are going on that the previous way of understanding the sacrament cannot respond to; but a different, more adequate interpretation is not yet in place. In other words, we are betwixt and between, aware that we cannot go back, yet not knowing in which direction we should proceed.

In such a situation, the old and the new are mixed together in strange, even contradictory ways. As I analyze and criticize the sacrament of confession or reconciliation in this book, I will sort out various currents and evaluate them on the basis of their ability to be a critical and constructive force with regard to the problems U.S. individualism has raised.

What follows, therefore, presupposes a close connection between the Roman Catholic experience of morality and the sacrament of penance or reconciliation, and it presumes that the sacrament is presently in an anomalous situation. Through a brief tracing of the history of the sacrament, I will indicate how the Roman Catholic understanding of morality as refracted through the sacrament of penance can implicitly support rather than challenge the issues presently facing U.S. individualism.

The form of the sacrament of penance to which we are accustomed dates back officially only to the Fourth Council of the Lateran in 1215. This is not to say that the sacrament did not exist prior to that date; rather, it was at that time that the present ritual received official sanction.

In the early church, the sacrament took the form of Canonical or Public Penance. Only certain sins, judged by the community to be of especially grave import, were the subject matter of this public ritual; other sins were forgiven through personal prayer, fasting, attending the eucharist, etc., without the need for the sinner to atone publicly.

Gradually, the severity of the demands made by the sacrament increased until, by the sixth century, people would

---

[4]Thomas S. Kuhn, *The Structure of Scientific Revolutions*, 2nd ed. (Chicago: The University of Chicago Press, 1970), chapter 6. For a discussion of the relation of Kuhn's thesis to theology, see T. Howland Sanks, *Authority in the Church: A Study in Changing Paradigms* (Missoula, MT: Scholar's Press, 1974), especially pp. 103-108, 129-140.

receive it only in their later years, or even only on their death-bed. Meanwhile, in the British Isles (especially in Ireland), isolated from the Mediterranean church, another form of the sacrament was developing: private confession. This ultimately evolved into what is for us the familiar ritual of the penitent's self-accusation to the priest, the administering of a penance, and the immediate granting of absolution. It could be received any number of times, and became part of people's regular religious life.

Even though the system of private penance began as early as the fifth century, it was slow in being accepted by the church at large. In fact, as it spread from the British Isles to the continent, it remained very much in conflict with the original practice of the early church, despite the fact that the latter was little used. In 589, for example, the Third Council of Toledo denounced private penance in no uncertain terms, using such words as "detestable" and "abominable."[5] Not until 1215, at the Fourth Council of the Lateran, was it accepted as the official practice of the church.

This date is especially significant, given our earlier discussion about the twelfth-century discovery of the individual in the West which paved the way for individualism. As Colin Morris points out, the practice of private confession was closely linked with this discovery.[6] Starting in the eleventh century, penitential hymns emphasizing the need for inner penance became popular. Along with this, attention began to focus more and more on the intention behind an action. It was not sufficient simply to say that an action had been performed; the reason or motive the agent had for doing so should also be taken into account. In 1135, Abelard wrote in his *Ethics: or, Know Yourself* that moral judgments are based not on the act itself or on the will's intention but on the mind's consent.

> The doing of deeds has no bearing upon an increase of sin and nothing pollutes the soul except what is of the soul,

---

[5]Cited in Ladislas Orsy, *The Evolving Church and the Sacrament of Penance* (Denville, NJ: Dimension Books, 1978), pp. 38-39.

[6]Morris, p. 75.

that is, the consent which alone we have called sin, not the will which preceeds it nor the doing of the deed which follows.

In fact we say that an intention is good, that is right in itself, but that an action does not bear anything good in itself but proceeds from a good intention.[7]

The type of self-examination this required had a strong influence on the self-reflection and self-consciousness connected with the discovery of the bounded, separate individual. And the ruling of the Fourth Lateran Council that every member of the church over the age of discretion must receive the sacrament of penance at least once a year structured this into the rhythm of people's lives.

Not only did this serve the development of self-consciousness but it also focused the individual's attention primarily on the confines of his or her own life. For, at issue was whether or not that action was consciously and intentionally done. This can effectively narrow the scope of an individual's responsibility, excluding from it unconscious involvements

---

[7]Peter Abelard, *Peter Abelard's Ethics*, trans. D.E. Luscombe (Oxford: Clarendon Press, 1971), pp. 23, 25, 53. Le Goff brings out well the impact this emphasis on consent had on the sacrament of penance. "...[T]he important point is that guilt (*culpa*), which normally leads to damnation, can be pardoned through contrition and confession, while punishment (*poena*), or expiatory castigation, is effaced by 'satisfaction,' that is, by completing the penance ordered by the Church. If contrition and/or confession have taken place but penance has not been undertaken or completed, whether voluntarily or involuntarily (e.g., because death intervenes), the punishment (*poena*) must be completed in purgatorial fire, i.e., from the end of the century onward, in Purgatory.

"Henceforth all spiritual and moral life centered on the search for intentions, on the examination of what was voluntary and what was involuntary, on the deed committed knowingly as opposed to the deed committed out of ignorance. The notion of personal responsibility was thereby considerably expanded and enriched. The pursuit of sin became part of 'an internalization and personalization' of moral life, which called for new penitential practices. What was now sought more than internal proof was confession; what counted more than punishment was contrition. All this led to the attribution of fundamental importance to confession—confession whose nature was transformed." Jacques Le Goff, *The Birth of Purgatory*, trans. Arthur Goldhammer (Chicago: The University of Chicago Press, 1984), p. 214. While the focus on intention was a great development in morality in the twelfth century, it is a problem today, as I have indicated, because it can lead to a diminution of responsibility.

in forces for good and ill operative within society. (While this limitation on responsibility does not *ipso facto* rule out of moral court a concern for the social sphere, it can easily be interpreted that way when presented within U.S. culture when the ties between the individual and society have been loosened.)[8]

In addition to emphasizing self-reflection and the intention of the agent, the practice of private confession also bound the individual very closely to an external authority. The penitent was to confess to a priest, who, in his role as confessor, was much more than just a passive listener. The Council of Trent in the sixteenth century made this abundantly clear:

> For, when He was about to ascend from earth to heaven, our Lord Jesus Christ left priests to represent Him ... as *presiding judges* to whom all mortal sins into which the faithful of Christ would have fallen would be brought that they, in virtue of the power of the keys, might *pronounce the sentence* of remission or retention of sins.[9]

The philosopher Michel Foucault makes an interesting comment on this role of the priest:

> If one had to confess, this was not merely because the person to whom one confessed had the power to forgive, console, and direct, but because *the work of producing the truth was obliged to pass through this relationship* if it was to be scientifically validated. The truth did not reside solely in the subject who, by confessing, would reveal it wholly formed. It was constituted in two stages: present but incomplete, blind to itself in the one who spoke, it could only reach completion in the one who assimilated and recorded it. It was the latter's function to verify this obscure truth: the revelation of confession had to be cou-

[8]At the time, this emphasis on self-examination was a positive development in light of the extrinicism of the penitentials which based guilt on an evaluation of external behavior.

[9]Jesuit Fathers of St. Mary's College, *The Church Teaches* (St. Louis, MO: B. Herder Book Co., 1955), p. 309.

pled with the decipherment of what is said. The one who listened was not simply the forgiving master, the judge who condemned or acquitted; he was the *master of truth.* His was a *hermeneutic function.* With regard to the confession, his power was not only to demand it before it was made, or decide what was to follow after it, but also to constitute a discourse of truth on the basis of this decipherment.[10]

In performing this hermeneutic or interpretive task, the priest was not left to his own devices or whims. The church carefully instructed and guided him in making his judgments.[11]

Thus, two contrasting and interwoven dynamics were present in this system of private penance. There was, first of all, the penitent's self-reflection and introspection, calling attention to the need to consider the motive behind the action performed. Second, however, prominent place was given to the judgment of the confessor who set the confession of the penitent over against the impersonal demands of the church, and who made the final judgment whether the penitent was in need of forgiveness and worthy of absolution.

These contrasting and interwoven dynamics are also apparent in the development in moral thought at this time which was important to the evolution of the ritual of private penance. Of particular note here is the philosophical school called nominalism, which William of Ockham (c. 1285—1334) is credited with founding. Ockham reacted against the "realism" of scholasticism which held that universals exist independent of the mind and can be known. In other words, according to realism, we do not just recognize Bob and Carol and Ted and Alice, but are able to know the human nature common to these individuals.

For Ockham, the mind can know only individual objects. From these individual objects, the mind intuits an idea of

[10]Michel Foucault, *The History of Sexuality,* vol. 1; *An Introduction,* trans. Robert Hurley (New York: Random House, 1980), pp. 66-67. Emphasis added.

[11]See Bernard Cooke, *Ministry to Word and Sacraments* (Philadelphia: Fortress Press, 1976), p. 472.

what they have in common, and to this assigns a name. But that name in no way refers to something independent of the mind, like a human essence, for no such thing exists, only individual beings. This way of perceiving reality in turn carried over to Ockham's understanding of morality. The core of his moral thought "lies in his conception of freedom as radically indeterminate, completely self-autonomous and absolutely self-determining, with no 'outside' input into its decision-making."[12] Since only the singular is real, morality is centered on the individual with negative freedom deciding what should be done in a particular situation.

But God is no less radically free in determining the content of morality. God, in Ockham's thought, is not bound by the nature or the essence of anything in deciding what is right or wrong, moral or immoral. "God can make even blasphemy good and meritorious. He can command man to hate him and reward him for doing so."[13] In other words, something is right or wrong because God so commands; God does not command in this way because something by its very nature is right or wrong.

> Since there can be no intrinsic prior determination of morality, either in God or in the nature of things, the whole of morality becomes dependent on God's will and the whole of morality . . . lies in doing God's will. Thus obligation (i.e., the obligation of law) is made essential and central to morality.[14]

Ockham's emphasis on obligation and law deeply affected the direction of Roman Catholic moral thought. It was a factor—an important one—contributing to the church's authoritarianism in this area. Obligation was accepted as the

---

[12]Servais Pinckaers, "Ockham and the Decline of Moral Theology," *Theology Digest* 26/3 (Fall, 1978): 240.

[13]Ibid.

[14]Ibid. For a discussion on the implications of a morality of obligation, see Servais Pinckaers, *Le Renouveau de la Morale* (Tournai, Belgium: Casterman, 1964), pp. 26-31.

core of morality; moral laws were set forth by the hierarchy, then catalogued and explained in catechisms and moral manuals.[15] Certain types of action, described in isolation from the lives of particular individuals, were declared sinful and rated as to their seriousness. At the same time, individuals were directed to examine their conscience as to whether they had committed any of these actions and with what interior motivation. But even these decisions and judgments on the morality of the act and the quality of the interior motivation had to be submitted for final review to the authoritative interpretation of the priest who functioned in effect as an external observer. Thus, the interplay once again of internal self-awareness on the one hand and external judgment and authority on the other.

Consider the impact of such an approach on the sacrament of penance and on moral decision-making in the context of U.S. individualism. As noted earlier, when the individual-society tie is loosened, this individualism can lead us to limit our attention to our personal world. And while freedom is a primary defining characteristic of us as individuals—freedom from external force and especially from the external, arbitrary will of the government—we are very much subject to the faceless and impersonal power of the majority opinion. Each of us falls under the eye of the impartial spectator who judges the appropriateness of our action.

Such a context can in turn have a strong impact on how the Roman Catholic tradition is interpreted. Those aspects of Roman Catholic morality (particularly as mediated through the more traditional aspects of the sacrament of penance) that are congruent with the individualism of U.S. culture stand out. Again, I want to emphasize that the sacrament of penance as it has been more traditionally understood and celebrated is not itself individualistic. But it contains elements that, when

[15]"Freedom and law, practical reason (what later moralists will call "conscience"), free acts or cases of conscience (casuistry), and, at the center, obligation—these are the constitutive atoms of the nominalist system. We readily see the principal traits that will form the later moral manuals. Only the emphasis on sin is missing. But subsequent to Trent, this too will come to the fore." Pinckaers, "Ockham and the Decline of Moral Theology," p. 241.

experienced within an individualistic culture, make it seem to be so. And these elements are to the fore of people's awareness precisely because they fit in so easily with culture's main currents. Thus, Roman Catholicism can seem to go along naturally with the morality of U.S. individualism, and vice versa. As a result, Roman Catholicism ends up implicitly legitimating a system which, in fact, it strongly questions.

This close fit between Roman Catholicism and individualism is being challenged by some of the changes resulting from the reform of the sacrament of reconciliation. Moving the celebration of the sacrament outside the confessional box into a reconciliation room where priest and penitent talk face-to-face is an important advance; so too is the identification of the priest as *celebrant* of the sacrament. Both can undercut, or at least diminish, the perception of the priest as judge, as impartial external observer. But much more needs to be done to develop conceptually and implement a definition of the priest's role as other than that of judge. Until we do so, that perception of the confessor will continue to hover in the background.

A further challenge to the connection between Roman Catholicism and individualism is the introduction of the communal celebration of penance with general absolution. This offers an important opportunity for bringing out the social nature of sin as well as the communal aspects of forgiveness. Unfortunately, however, this social dimension can be easily lost to sight, since this manner of celebrating reconciliation takes place only in accidental circumstances (that is, when there are not enough priests to hear individual confessions). As such, it tends to be seen as an addendum to private confession rather than as a significantly different form of celebration.

Nominalism has also opened Roman Catholicism to an individualistic interpretation by making the obligation of law the center of morality. Laws can spell out better what must be avoided than what must be done. When we examine our conscience from such a negative standard—"did I do anything wrong?"—expectations of ourselves are greatly reduced. We can be satisfied that we are good because we have done no wrong. Or, to make it more specific, we can say we have been loving people so long as we have not hated anyone. That is minimalistic.

The promotion of the Ten Commandments as the framework for the examination of conscience has fostered this minimalism. Such a framework marks out the forbidden territory and asks us whether or not we have strayed into it by word or deed. But replacing the Commandments with the Beatitudes leads to dramatically different results. It is one thing to be faced with the question: Did you have "bad thoughts" and did you "take pleasure" in them? It is quite another to be challenged with: "Did you hunger and thirst after justice?" To the first question we can answer a straightforward "yes" or "no." But the second allows for no such simple response; and even after a tentative affirmative answer is given, we are called upon to stretch ourselves further.

The minimalistic approach to morality generated by nominalism fits in well with, and even promotes, some of the negative effects of individualism. As noted earlier, individualism leaves us with an empty self. Assigning the self only rights, negative freedom and wants, it leaves the individual with no substance. The effect of nominalism on Roman Catholic morality does nothing directly to offset this; in fact, it can support it. Particularly is this true if moral laws are understood as based merely in the fiat of the authority promulgating them and not in what is demanded of us by our very nature. After we have questioned our consciences about the Ten Commandments, what do we know about ourselves? To be sure, we have determined whether or not we are rule-breakers. But even if we are, what difference does it make? What does that say about the substance of our personhood? Not much, it would seem, especially when, as popularly understood, we only have to go to confession to have things set right. The effects of our disobeying one of the Commandments cannot sink too far into the substance of our being if they can be removed so quickly.

Here again, intimations of something different arise in the reform of the sacrament of reconciliation. In our examination of conscience and confession, at times we are encouraged to look more broadly at our lives. In taking stock of what we have done and who we are, the Beatitudes are set before us;

and we are reminded of the demands of social justice. All of this offsets the minimalism of the past. But that past has not totally receded. It hangs on in lingering doubts and guilt feelings, in an emotional sense that the Ten Commandments, especially the sixth and the ninth, are still the bottom line. In other words, in the "anomalous" situation in which we find ourselves, the traditional still retains a great deal of its power.

### Personal and Social Morality in Roman Catholicism

A second area where the policy and practice of Roman Catholicism can fit in well with the individualism of the United States and can end up, albeit unconsciously, supporting and legitimating its problems is the dichotomy between the Roman Catholic teaching on social justice and its teaching on personal morality.[16]

The nature of this dichotomy can be seen by comparing the *Declaration on Certain Questions Concerning Sexual Ethics* issued by the Vatican in 1976 with Pope Paul VI's apostolic letter, *A Call to Action*, written in 1971 on the occasion of the 80th anniversary of Pope Leo XIII's great social encyclical *Rerum Novarum*.[17]

The 1976 document on sexual ethics, after noting the power of the human reason to grasp "immutable laws in-

---

[16]On the nature and implications of the division between personal and social morality within the Roman Catholic church, see Paul J. Surlis, "The Moral Theologian as Analyst," *Proceedings of the Catholic Theological Society of America* (Bronx, NY: Catholic Theological Society of America, 1981), pp. 148-154. See also, Kenneth R. Overberg, *An Inconsistent Ethics?* (Lanham, MD: University Press of America, 1980). During the 1980 synod on the family, a group of French bishops made the following statement: "On the theoretical level, it would be necessary to overcome the dichotomy between the rigidity of the law and pastoral flexibility following analogically the manner of formulation of the Church's social doctrine, without linking too intrinsically the question of means to the promotion of fundamental values, and using prudence in making moral judgment on the means." Quoted in *The Catholic Review*, October 17, 1980.

[17]My primary concern here is not to critique these particular documents but to use them to bring out the dissonance in the Roman Catholic approach to personal and social morality.

scribed in the constitutive elements of human nature"[18] and the right of the church to interpret officially these laws, makes the following statement:

> ... masturbation is an intrinsically and seriously disordered act.
>
> The main reason is that, whatever the motive for acting in this way, the deliberate use of the sexual faculty outside normal conjugal relations essentially contradicts the finality of the faculty.[19]

The document then goes on in a pastoral vein to say that, while the incidence of masturbation remains objectively an intrinsically disordered act, subjectively there can be excusing reasons for not judging it a serious fault. And it concludes by counselling those measures against masturbation "which Christian asceticism from its long experience recommends for overcoming the passions and progressing in virtue."[20]

Pope Paul VI's 1971 apostolic letter on social justice takes a different tack. It too establishes principles on the basis of human experience rather than scripture. But rather than seeking these principles in the functions and purposes of a particular part of the body as was the case in the document on sexual ethics (viz., the genital organs), the apostolic letter looks to the total person and to the "aspirations" of the person.

> While scientific and technological progress continues to overturn man's surroundings, his patterns of knowledge, work, consumption and relationships, *two aspirations* persistently make themselves felt in these new contexts, and they grow stronger to the extent that he becomes better

[18]Sacred Congregation for the Doctrine of the Faith, "Declaration on Certain Questions Concerning Sexual Ethics." *Love and Sexuality*, ed. Odile M. Liebard (Wilmington, NC: McGrath Publishing Company, 1978), sec. 4, p. 432. Hereafter referred to as "Declaration on Sexual Ethics."

[19]Ibid., sec. 9; Liebard, p. 436

[20]Ibid., sec. 9; Liebard, p. 437.

informed and better educated: the aspiration to *equality* and the aspiration to *participation*, two forms of man's dignity and freedom.[21]

Having established these principles, however, the pope does not see it within his competence to provide solutions to the plurality of problems besetting humankind throughout the world.

> In the face of such widely varying situations it is difficult for us to utter a unified message and to put forward a solution which has universal validity. Such is not our ambition, nor is it our mission. It is up to the Christian communities to analyze with objectivity the situation which is proper to their country, to shed on it the light of the Gospel's unalterable words and to draw principles of reflection, norms of judgment and directives for action from the social teaching of the Church.... It is up to these Christian communities, with the help of the Holy Spirit, in communion with the bishops who hold responsibility and in dialogue with other Christian brethren and all men of good will, to discern the options and commitments which are called for in order to bring about the social, political and economic changes seen in many cases to be urgently needed.[22]

[21]Paul VI, "A Call to Action," para. 22; Gremillion, p. 496. Emphasis added.

[22]Ibid., para. 4; Gremillion, p. 487. This is the approach taken in the U.S. Roman Catholic bishops' pastoral letters on war and peace and on the U.S. economy. In both instances, they set forth the general principles that underlie the Roman Catholic stance, then they apply these on the basis of prudential judgments. In so doing, the bishops leave open the possibility of discussion and debate both within the church and between the church and civil society. In the pastoral on war and peace, the bishops state: "In this pastoral letter, too, we address many concrete questions concerning the arms race, contemporary warfare, weapons systems, and negotiating strategies. We do not intend that our treatment of each of these issues carry the same moral authority as our statement of universal moral principles and formal Church teaching. Indeed, we stress here at the beginning that not every statement in this letter has the same moral authority. At times we reassert universally binding moral principles (e.g., noncombatant immunity and proportionality). At still other times we reaffirm statements of recent popes and the teaching of Vatican II. Again, at other times we apply moral principles to specific cases.

The pope concludes by noting that, after this consultation by the local church has been completed, it may well happen—and not inappropriately so—that people will arrive at different conclusions and see themselves called to different commitments. In other words, there is the distinct possibility for true pluralism in the church.[23]

Significant differences are apparent here. While in both documents there is a recognition of the power of human reason to get insight into human flourishing and to establish principles for the attainment of that goal, the powers of human reason are perceived as dramatically greater in matters of personal ethics than in questions of social justice. The principles that guide a Roman Catholic's attitude toward masturbation are clear and concise: they are immutable, unconditioned by culture and history, and immediately applicable to the concrete situation in which the decision is made. The principles which guide the Roman Catholic conscience in analyzing and deciding about social issues, however, have only become apparent with the social changes caused by technological development. These principles tend to be more general in nature; they are to be applied only after a joint effort of Christians and all people of good will to discern the signs of the times; their application is affected by the specifics of history and culture.

As a result, matters which fall under the umbrella of personal morality are removed from any substantial relation to society. The fact that individuals live within a certain time-

---

"When making applications of these principles we realize—and we wish readers to recognize—that prudential judgments are involved based on specific circumstances which can change or which can be interpreted differently by people of good will (e.g., the threat of 'no first use'). However, the moral judgments that we make in specific cases, while not binding in conscience, are to be given serious attention and consideration by Catholics as they determine whether their moral judgments are consistent with the Gospel." National Conference of Catholic Bishops, *The Challenge of Peace: God's Promise and Our Response* (Washington DC: United States Catholic Conference, 1983), para. 10, page 5. See also, National Conference of Catholic Bishops, "Economic Justice for All: Catholic Social Teaching and the U.S. Economy," *Origins* 16/24 (November 27, 1986): 426.

[23]Paul VI, "A Call to Action," para. 50; Gremillion, pp. 510-511. See also, *The Challenge of Peace*, p. 3.

and locality-frame has implications for the way they will dispose of property and be involved in political structures, but not for the way they will understand and live out their sexuality. This drives a sizable wedge between the personal and social dimensions of life.

A dichotomy is also evident in the theological framework within which these two dimensions of morality are discussed. Philip S. Land[24] notes a definite development in Roman Catholic social thought under Pope Paul VI. While *Ecclesiam Suam*, his 1964 encyclical on the relation of the church to the world, "smacked heavily of 'salvation dialogue,' which suggested a certain otherworldliness," *A Call to Action* emphasized the structural foundations for exploitation and underdevelopment and the need for political involvement to establish justice. The this-worldly aspect of life and the sociopolitical dimension of this world are in the foreground.

Personal morality, however, divorced as it is from the social aspects of existence, seems to fall (if not explicitly, at least by default) under the aegis of the otherworldly. For, while the Vatican declaration on sexual ethics indicates concern for the social consequences of the present corruption of morals, there is no invitation for Roman Catholics to join with others to seek a solution. Indeed, the Vatican declaration on sexuality states that "whatever the force of certain arguments of a biological and philosophical nature, which have sometimes been used by theologians, in fact both the Magisterium of the Church—in the course of a constant tradition—and the moral sense of the faithful have declared without hesitation that masturbation is an intrinsically and seriously disordered act."[25] Solutions are to be found in the immutable values inherent in human nature which are discovered by reason and authenticated by the church. Nor is there any clear indication how the stance toward masturbation, for example, is to help rebuild society—much less how it is to be a salvific force in the world, contributing to the establishment of God's Reign of peace and justice on earth.

---

[24]Philip Land, "The Social Theology of Pope Paul VI," *America* 140 (May 12, 1979): 392-394.

[25]"Declaration on Sexual Ethics," sec. 9; Liebard, p. 436.

This dualism in the Roman Catholic perspective on morality opens the door to the possibility of some unwelcome consequences. Issues of social justice by their nature tend to intimidate: problems are often of such enormity and complexity that possible solutions extend beyond our abilities as individuals and involve a time frame that exceeds our individual lifespan. They can only be addressed through the combined wisdom and efforts of a group. The manner in which the Roman Catholic church addresses issues of social justice acknowledges this. The approach taken to matters of personal morality, however, simply places the burden on, and leaves it with, the individual. And if the latter approach represents the way in which people are accustomed to think about and deal with morality, questions of social justice will necessarily appear foreign and foreboding—too much so to be given serious consideration. Or questions of social justice may appear as totally outside the parameters of morality.

A further possible consequence is that people can be lulled into an authoritarianism and a legalism in matters of personal morality. The way in which the church speaks about an issue in the area of sexuality, for example, contrasts sharply with the way it addresses problems in the economic sphere. The difference might be termed one of command-language versus principle-language. Specific, concrete commands or laws are laid down to direct our sexual behavior; but in economic or political or legal matters, more general guidelines or principles are offered to help us reach concrete decisions. As a result, we are called upon to take a more active, a more substantive role in matters of social justice; but on issues of personal morality, we are more the passive recipients of specific moral directives.

As Paolo Freire has pointed out, however, the more people are rendered passive while being taught, the more apt they are to be passive in relation to the world in which they live.[26]

---

[26]"It is not surprising that the banking concept of education regards men as adaptable, manageable beings. The more students work at storing the deposits entrusted to them, the less they develop the critical consciousness which would result from their intervention in the world as transformers of that world. The more completely they accept the passive role imposed on them, the more they tend simply

Does not the same hold true for the church? If we are kept passive within the church because of an authoritarian approach to personal morality, how are we suddenly to become active and creative when dealing with the problems of the world?

Whether or not these negative possibilities are, in fact, actualized is conditioned by the situation in which the teachings of the church are communicated. Communication is dialogical; it requires both a speaker and a listener. What actually is communicated depends upon the nature of the message transmitted; but it is equally affected by the mindset of the listener. In the case at hand, the mindset of the American audience is determined by the problems connected with U.S. individualism spoken of earlier. The loosening of the ties of the individual to society can easily result in church statements on personal morality being taken with utmost seriousness while pronouncements on social justice are seen as optional or even irrelevant. Furthermore, the conformism and authoritarianism arising in U.S. individualism easily tunes our ear to the authoritarian and legalistic elements in official Roman Catholic morality, thus further underscoring personal over social moral concerns.

The effect of this American way of hearing was apparent in the selective attention paid to the speeches of Pope John Paul II when he journeyed to the United States in October 1979. What was it that captured people's attention, Roman Catholics and non-Roman Catholics alike? Birth control, abortion, the role of women in ministry in the church received all the headlines and more than likely continue to be foremost in people's memory. But in his homily during the Mass at Yankee Stadium, the Pope said:

> We must find a simple way of living. For it is not right
> that the standard of living of the rich countries should

to adapt to the world as it is and to the fragmented view of reality deposited in them.

"The capability of banking education to minimize or annul the students' creative power and to stimulate their credulity serves the interests of the oppressors, who care neither to have the world revealed nor to see it transformed." Paulo Freire, *Pedagogy of the Oppressed* (New York: Herder and Herder, 1970), p. 60.

seek to maintain itself by draining off a great part of the reserves of energy and raw materials that are meant to serve the whole of humanity. For readiness to create a greater and more equitable solidarity between peoples is the first condition of peace.[27]

That seemed to make little impression.

This same attitude has also become apparent in the reaction of more than a few Roman Catholics to the pastoral on war and peace and the pastoral on the U.S. economy by the U.S. bishops. They see these statements as an unwarranted and illegitimate intrusion of religion and morality into the public arena. Religion and morality should be restricted to concern for the personal spiritual welfare of individuals.

The result, I believe, is that the Roman Catholic Church can easily become its own worst enemy. Because of the dichotomy in its approach to morality, it can end up implicitly fitting into and supporting U.S. individualism and the problems it presently faces in spite of the fact that its tradition runs in a very different direction.

This sets the agenda for the Roman Catholic church in the United States. If we are to take up Pope Paul VI's challenge of addressing responsibly the problems that beset us as a nation, part of the solution has to include a way of speaking about morality that does not compromise and misdirect our efforts. We have to find an approach to morality that strengthens the ties between the individual and society, thereby responding critically and constructively to the problems raised by U.S. individualism.

This book represents an attempt on my part to contribute to that project. Specifically, I am addressing the moral life and moral decision-making, seeking to show that there is a social dimension to all aspects of these, even those aspects that appear to be only personal and private in nature. By emphasizing solidarity and participation rather than the individual and freedom, I am by no means introducing some-

---

[27]Pope John Paul II, "Special Sensitivity Toward Those in Distress," *Origins* 9/19 (October 25, 1979): 311.

thing totally alien to the experience of people in the United States. The goal is to find a way of defining the individual that emphasizes the belongingness rather than the separateness of the person.

I am addressing the problem of U.S. individualism within the context of a discussion of the fundamental dimensions of the moral life and moral decision-making because I believe this is the best way to get at the roots of the difficulty. We can continue to issue proclamations, establish diocesan and parish Justice and Peace commissions, teach, give congressional testimony, declare how important matters of social justice are all we want. But until we get at the root cause of our selective hearing that either makes us in the U.S. deaf to such matters or else leads us to interpret these matters as being only secondary and optional, the social dimension of morality will remain at the periphery rather than at the core of Roman Catholic existence.

# PART TWO:

## The Goal of Morality

# 4

# Virtue: The Goal of Morality

The point of departure of this book—the point where we discovered the cause of the aching feet—is U.S. individualism as discussed in part one. Part two might well be termed the point of arrival. Its purpose is to set forth the goal of the moral life and of moral decision-making. The reason for talking about what is actually the conclusion of this book at this time is that it provides a natural and needed bridge to what follows. The goal of the moral life and of moral decision-making takes its specificity from the particular problems to which it is responding. But only as we are clear about the goal can we establish the means to achieve it.

Thus this section, which includes both a positive (virtue) and negative (sin) discussion of the goal, sets the stage for the remainder of the book which lays out the tools for addressing the moral life and moral decision-making in response to the problems raised by U.S. individualism. In particular, we are concerned here to strengthen the relation of the individual to society and to establish a more substantive self.

In establishing the nature of this goal, three major questions present themselves: (1) Is the goal primarily negative or positive; i.e., are we mainly concerned about what is to be avoided or about what is to be done? (2) Is the goal primarily single-act-oriented or character-oriented; i.e., is our principal focus on the specific actions we perform or on the overall pattern of our life?[1] (3) Is the goal primarily personal (in the

---

[1]This is sometimes described as a choice of being over doing. I am uncomfortable

sense of private) or social; i.e., to what degree, if any, should the social dimension of morality figure into our moral life and moral decision-making?

The basis of these questions is, of course, the problems individualism raises for morality at the present time and the ways Roman Catholic thought and practice can contribute to these problems. Individualism, insofar as it is limited to emphasizing individual rights, concern for justice, and pursuit of self-interest, leaves the self empty. The tendency toward minimalism in some aspects of Roman Catholic thought, as influenced by nominalism, not only fails to challenge this emptiness, it can support it by leading to the same result. Thus the goal of morality is best conceived in positive terms.

In considering whether the focus should be on discrete actions or on our overall life pattern, we must keep in mind the "dis-integrative" effect of individualism. Concerned to leave the self at liberty to choose among whatever options present themselves, and influenced by the methodology of modern science, individualism leads us to look at our lives in separate, discrete phases. If we fail to consider the continuities in our history, we can lose our overall identity; focusing solely on particular options immediately present before us, we forget how much we are influenced by the patterns of our past life and of our society. Roman Catholic thought on morality, as affected by nominalism, has likewise emphasized individual actions rather than overall patterns. Examination of conscience has tended to concentrate on isolated pieces of behavior, thus promoting the same effects as individualism. Therefore, a character-oriented, rather than a single-act-oriented morality will be advanced here.

Finally, not only should the goal of the moral life and of moral decision-making be positive rather than negative and character-rather than single-act-oriented, it should also attend primarily to the social, but without losing sight of the personal dimensions of life. As noted in part one, U.S. individualism has loosened the ties between the individual

---

with that description because it can leave the impression that our transaction with the environment is a secondary factor in our lives and that our identity is established somehow prior to our action rather than through it.

and society. This has been supported by the Roman Catholic Church's strong emphasis on personal morality. Such an emphasis implicitly gives the message that the personal sphere of life requires our constant attention, but that the social sphere is less important and more optional—that it can pretty much get by on its own. In point of fact, however, the social good has not taken care of itself. And so, in setting a goal for the moral life and for moral decision-making appropriate for the age and culture in which we live, it is essential that the social dimensions of morality and the demands of social justice be made explicit and brought to the fore.

Roman Catholicism has also implicitly supported loosening the individual-society connection by its own differences of methodology and emphasis in discussing personal and social morality. Therefore, not only must the social dimensions of morality be highlighted, but this must be done in a way that brings out the essential connections between the personal and the social.

These three dimensions of the moral life and of moral decision-making—that they be positive, that they address the totality of the person and not be limited to abstractions of individual actions, and that they make explicit the social dimension of morality and its connection with the personal—are best responded to, in my judgment, by a virtue ethic, that is, by a theory of ethics which sets virtue as the goal of the moral life and of moral decision-making. The task now is to spell out what that means.

## Problems of a Virtue Ethic

Defining virtue is no simple matter. Not only are there different interpretations of virtue, some of which contradict one another, but serious questions also have been raised about the very possibility of considering morality from a virtue perspective.

To begin, what does it mean to talk about virtue as the goal of the moral life and of moral decision-making? Would it not be better to say that virtue is a means toward something else? If virtue is the goal, do we end up acting to uphold our virtue? But that can lead to a pretentiousness and self-right-eousness that is overbearing; and besides, it keeps our attention on the self rather than on the relation of the individual to society.

Viewing virtue as a means rather than a goal helps answer these problems; but it raises others. If virtue is simply a means, so too is the self. For virtue, I shall argue, really means character; it is who we are, not something we have. Thus, to make virtue a means is to assign the self merely instrumental value.

Making virtue the goal of morality highlights the fundamental unity between the person and his or her actions. As Dewey points out,

> Selfhood or character is thus not a *mere* means, an external instrument, of attaining certain ends. It *is* an agency of accomplishing consequences, as is shown in the pains which the athlete, the lawyer, the merchant, takes to build up certain habits in himself, because he knows they are the causal conditions for reaching the ends in which he is interested. But the self is more than an external causal agent. *The attainment of consequences reacts to form the self.*[2]

This unity of self and action is likewise a unity of self and world: because of who we are, we affect the world in a certain way; and because of what the world becomes, it affects who we are. And so virtue is not a private matter.

To make virtue the goal of morality, then, is to highlight the primary importance of the interaction between the self and its environment, and to call for a certain quality to that interaction. (What exactly that quality is will be discussed later in this chapter.) As such, virtue is the goal of morality, not as the immediate purpose of our actions but as their effect. In that, it is like happiness. The more we seek happiness directly, the more it eludes us. But if we go about our

---

[2]John Dewey, *Theory of the Moral Life* (New York: Holt, Rinehart and Winston, 1960), pp. 149-150. Emphasis added in the last sentence.

lives in the best manner we can, happiness is usually present to us. According to Dewey, happiness "is *not directly an end of desire and effort*, in the sense of an end-in-view purposely sought for, but is *rather an end-product*, a necessary accompaniment, of the character which is interested in objects that are enduring and intrinsically related to an outgoing and expansive nature."[3] We are concerned about our virtue or character, then, not as an end in itself but because of its import for who we are and so for how we interact with the environment. And because of this import, virtue has a fundamental moral significance.[4]

Second, virtue raises theological questions. Protestants, for example, have serious doubts about using the language of virtue to speak about morality. For them, it smacks of Pelagianism, that is, of the attempt by human beings to save themselves through their own efforts. Frederick S. Carney speaks about an "acquiremental view of virtue" in which "one 'justifies' himself through the diligent performance of a great number of compartmentalized 'good works.'"[5] This view, according to Carney, was evident in Catholicism at the time of the Reformation and, interestingly, in eighteenth-century Protestantism.

Rather than dismiss a virtue ethic completely, however, Carney also points to a "relational theory" of virtue which, he says, is implied in Luther's doctrine of justification by faith. According to this theory, "man's virtue is understood to be a product not of his own achievement, but of his acceptance in faith of the justifying relation God freely offers him, and of his consequent acceptance in love of a servant relation with his fellow man."[6]

This relational theory of virtue is by no means foreign to Roman Catholicism, although it is interpreted differently.

[3]Ibid., p. 46. Emphasis added.

[4]See Stanley Hauerwas, *Vision and Virtue* (Notre Dame, IN.: Fides Publishers, 1974), p. 67.

[5]Frederick S. Carney, "Deciding in the Situation: What is Required?" in *Norm and Context in Christian Ethics*, eds. Gene Outka and Paul Ramsey (New York: Charles Scribner's Sons, 1968), p. 14.

[6]Ibid.

Aquinas, for whom virtue was the center of ethics, did not see the moral life as a series of separate, compartmentalized actions performed by the individual for his or her self-justification. Rather, he set forth an ethic of virtue concerned not with actions performed repeatedly, but with "virtues and vices and other like habits, which are the principles of human acts."[7] The moral or cardinal virtues require human effort, and human effort is an important factor in their development. But they must be directed toward our last end, which is God; and, for that, we stand totally in need of God. ". . .[V]irtue which directs man to good as defined by the Divine Law, and not by reason, cannot be caused by human acts, the principle of which is reason, but is produced in us by the Divine operation alone."[8] We cannot attain God on our own; but we at the same time cannot remain passive.

At present, a virtue ethic is receiving much more attention from Protestant than Catholic theologians.[9] Catholic theologians, however, are working to overcome a "compartmentalized" morality, although they are doing so more under the rubric of fundamental option[10] than of virtue. And they are

---

[7]Saint Thomas Aquinas, *Summa Theologica*, trans. Fathers of the English Dominican Province (New York: Benziger Brothers, 1948), I-II, 49.

[8]Ibid., I-II, 63, a.2.

[9]See John W. Crossin, O.S.F.S., *What Are They Saying About Virtue?* (New York: Paulist Press, 1985). For a discussion of virtue from a Roman Catholic perspective, see Joseph Pieper, *The Four Cardinal Virtues* (Notre Dame, IN.: University of Notre Dame Press, 1966); Paul J. Philibert, O.P., "Lawrence Kohlberg's Use of Virtue in His Theory of Moral Development," *International Philosophical Quarterly* 15 (December 1975): 455-479; idem, "Conscience: Developmental Perspectives From Rogers and Kohlberg," *Horizons* 6/1 (1979): 1-25.

[10]The theory of fundamental option or fundamental orientation holds that our actions are not separate, isolated events without a significant effect on our person. They follow from our fundamental orientation, and, in turn, are formative of that orientation. Curran explains it this way: "According to the Thomistic teaching there are many particular individual choices that a man makes. Some choices, for example, choice of a vocation, are more basic than others. The more fundamental choices guide and direct other individual choices. Ultimately, there are only two possible fundamental options—the love of God or the love of a creature, which in the last analysis is self. Man either chooses God as his ultimate end and directs all his activity toward God, or he chooses self and directs all his activity toward self. A particular individual action has meaning insofar as it makes incarnate and intensifies the fundamental option." Charles E. Curran, *A New Look at Christian Morality* (Notre Dame, IN: Fides Publishers, Inc., 1970), p. 204. See also, John W. Glaser,

addressing the issue of self-justification by reintegrating the discussion of morality into the broader theological enterprise.[11] Thus, rather than being solely the result of human effort, the moral life is first and foremost grounded in the redeeming power of God as revealed through the life, death, and resurrection of Christ. This power guides our life, providing a vision through which we interpret our world. It is in thankful response to the great gift of redemption that we seek to fashion our lives and our world in accordance with the "image and likeness" in which we were created.

## Defining Virtue

What, then, is virtue? In looking for a definition, we move from the general to the particular, marking out the boundaries of the area we will search, then zeroing in on the subject of our investigation. The boundaries are set by three concerns.

(1) Lawrence Kohlberg, widely known for his work in the theory of moral development, alerts us to the problems of what he terms the "bag of virtues approach." According to Kohlberg, the discussion of virtues usually involves a list of positive personality traits that are drawn up by one group and then foisted off on someone else.

> The objection of the psychologist to the bag of virtues is that there are no such things. Virtues and vices are labels by which people award praise or blame to others, but the ways people use praise and blame toward others are not

---

S.J., "Transition Between Grace and Sin: Fresh Perspectives," *Theological Studies* 20/2 (June 1968): 260-274; O'Connell, chapter 6. For a critique of O'Connell's position, see Stanley Hauerwas, *The Peaceable Kingdom* (Notre Dame, IN.: University of Notre Dame Press, 1983), pp. 40-44. For a statement of the official Vatican position on fundamental option, see "Declaration on Sexual Ethics," sec. 10; Liebard, pp. 437-438.

[11] See Franz Böckle, *Law and Conscience*, trans. M. James Donnelly (New York: Sheed and Ward, 1966), pp. 21-49.

the ways in which they think when making moral decisions themselves.[12]

The "bag of virtues approach" to morality results in moral education becoming indoctrination, and this, in turn, undermines the ability and the willingness of the individual to take a responsible place within society.[13]

While moral indoctrination and its effects are indeed unacceptable, even more problematic is the disjointed picture the "bag of virtues approach" presents of what it means to be human. An individual is encouraged to incorporate a particular virtue in one aspect of life, to realize another virtue in a second aspect, to bring a third aspect under the control of a third virtue. How these virtues interrelate—if, in fact, they do—is not considered. But one of the primary difficulties U.S. individualism presents is the need to account and provide direction for the unity and integrity of the self.

(2) While the focus in defining and describing virtue is on the unity and integrity of the individual, this must not lead us to isolate the individual from the world within which he or she exists. If we do so, we may address the issue of the substance of the self raised by U.S. individualism, but we have not strengthened the individual's ties with society. We could end up with a sort of "moral invisible hand," presuming that as long as the individual is tending well his or her own bailiwick, the world itself is automatically getting better. We have no proof this will actually happen; in fact, we have much historical evidence to the contrary. We must, therefore, make explicit the nature of the ties and interactions that will lead to the development both of the self and of the world.[14]

(3) On the other side of the coin, just as we cannot presume that the world will automatically benefit from personal de-

---

[12]Lawrence Kohlberg, *The Philosophy of Moral Development*, vol. 1, *Essays on Moral Development* (San Francisco: Harper and Row, 1981), p. 34.

[13]Ibid., pp. 31-33.

[14]Character is "the personal achievement of a stable and fruitful relationship with one's natural and social environment." Robert Johann, *Building the Human* (New York: Herder and Herder, 1968), p. 144.

velopment, so too we cannot take it for granted that concern for others and for society is all that is needed to make the individual flourish. Kohlberg's theory brings this out well. While Kohlberg argues against a "bag of virtues approach," he does not want to throw out virtue completely. But he limits the goal of the moral life to a single virtue: justice.

> A moral obligation is an obligation to respect the right or claim of another person. A moral principle is a principle for resolving competing claims: you versus me, you versus a third person. There is only one principled basis for resolving claims: justice or equality. Treat every person's claim impartially regardless of the person. A moral principle is not only a rule of action but a reason for action. As a reason for action, justice is called *respect for* people.
>
> Because morally mature people are governed by the principle of justice rather than by a set of rules, there are not many moral virtues, but one.[15]

To see morality as primarily a matter of resolving competing claims and justice as the only virtue is to continue the problems raised by individualism, not solve them. It does nothing to strengthen the individual-society ties and it leaves the individual empty. An adequate understanding of virtue has to relate the individual to society in a way that indeed honors the individual's responsibility to society but that does it in a way that also gives substance to the individual's life.

(4) Finally, the discussion of virtue cannot remain at the level of abstraction. It should set forth a vision of self and world that addresses the problems of the times. Thus, in establishing a virtue ethic, it is necessary to make clear what virtue specifically and concretely means in terms of the nature of the times. In this instance, we have to look for an understanding of virtue that responds to the problems raised by U.S. individualism.

Within these boundaries, we can develop a definition (or better, a description) of virtue. First of all, in seeking to

---

[15]Kohlberg, pp. 39-40.

maintain the integrity and unity of the person, we do well to follow Stanley Hauerwas and speak about *character* rather than virtue because it carries less problematic connotations. He distinguishes between the term "character traits" which evokes a discussion about distinctive features or qualities of a person's life, and "having character" which "indicates a more inclusive and unitary concept."[16] It is character used in the latter sense that best typifies the notion of virtue we are after here—a fundamental qualification and formation of who we are as person.[17]

Speaking about virtue as character, however, does not mean that virtues are dispositions to act in particular ways. As Gilbert Meilander points out, "Virtues offer no preconceived blueprint for human life."[18] They are more in the nature of "skills which suit us for life generally, not just for some particular activity."[19] But these skills are not just techniques. They are like the skills which separate the true artist from the one who paints-by-number: skill understood not as teaching us how to do certain things but as empowering us as a person. Virtue as character, then, refers to the integrity and empowerment of who we are.

Second, the form and development of this virtue-as-character has to take into account the interconnection between self and society. Erik Erikson brings this out well. Defining virtue as the *"inherent strength or active quality"*[20] of the human ego, he places the development of such strength within a broad social context. "For man's psychosocial survival is safeguarded only by vital virtues which *develop in the interplay of successive and overlapping generations, living together in organized settings."*[21]

---

[16]Hauerwas, *Vision and Virtue*, p. 55.

[17]As such, there is no bag of virtues any more than we are just a bag of bones. The best of Roman Catholic thought has traditionally moved in this direction.

[18]Gilbert C. Meilander, *The Theory and Practice of Virtue* (Notre Dame, IN: University of Notre Dame Press, 1984), p. 8.

[19]Ibid.

[20]Erik Erikson, *Insight and Responsibility* (New York: W. W. Norton and Company, Inc., 1964), p. 113. Emphasis in original. See also, Alasdair MacIntyre, *After Virtue* (Notre Dame, IN: University of Notre Dame Press, 1981).

[21]Erikson, p. 114. Emphasis added.

Not only do they develop within society, but they are meant to redound to the benefit of society also. They strengthen the self; and through that strengthening as well as through the particular ways they unify the self, they also build up society. In making virtue the center of the moral life and of moral decision-making, then, we have to describe those qualities of character that integrate and empower the self in a way that contributes to the good of the world.

Finally, the description of those qualities must be historically specific, addressing and offering a constructive alternative to the problems that U.S. individualism causes. John Dewey is helpful here. Virtue is a focal point of his theory of ethics; and his discussion of ethics in general and of virtue in particular is shaped by an abiding interest in overcoming the destructiveness of individualism.[22]

In describing virtue, Dewey relies on the classical theory of what are known as the cardinal virtues. These, he argues, refer not to particular forms of behavior a person should pursue but to those qualities that should characterize every aspect of the life of a society and of an individual. And, while Dewey does not make this explicit in his discussion, the particular slant he takes on each of the cardinal virtues is dictated by the desire to find an alternative to individualism. As such, Dewey is an especially important resource here.

Following his guidance, we concretize the description of virtue by considering the four cardinal virtues—temperance, justice, fortitude and prudence; then, to make explicit the christian foundations of what we are about, we will conclude with a discussion of the three theological virtues—faith, hope, and charity—showing how they are the grounding for a vision of the self and society that can liberate and redeem us from the problems caused by U.S. individualism.

---

[22]See Thomas F. Schindler, "John Dewey on Individualism: Toward an American Religious Socialism," (Ph.D. dissertation, The University of Chicago, 1978).

## The Cardinal Virtues

### Temperance

U.S. individualism, as we have seen, has loosened the ties of the individual to society, leaving the self isolated; and because the self, as defined by individualism, lacks adequate substance, the individual is unable to recover and restore the needed connections. Virtue, then, if it is to be a contributing factor in liberation and redemption, must bring *substance* and *wholeness* to the person and to society at large. Temperance is the dimension of character or the quality of the virtuous person and the virtuous society addressing this issue.

Temperance has had bad press. Because of the uses made of this term in the past, it conjures up images of Carrie Nation marching into a Kansas saloon and smashing up the place with a hatchet. Or it has overtones of repression, especially in the area of sexuality. In a recent book on the virtues, for example, the author notes in the section on temperance that "men are so variously and exquisitely lecherous: they must have their 57 varieties." He ends with this comment:

> Let us turn from there to better themes; breathe the air of mountain heights rather than fetid stress. Marriage is a great good but not the best: virginity, a total consecration to the love of God that excludes human sexual love is the best, the most glorious victory over our corruption.[23]

We have here shades of St. Jerome's famous statement: "I praise marriage and wedlock; but only because they beget celibates; I gather roses from thorns, gold from the earth, pearls from shells."[24]

Temperance, as I am using the term in this book, does not

---

[23]Peter Geach, *The Virtues* (Cambridge: The University Press, 1977), pp. 146, 148, 149.

[24]Quoted in James Nelson, *Embodiment* (Minneapolis, MN: Augsburg Publishing House, 1978), p. 52.

refer to some inner struggle in which a dramatic battle between the forces of good and evil is played out. It does not signify the repression of one dimension of our person. It has the positive meaning and goal of introducing integrity and unity into our lives.

The reason integrity and unity have to be sought is that they are not present at birth. We are born as highly plastic individuals. Our genetic make-up predisposes us in certain directions; but we must use the materials of our culture to fashion the specific content of our person. These materials include role models, values, language, modes of thinking, etc. In establishing an identity, we not only have to bring specificity to the various dimensions of self; we must develop an overall unity in who we are as individuals. It is this unity and integrity that the virtue of temperance addresses.

To achieve this unity and integrity, temperance requires restraint and self-control. Passion and emotion have to be restrained and controlled; but this does not mean they must be repressed—as we have often been led to believe in the past. The problem "is rather that tendency of desires and passion so to engross attention as to destroy our sense of the other ends which have a claim upon us."[25] We can become so engrossed in, or so engrossed by, some particular object that we lose the forest for the trees and so fail to develop integrity—to bring unity to our lives.

It is not just the objects of passion and emotion, however, that engross us in this way. In fact, if there is one thing that is out of control and needs restraint at the present time, it is reason—at least reason the way it is understood and put to use in our culture. This seems surprising, since reason has generally been held up as the means to bring about the necessary control in our lives.

As Philip Slater points out, however, our society is typified by a "technological impulse—that is, the tendency to give material rather than interpersonal form to psychic impulses."[26] Technology is the result of a rigorous use of reason

---

[25]John Dewey and James Tufts, *Ethics* (New York: Henry Holt and Co., 1926), pp. 365 366.

[26]Slater, pp. 11-12.

for purposes of control and domination. We have so developed our technological ability that we can give material form to any of our imaginings. As a result, in Slater's colorful language, we pollute our environment with our "psychic excretions."[27] We are threatened, then, not by a tidal wave of emotion, but rather by the lack of those emotions—love, care, response to beauty—necessary to bring wholeness and integrity to the life of the individual and of the surrounding world.

If restraint and control are needed to temper our lives, how is this to be achieved? To begin, we should not envision the goal of this virtue to be a stoic whose life is basically quiescent, with all internal dimensions carefully balanced, and with no compelling or absorbing external commitments. Positively, temperance requires *reverence*: reverence in the sense of seeing the part in relation to the totality. Not only does this not rule out commitments—forceful, single-minded dedications; it, in fact, requires them. For it is precisely in the dedication of ourselves to certain causes or ideals or persons— especially in those cases where that dedication affects the totality of our lives—that we establish integrity and unity in who we are.[28] Through such commitments we organize and prioritize our energies; we pull our lives together.

Thus, in acting out of reverence by making commitments, it is never a matter of choosing between either seeking self-fulfillment or sacrificing ourselves for others. To temper our lives, i.e., to establish integrity in our lives so as to find meaning and flourishing, requires that we give ourselves to something or someone else. What is at issue is the nature and quality of the object or person for whom we make this sacrifice or dedication. According to John Dewey, that which absorbs us can do so justifiably "only if it expresses the

[27]"Our psychic excretions, in other words, show an annoying tendency to become part of our real environment, so that we are forced to consume our own psychic wastes in physical form. Instead of being recycled, as they are in emotional exchanges between people—thus keeping the level of psychic poison relatively constant—their materialization leads to increasing poison accumulation." Ibid., p. 11.

[28]See Eric Mount, *Conscience and Responsibility* (Richmond, VA: John Knox Press, 1969), p. 68. See also, Gordon W. Allport, *Becoming* (New Haven: Yale University Press, 1955), p. 29.

entire self."[29] Paul Tillich, addressing the issue in much the same way from a more explicitly theological perspective, puts it this way:

> Genuine sacrifice fulfills rather than annihilates him who makes the sacrifice. Therefore historical sacrifice must be surrender to an aim in which more is achieved than just the power of a political structure or the life of a group or a progress in historical movement or the highest state of human history. Rather, it must be an aim the sacrifice for which produces also the personal fulfillment of him who surrenders himself. . . . Wherever historical sacrifice and the certainty of personal fulfillment are united in this way, a victory of the Kingdom of God has taken place. The participation of the individual in historical existence has received ultimate meaning.[30]

Here a word of caution is in order. Calling for dedication to a person or an object that is worthy of us does not mean that the ordinary, small events of daily life are unimportant for the virtue of temperance. Reverence enables us to see the significance of the particular and the immediate because it sees beyond them to the larger whole within which they exist. Or better, reverence sees within the particular and the immediate the larger whole of which they are a part. According to Dewey, the very meaning of reverence is the

> recognition of the unique, invaluable worth embodied in any situation or act of life, a recognition which checks the flippancy of surrender to momentary excitement coming from a superficial view of behavior. . . . The consciousness that every deed of life has an import clear beyond its immediate, or first significance, attaches dignity to every act.[31]

[29]Dewey and Tufts, p. 366.

[30]Paul Tillich, *Systematic Theology* (Chicago: University of Chicago Press, 1967), vol. 3, pp. 392-393.

[31]Dewey and Tufts, pp. 366-367.

Describing temperance in terms of integration through commitment clearly indicates that this virtue, while mainly focused on the individual, is not merely a personal, privatized reality. Temperance is concerned with the unity and integrity of the individual, not just for the internal good of the self, but more importantly for the quality of the interaction between the individual and his or her environment. Because there is wholeness within us, we can bring wholeness to our world.

But there is more to the social nature of temperance than that. We cannot overlook the fact that, even as we create our world, our world creates us. Our personality and identity are not present at birth; they gradually develop under the influence of culture. And, while we are not simple clones of our society, we are heirs, for good and ill, of its particular definition of human reality.

Thus, if we are concerned about integrity and unity in the life of the individual, society must be questioned about its influence and support for this endeavor. What are the values it presents to its members? Do these encourage the integration and development of the various dimensions of the human person? What are the ideals, the roles, the models which society holds out to its members as objects of commitment? Are they of such a nature as to engage the entire person and bring personal integrity?

I have already mentioned a negative example of this. "Technological rationality," an integral part of individualism, overemphasizes the use of reason to manipulate the world, while it underplays the emotive dimension which brings with it care and concern. Thus, it discourages the establishment of unity and integrity in our lives. And commitment to it does not lead to a sense of ultimate meaning through participation in the great and small events of our world—which Tillich points to as necessary.

This is not to say that we should do away with all technology. But we must be mindful that technological rationality, while essential, can introduce highly destructive dynamics into society if it becomes an independent and self-authenticating reality. When that rationality is joined with the feeling of insecurity raised by individualism, it too easily becomes "reasonable" to continue the vertical and horizontal development of the arms race, to talk about "winning" a nuclear war, to justify contemptuous neglect of the poor in the name of national security and of an economic theory, to accept every new piece of technology as "progress."

These policies and practices are "reasonable" in the sense that reasons can be given for our thinking and conclusions, and these reasons can be backed up with impressive theories and statistics. Even more, they are "reasonable" because quite simply they make sense to us in U.S. society without a great deal of proof. But holding them reasonable on these grounds fails to take into account those factors which classically have been identified with the "reasonable": "Is this kind of action abusive of my person, or of the person of another person? If it is, then it is an immoral kind of activity and, in general, should not be approved or done."[32]

Another area where a society structured on individualism encourages disintegration is in its emphasis on negative freedom. As noted earlier, a primary element of the person in individualism is the absence of coercion. The ideal is an individual who has a full range of options from which to choose. Such freedom can easily undermine commitments which by their very nature limit our options and make demands on us. This fact is vividly apparent at parties for men about to get married. At some point, someone usually lifts a bottle of beer in toast to this poor guy who is in his last days or hours of freedom. Given the high regard in which freedom in held within our society, this can have a devastating effect on commitments made for a lifetime.[33]

Finally, it is appropriate to say a few words about sexuality, since that has been so closely identified with temperance. The issue has at times been formulated something like this: in what ways does society aid and abet the uncontrollable and uncooperative nature of our sexuality which is the

---

[32]Vernon J. Bourke, *Ethics in Crisis* (Milwaukee: The Bruce Publishing Company, 1966), p. xix.

[33]For a discussion of the impact of individualism on commitment, see Bellah et al., chapters 4 and 6.

result of its corrupted nature at birth? Such an approach, if what has been argued up to this point is correct, can only exacerbate the problems caused by individualism; it does not solve them. First of all, the ideal it holds out is the restriction of sexuality; but restriction by itself does nothing to bring unity to a person's life. Second, it suggests reason as the means for gaining control over our sexuality; but such a suggestion overlooks the fact that in our society reason primarily takes the form of technological rationality—a type of reason unable by itself to bring integration to our lives.[34] Finally, such an approach fails to take into account the specific cultural roots undermining the commitment which sexuality needs to become an integrated dimension of a unified person.

A different set of concerns arises when the issue of sexuality is addressed in light of the definition of temperance offered here. Dan Sullivan, citing the psychologist, W.R.E. Fairbairn, provides the context.

> Eros is really an integral dynamism of the mind and . . . it aims, not at pleasure of the senses, but at something more commensurate with its source in the whole person, namely, union with the other person as person. . . . It is only when one's history of not being authentically loved as a whole person, and not being able to love wholly, becomes relatively unbearable, that, as Fairbairn states, "the inherent libidinal drive toward the object (person) leads to . . . aberrant reactions."[35]

[34]In this regard, it is interesting to take note of what Rollo May calls the "new puritanism" infusing U.S. culture, despite our seemingly open attitude toward sexuality. "I define this new puritanism as consisting of three elements. First, *a state of alienation from the body.* Second, *the separation of emotion from reason.* And third, *the use of the body as a machine.*" Rollo May, *Love and Will* (New York: W.W. Norton and Company, Inc., 1969), p. 45. On the effects of the "rationality of domination" on sexuality, see Herbert Marcuse, *Eros and Civilization* (New York: Random House, 1955).

[35]Dan Sullivan, Forward to *The Anthropology of Sex* by Abel Jeannière (New York: Harper and Row Publishers, 1964), pp. 22-23. Quotation is from W.R.D. Fairbairn, *Psychoanalytic Studies of the Personality*, 2nd ed. (London: Tavistock, 1962). See also, Karl Rahner, "The Current Conception of Concupiscentia," in *Theological Investigations*, trans. Cornelius Ernst, O.P. (Baltimore, MD: Helicon Press, 1963), pp. 347-382.

Sexuality, then, does not come as a ready-made, evilly oriented dimension of our person that can be allowed expression only in tightly controlled and closely circumscribed situations. Like other aspects of our person, at birth it has a highly malleable form that is shaped in light of the role identities, values and definitions of our culture. What, then, within our culture contributes to an individual "not being authentically loved as a whole person, and not being able to love wholly," and, therefore, turning to aberrant relations? Is it indeed our culture's permissive attitude toward genital activity?

The more basic problem with sexuality in our culture, in my judgment, is to be found in the malformed gender identities that we present to our children and live out ourselves; and in the disvaluing of our bodily existence, with our emphasis on the mind and our view of the material as that which can be manipulated to serve our wants. If my judgment is correct, then an approach to sexuality which continues to insist on restraint understood as repression only fuels the problem. Restraint indeed is needed, but restraint that leads to integration, not to excommunication.

The Roman Catholic tradition is a great resource for developing the virtue of temperance. It maintains the classical understanding of reason which allows reason to consider moral questions (should we do this?) and does not confine it merely to technique (how do we do this?) Through its deep appreciation of symbols especially in liturgy, it engages human feelings and emotions in a powerful way. It has recognized the destructiveness caused by the undercutting of commitments and relationships, and has sought to address that.

Still, there is a potential down-side to the Roman Catholic tradition. While the church appeals to emotion in liturgy, its official documents betray a distrust of emotion in other areas—most particularly, in sexuality. Passion and desire are to be controlled and reason is to be master. When sexuality is identified primarily with genitality and when celibacy is held up as the ideal, control can easily be interpreted as repression.

While recent Vatican statements have spoken of the basic

goodness of sexuality, negative elements from the past continue to be in evidence.[36] On top of that, these negative elements remain strongly rooted in the Roman Catholic ethos and will not easily disappear.

This distrust of emotions and the felt-need to repress them can easily be read in the U.S. context as supporting the position of individualism. So also the placing of reason in control over the emotions—even though the type of reason is not the same. Universal messages are understood in light of the local language. If that message is to bring meaning and flourishing to life, it must not only be properly translated from Latin to the vernacular; it must be framed so as to address head-on the destructive forces at work.

In summary: my argument that individualism is a primary "sign of the times" in the United States, the issue which unifies and clarifies the other problems facing our society, has determined the way in which I have defined temperance. As noted earlier, individualism loosens the ties of the individual to society and fails to provide the self with adequate substance. The meaning given to temperance has been in response to that. Temperance moves us to find a way of coordinating and interrelating the various aspects of our being so that (1) there is a unity and integrity to life that does justice in as full a manner as possible to all dimensions of our person, and (2) we can interact with our environment in a unified and unifying way.

While temperance concentrates primarily on the individual, it is essentially social as well. It challenges society to

---

[36]For example, section 11 of the "Declaration on Sexual Ethics" states: "The virtue of chastity, however, is in no way confined solely to avoiding the faults already listed. It is aimed at attaining higher and more positive goals." (Liebard, p. 439.) Compare this call for a positive approach to chastity with the means recommended for "living a chaste life" in section 12: ". . . discipline of the senses and the mind, watchfulness and prudence in avoiding occasions of sin, the observance of modesty, moderation in recreation, wholesome pursuits, assiduous prayer and frequent reception of the Sacraments of Penance and the Eucharist." (Liebard, p. 442.) For a more positive approach to sexuality see Bishop Francis J. Mugavero, "Sexuality—God's Gift," *Catholic Mind* (May 1976): 53-59; Lisa Sowle Cahill, *Between the Sexes: Foundations for a Christian Ethics of Sexuality* (Philadelphia: Fortress Press/New York: Paulist Press, 1985); Philip S. Keane, *Sexual Morality: A Catholic Perspective* (New York: Paulist Press, 1977); Nelson, *Embodiment.*

provide its members the material out of which such unity and integrity can be achieved and to encourage and support that goal. And it calls upon the church to mine its tradition for the resources it has, while at the same time being critically conscious of the ways it can support aspects of a culture which are in fact opposed to that tradition.

Thus, temperance is not just one item in a "bag of virtues"; nor does it lay out a particular program of life. It is a general aspect of our character, affecting how we see and interact with our world—a general aspect integrating and empowering ourselves and bringing wholeness to our environment.

## Justice

The cardinal virtue of justice is as problematic as temperance because of the connotations the term evokes. The difference is that while the images associated with temperance make it appear outdated and irrelevant, the meanings associated with justice in our culture serve to support individualism and are readily accepted as the centerpiece of our social existence. Any politician who would run for office with the concerns of the Women's Temperance League as his or her primary platform would be viewed as quaint and quixotic. But a politician who campaigns for greater justice is taken with great seriousness and hardly has to explain his or her stance.

What does justice connote within the individualism of U.S. culture? What images does that word call forth? In individualism, people are treated justly if their rights are respected. According to these rights, we as individuals can properly make a claim on pursuing our interests to the extent of our abilities and on enjoying the results of our initiative and effort. In short, we have a right to earn what we can, and to make use of what we earn as we see fit.

As a result, society becomes, in the words of C.B. Macpherson, "a lot of free equal individuals related to each other as proprietors of their own capacities and of what they have acquired by their exercise."[37] When we think of justice, we

---

[37]C.B. Macpherson, *The Political Theory of Possessive Individualism* (London:

focus primarily on situations where we buy and sell things, where we enter in contractual agreements with others. Justice is concerned that each individual be treated with respect; and this requires that an individual deal honestly and be dealt with honestly in any exchanges. Thus, insofar as we get what we pay for and pay for what we receive, justice has been accomplished. Should we receive something not earned or give something to another not paid for, that is charity, not justice.

Thus, the justice of individualism is a sometime thing, dealing only with certain types of relations with others. It comes into play during times of "exchange between proprietors."[38] While such occurrences are an important part of society, they are not the sum of our lives nor the totality of our relations with others.

Justice considered as a cardinal virtue and a dimension of the virtuous person and the virtuous society is interpreted differently—in a way that responds constructively to the problematic aspects of individualism. As a cardinal virtue, justice is understood and applied more broadly. It qualifies all we are and do.

The specific qualification that justice introduces into our lives is a concern for the *common good*, a principle central to the Roman Catholic tradition.[39] Both components of this concept are important.

(1) The "good" of the common good refers to the realization of basic human needs. The good is that which fulfills some dimension of our humanity. Such an approach stands in contrast to the presupposition of individualism that we as individuals have the right to pursue personal interests or wants so long as that does not prevent others from doing likewise. These interests or wants are simply personal pre-

Oxford University Press, 1972), p. 3. On the same point, see Adam Smith, *The Theory of Moral Sentiments* (New Rochelle, NY: Arlington House, 1969), p. 195.

[38]Macpherson, p. 3.

[39]For a discussion of the common good, see Pope John XXIII, *Pacem in Terris*, paras. 53-66; Gremillion, pp. 213-216; Jean-Yves Calvez and Jacques Perrin, *The Church and Social Justice* (Chicago: Henry Regnery Co., 1961), pp. 114 ff.; Merle Longwood, "The Common Good: An Ethical Framework for Evaluating Environmental Issues," *Theological Studies* 34 (September 1973): 468-480.

ferences which are valid simply because they are ours. If other individuals have different interests and wants, those are equally valid. Whether or not these interests and wants advance our humanity is not an issue that can be addressed.

This is so because individualism, as I pointed out in part one, limits the scope of reason to helping us realize our individual wants; it does not see reason as undertaking the substantive task of discovering the basic requirements of our humanity.

On the other hand, when justice is defined as regard for the common good, it presupposes that our essential human needs can be known; and, more than that, it requires that concern for the realization of those needs qualify all aspects of our personal and social existence.

This, in turn, affects how we perceive society. For the relationship between people, then, is not fundamentally a transaction between individuals, each with a right to pursue personal interest so long as one does not interfere with another's similar pursuit. It is an interaction between people sharing certain basic needs that have to be met if their humanity is to be honored.

In our relationship with others, then, we cannot be satisfied simply to say that we have not harmed someone, that we have not violated another's rights; nor can we be content to restrict our responsibility to those areas where others have a juridical claim on us. The approach taken here in response to individualism emphasizes the multiple ties that bind us together—our essential sociality—and the obligations those ties make on us. We bear responsibility for the human flourishing of others; and it is only as we address that responsibility that our own life flourishes.

Moreover, since not just human beings are at issue here but the interaction between persons and their environment, the focus of justice extends as well to the nonhuman world to which we are inextricably tied. The nonhuman world cannot be treated merely as a malleable mass to be shaped in whatever form we wish. We must take into account its need to survive and flourish.

(2) Just as importantly, this concern for human good must include the *common* good. The term "common" can be no

less foreign to an ear shaped by individualism than is the term "good." Individualism sees society as an aggregate of individuals, each an entity unto itself, bound together by self-interest. A bus stop images this view well: a group of people with nothing more tying them together than waiting to use the bus, each for his or her own purposes. For such a view, society is merely a mental fiction with no reality over and above its several discrete members. On that basis, the utilitarian principle of the greatest good of the greatest number makes a great deal of sense: since the personal interests of individuals are the starting point and since society is simply an aggregate of those individuals, seeking to realize the widest range of such interests is the ethical challenge.

The strong current of voluntary cooperation and participation evident in U.S. culture does not offset the bus-stop image. True, it indicates a willingness of individuals to work together. But the voluntary nature of this cooperation means that it is still an effort by an aggregate of individuals, not an effort by a group of people who feel themselves bound together by something deeper or more encompassing.

The common good as the central component of the cardinal virtue of justice points not only to the basic needs shared by the individual members of society; it presumes there is a reality to society over and above the individuals who compose it; and it demands that the good of this whole, which is more than the sum of the parts, be attended to.

As a bus stop reflects the society of individualism, the family is an appropriate symbol for the common good as described here. The family is obviously comprised of individuals; but there is a spirit and a dynamic—a reality—to the family that is more than just the sum total of the separate contributions of each member. The family is founded on interrelationship and interdependence, not on voluntary participation; it offers a place where life can flourish, where strengths can be built on, and where people can dare to be vulnerable. The spirit and dynamic of the family can, of course, be either positive or negative. Justice as a cardinal virtue is the disposition moving us to support the positive and to work to change the negative.

Thus, the scope of justice is broadened further still. In

addition to concern for the needs of individuals, we must work for the *common* good, that which contributes to the unity of society and to the needs of that unified whole. This is especially imperative in a society such as ours where individualism has loosened the ties of the individual to society.

The unity essential to the common good requires, first of all, that we be willing to look beyond the protection and satisfaction of our individual rights. For, if individual rights remain our primary concern, we will lose sight of the good of society as a whole.

We have to do more, however, than just get beyond protecting our rights; we must be willing at times to sacrifice those rights.[40] From the perspective of individualism, such a statement will probably be seen as heresy. But from the perspective taken in this book, it is simply an acknowledgement of a basic fact of life: without society, we could not exist as persons;[41] we are simply owning up to a debt that can never fully be repaid.

In that sense, the term "sacrificing rights" can actually be misleading inasmuch as it has individualistic overtones. The reality to which this points might better be discussed under the rubric of reverence: seeing the part in relation to the whole.[42] The part (or the individual) cannot be submerged into the whole (or society); but the part has to understand that it can flourish only as it exists within a whole that itself is truly alive and flourishing.

Viewing justice as requiring a concern for the common good addresses two fundamental problems raised by individualism. First, it helps us move beyond the split between private and social morality. Such a concern opens our eyes to the fact that in society the whole is more than the sum of the parts. As such, concern for the common good forces us to realize that life cannot be divided up neatly into a personal, private segment on the one hand, and a social, public segment on the other.

---

[40]Pope Paul VI, "A Call to Action," para. 23; Gremillion, p. 506.

[41]This point will be discussed more fully in chapter 6.

[42]Gloria Albrecht brought this to my attention.

The public sphere of human existence is the matrix within which our personal life is carried out, and without which our personal life is impossible. Our personal life in turn either contributes to the continuance of that matrix or it becomes a voice, however small, raised for its change. Thus, how we carry out our personal lives is a matter of social justice. But likewise, concern for social justice is not limited to enormous institutions and structures seemingly far removed from the commonplaces of everyday: it is a dimension of everything we do.

Therefore, in discussing the morality of sexuality, for example, we cannot confine our attention solely to the personal actions of individuals. Such a discussion within U.S. culture almost inevitably is limited to a consideration of genitality. We should broaden the point of reference to include also the issue of gender roles: what is the moral significance of what our culture associates with being male and female? Once we do that, however, the issues raised by sexuality cannot be limited to questions about procreation. For, as the women's movement has brought so forcefully to our attention, our culture's definition of what it means to be male and female has had a great impact not only on our personal lives, but on social structures and on the ways we interact with the physical world as well.[43]

And to follow through on another example discussed earlier, we cannot set aside the issue of "technological reason," holding that it is none of our business. It is our business— our *personal* business. This type of rationality plays a central role in our society and as such cannot help but impact our person and the way we relate personally with other. We were not immaculately conceived or born or educated!

The goal of technological rationality is mastery; and the delusion it generates is that mastery will lead to pleasure and self-satisfaction. This affects not just how we deal with earth's resources but also with each other. According to Slater, "The

---

[43]For a discussion of how the masculine gender identity negatively affects the ecology, see Rosemary Ruether, *Liberation Theology* (New York: Paulist Press, 1972), chapter 8; idem, *Sexism and God-Talk: Toward a Feminist Theology* (Boston: Beacon Press, 1983), chapter 3.

desire lying at the root of the compulsive striving for mastery is that someone will love me without my having to do anything to bring it about, that I shall receive gifts without having to ask, and that pleasure will come to me that I did not expect or seek."[44]

Second, concern for the common good addresses U.S. individualism by giving rise to a deeper and broader sense of responsibility. As I pointed out earlier, individualism narrows responsibility for actions to what is knowingly and willingly done. This severely limits our accountability. But if we begin with the presupposition that we are closely tied to one another within a social matrix, we have to ask whether this understanding of responsibility is adequate. If I cannot be content merely to do you no harm, I have to ask about the various ways in which I affect your life for good or ill. It quickly becomes apparent that I impact your life through more than just what I knowingly and willingly do.[45]

Dewey is helpful in understanding this broader sense of responsibility. Responsibility, he says, refers not to the past but to the future. Whether things might have been different is nothing more than a theoretic question: the past remains what it is. The future however, does not have to be a simple repetition of the past. It can be different *if* we become responsible; that is, if we respond differently.

> A human being is held accountable in order that he may learn; in order that he may learn not theoretically and academically but in such a way as to modify and—to some extent—remake his prior self.... The performance of an act which brought injury to others, that he did not

---

[44]Slater, p. 14.

[45]"Because thinking is embodied in man's immediate dealing with the world, it contains also an attitude toward this world. For example the way in which a driver manipulates his car can reveal a careless attitude, lack of respect for other users of the road, or selfishness. Such an attitude does not arise from deliberate reflection but is usually connected with the person's temperament and mentality. The person himself is probably not even clearly aware of his attitude. Yet he remains responsible for it, for, no matter how ambiguous his freedom may be, it nonetheless is true freedom." Remy Kwant, *Phenomenology of Social Existence* (Pittsburgh, PA: Duquesne University Press, 1965), p. 6.

mean or intend the act, is of no significance, save as it may throw light upon the kind of response by others which will render him likely to deliberate next time he acts under similar circumstances. The fact that each act tends to *form*, through habit, a self which will perform a certain kind of act, is the foundation, theoretically and practically, of responsibility. We cannot undo the past; we can affect the future.[46]

Justice has to be broadened spatially as well as temporally. Since the world in which we live is a part of us ever as much as we are part of it, there are no limits on the responsibility we bear for that world. We are inextricably intertwined in both its good and evil; we must take into consideration our response to that involvement whenever we assess our accountability. We are able, to be sure, to act on only a small segment of that responsibility. But that does not mean we can hold ourselves aloof, either because of apathy or self-righteousness, from those areas to which we do not respond.

The Roman Catholic tradition has a rich store to draw upon in promoting the virtue of justice as the common good. It has been a principal repository of the classical concept of the common good as presented here. It has held tenaciously to the idea of society as more than just an aggregate of individuals both theoretically in its pronouncements and practically in its organization as a church. And it has refused to accept the limited meaning of justice propounded by the classical liberal tradition. Instead, it has called us to look beyond our rights and acknowledge the multiple ties that bind us to our brothers and sisters the world over—ties that require us to reach out with a helping hand to others, but also to admit how much we ourselves stand in need and have to learn.

At the same time, this rich tradition can all too easily be lost to sight and the church can, despite its best intentions and contrary tradition, be seen as accepting the more restricted notion of classical liberalism. This can happen be-

[46]Dewey, *The Moral Life*, pp 169-170.

cause of the split between private and social morality in some aspects of Roman Catholic thought—a split which plays into the similar dichotomy in individualism. As pointed out in chapter three, this split is the result of addressing private, personal matters such as sexual and medical issues in a way that differs significantly in methodology from the approach taken to political and economic matters.

The church can also be interpreted as backing an individualistic society because of its tendency to assess responsibility by the degree to which an action is knowingly and willingly done. This fits nicely with individualism. It also serves to promote the private-social dichotomy since there are few social problems for which we can hold ourselves responsible due to knowing and willing action on our part.

Justice, understood as concern for the common good, is closely related to temperance. Each seeks unity and integrity: temperance primarily within ourselves, justice primarily within society. Justice offers temperance the breadth of commitments necessary for us as individuals to realize as broad a range of our capacities as possible, and to do so with as much integrity as possible. Temperance provides justice with a safeguard against the temptation to social conformity. As indicated in part one, the sense of powerlessness and emptiness the individual has from individualism sets the stage for people to conform to the expectations of the majority. Temperance affords us as individuals an inner strength that is a bulwark against this. In addition, the sense of the common good which defines justice prods us to participate in society in ways that run deeper than voluntary cooperation. More than just something we willingly agree to do, it is grounded in a fundamental belief that we must do so to be true to our own humanity.

## Fortitude

Fortitude or courage, the third cardinal virtue, differs significantly from the first two. Temperance and justice look primarily to the substance of human existence, the nature of personal and social interaction with our environment; courage concentrates on the spirit needed for the realization of that substance.

In the words of Dewey, courage is "the energy of devotion."[47] If good is to be achieved, it is not sufficient simply to *recognize* what is integrative of the self and constructive for the common good. An intensive and active interest in the good is needed once the good has been identified. The virtue of courage supplies that. Thus, courage is part of every situation we face, of every decision we make, of every action we take. To quote Dewey once again, "courage is preeminently the executive side of every virtue."[48] Courage is the attention, intensity, and perseverance we bring to life in seeking the type of interaction that achieves unity and the common good.

That these energies are required brings out clearly the fact that the good we recognize and seek to achieve is not without its opposition. Realization of the good, especially of a highly significant good, always demands effort. Inevitably there are obstacles and counterforces. What, then, are the specific difficulties in a society defined by individualism?

As noted in the first chapter, one of the ambiguities of life within our society is that, while we believe strongly in the freedom and uniqueness of the individual, and while we are always ready to take up weapons to protect these values, we are nonetheless a conformist people. We watch carefully to keep intrusions by authority—especially governmental authority—to a minimum; but at the same time we guard against doing anything that would seem odd or out of the ordinary in the eyes of our neighbors, our friends, even strangers. This underlines the importance of the virtue of courage within our society, the importance of being able to carry through on what contributes to integration and the common good *in the face of opposition from those who expect conformity from us.*

Courage refers as well to *the power to stand up to forces within us* that are obstacles to realizing the good. Especially important in a society characterized by individualism is the

[47]Dewey and Tufts, p. 369.
[48]Ibid.

need to withstand evil. Withstanding evil here means more than just opposing and overcoming it. In the discussion on justice I mentioned the need for a broader sense of responsibility. I argued that we must accept responsibility for whatever we do, whether we act knowingly and willingly or not; and, still more, that we must accept responsibility for whatever evil exists in the world. To do so we have to overcome a need to be innocent, a need to try to find the high moral ground where we can hold ourselves to be without moral blame.

The price of such innocence is great indeed. To be innocent we have to divorce ourselves from a great deal of what we do and who we are. We have to limit our responsibility only to those actions done knowingly and willingly (actions which in fact comprise only a small percentage of our lives); we have to deny our essential connection with society, since through that connection we cannot help imbibe the currents, both good and ill, of our culture.

Only as we own our lives and our membership in society are we energized to act out of a broad sense of responsibility. In the words of Rollo May: "No matter how civilized an individual may pride himself on being, or how much he may deplore violence on the part of others, he must still admit that he is capable of this—or, if he is not, something important in his character has been suffocated."[49]

Courage, then, empowers us to stand up and be counted in the face of pressures for conformity and the drive to innocence that are a part of the individualism of U.S. culture.

This courage is essentially social. True, it resides in individuals. But we as individuals do not come to it on our own, nor can we resist and challenge the directions of society by ourselves, Lone-Ranger style. This courage is mediated to us through a community; and it is only because we know that others stand with and behind us that we dare to speak out and act.

But the community is (or should be) more than just a place where members plug in to have their courage charged

[49]May, p. 160.

up. After all, the community is not just an aggregate of individuals; it has a reality of its own. And part of that reality should be a spirit of courage—a dynamic drawing the group as a whole to insist upon and to work for an environment that promotes integrity and the common good.

The Roman Catholic tradition can be very helpful in developing and supporting the dimension of courage in our character, in our interaction with the environment. First, as an international organization it keeps before its members a broad picture, thereby helping local churches get critical distance on the culture of which they are a part; and it can provide assistance when a local church challenges a culture. Second, its sacramental system can mediate to its members a sense of forgiveness, thus undercutting the drive for innocence and so allowing them to take on broader responsibilities.

Still, ambiguity is evident. Only recently have the Roman Catholic bishops in the United States started to challenge the policies of the U.S. government. Previously, because of suspicions about Roman Catholics' partriotism dating back to the founding of this country, a primary concern of the church was to show that being a Roman Catholic was not antithetical to being a loyal citizen of the U.S. Now, especially with their pastorals on war and peace and on the U.S. economy, the Roman Catholic bishops in this country have begun to criticize some national policies and practices. This has greatly encouraged people both inside and outside the church to speak out. But more still is needed. While the bishops have challenged aspects of U.S. society, they have not yet used the principles they set down to question the basic structures of U.S. society, merely some of its programs. As a result, their principles tend to remain general and somewhat abstract.

And, as was discussed in the first chapter, the traditional celebration of the sacrament of penance, with its juridical overtones, can leave us with an image of a judging, condemning God. Such an image of God moves us more to pursue innocence than to accept the burden of sinfulness that accompanies a broad sense of responsibility.

In brief, then, courage is the energy necessary to make real the good we see through temperance and justice. In particular, it is the power needed to withstand the forces for conformity and innocence. This courage, at once a personal and a social reality, requires the existence of an enabling community that itself is enlivened with courage.

## Prudence

Finally, we consider the cardinal virtue of prudence. The name of this virtue can be as misleading as temperance; it connotes, at least at the present time, the idea of caution, discretion, tact. While there is nothing inherently wrong with cautious, discrete, tactful behavior, this in no way describes what the classical cardinal virtue of prudence is all about.

Traditionally, prudence referred to the spirit with which decision-making is approached. The prudent person is one who makes decisions based on wise deliberations. As such, prudence occupies a place of primacy among the cardinal virtues, informing all the rest. If a person is to act temperately or justly or courageously, he or she has to do so in a prudent way. "Thus prudence is cause, root, mother, measure, precept, guide, and prototype of all ethical virtues; it acts in all of them, perfecting them to their true nature; all participate in it, and by virtue of this participation they are virtues."[50]

While continuing to recognize its place as primary among the cardinal virtues, I will offer a description of prudence that responds to some of the problems connected with U.S. individualism as pointed out in part one. To be more specific, I will show how prudence presents a constructive alternative to individualism's fragmentation of the self, its commutation of the moral life to discrete conscious decisions, and its overemphasis on reason.

To begin, it is helpful to follow Dewey's suggestion of calling prudence "conscientiousness."[51] That distances us from the connotations of timidity attached to the term "prudence," while at the same time helping us capture the essence

---

[50]Pieper, p. 8.
[51]Dewey and Tufts, pp. 418-423.

of this virtue. Conscientiousness according to Dewey has two dimensions: "sensitiveness" and "thoughtfulness."

Sensitiveness

As mentioned earlier, morality cannot be limited to the isolated, discrete decisions we make. To be understood, to have meaning, these decisions have to be interpreted in light of our biography. What does this action indicate about who we are, about where we are going? Moreover, in making a decision, we are not computer-like entities who, in some dispassionate, scientific way, analyze a particular situation into its various component parts; then bring to bear on them certain rules and principles; and finally, without an ounce of sweat or passion, arrive at decisions. Such a mode of acting is nonhuman, if not inhuman.

When we are involved in any situation, we come to it with a perspective, a framework within which to understand and evaluate it. This is so second-nature to us that we hardly advert to it. In fact, unless we stop and reflect on how we know and judge, we tend to assume we are like a camera or a tape recorder, simply recording things exactly as they are in the outside world, and making judgments in an objective and unbiased manner.

We reflect on our way of comprehending the world around us only after we are brought up short by the statements of others who understand and judge events differently. Our first reaction is that something must be wrong with *them*: how could anyone *possibly* see things that way? If we get beyond this, however, we come to realize that even though others are looking at the same goings-on as we are, they are viewing it from a perspective and interpreting it out of a framework different from ours.

Imagine, for example, what the reactions would be to a report on the news about a Ku Klux Klan cross burning if those reading the article were a racial bigot and a civil rights worker. Or imagine the differing responses that Betty Friedan and Phyllis Schlafly would have to an article in the paper that the income of women in this country is less than two-thirds that of men.

These two examples refer only to the effects our perspective has on our conscious reaction to things. Our unconscious actions, indeed the whole tenor and orientation of our lives, are no less affected. Craig Dykstra speaks of this perspective or framework under the heading of "imagination." For him, imagination is much more than a source of fantasy or flight of fancy, tuned in to enliven a dull moment.

> As human beings, we are bombarded constantly by sensations of light, touch, smell, sound, and taste. But these do not come to us nakedly. We receive them as beings who sense our own internal bodily movements in relation to them, and as beings who respond to these stimuli in the light of our memories, expectations, and affections. The work of the imagination is to compose all of these external and internal stimuli into meaningful and apprehensible wholes—in sum, into images.[52]

Because of these images we are able to place individual events and pieces of information within a larger context, thereby finding their meaning and significance. Thus, it is not just a matter of reading, for instance, about a cross-burning; through the images we have, we can interpret and understand that event.

These images, however, are more than just something that is happening in and to us. They are rooted in the formation and orientation of our person. Because of the type of person

---

[52]Craig Dykstra, *Vision and Character* (New York: Paulist Press, 1981), p. 77. Emphasis added. Hauerwas discusses this perspective or framework under the rubric of intention. Intention, he contends, is distinguished from purpose. Purpose refers to the cause-effect connection between an action and its result which is externally observable. "The concept of intention is confined in its application to language-using, reflective creatures who are able to characterize their own conduct, whereas the concept of purpose is not so limited. *Only men can be characterized as intending what they do, whereas animals may be said to have purposes.* Thus to argue that action is basically intentional is to point to the fact that action can only ultimately be described and understood by reference to the intention of the agent. Only the agent can supply the correct description of an action, whereas purpose can be characterized from the observer's point of view." Hauerwas, *Vision and Virtue*, pp. 56-57. Emphasis added.

we are, certain images are present and to the fore, determining how we see and relate to the world.

As the images by which we interact with our world change, our character changes. And, concomitantly, as our character changes, so too our images. "The imagination is foundational to all of our seeing, believing, feeling, and action; and any shift of its contours is also a transformation of ourselves as moral beings."[53]

The work of imagination in our lives attests to the fact that we do not approach any situation in a purely passive, purely receptive way. We are not just cameras and tape recorders. Because of who we are, we see and hear the world in a particular way.

It also shows that our lives are much more than pieces of behavior strung together like popcorn being readied for the christmas tree. There is a unity and a consistency to our lives that lays the basis of our identity: the way we know ourselves and the way others know us. When that unity and consistency is not there, or when it begins to deteriorate, anxiety appears and insanity threatens.

This unity and consistency grounding our identity is referred to as story or narrative.[54] To speak about the self as narrative does not mean that we go about telling tall tales about ourselves. Rather, it calls attention to "a concept of a self whose unity resides in the unity of a narrative which links birth to life to death as narrative beginning to middle to end."[55]

> Our character is the result of our sustained attention to the world. . . . Such attention is formed and given content by the stories through which we have learned to form stories to be told through us so that our manifold activities gain a coherence that allows us to claim them for our own.[56]

---

[53]Dykstra, p. 87.

[54]For a discussion of the place of story or narrative in ethics, see Dykstra, pp. 50-55; Hauerwas, *The Peaceable Kingdom*, pp. 17-34; idem, *Vision and Virtue*, pp. 68-89.

[55]MacIntyre, *After Virtue*, p. 191.

[56]Hauerwas, *Vision and Virtue*, p. 74.

Thus, imagination based on the understanding of self as narrative or story is what is meant by sensitivity. It is the quality of the way we attend to our world, of the way we relate and interact with it based on the type of person we are. This is absolutely foundational to the moral life: on this basis rests the majority of our life. Whatever we do as second nature, without thinking, finds its direction here. And even when we advert to what we are doing or take counsel with ourselves about what we are going to do, who we are establishes our point of departure for knowing the situation. Because of our identity, certain aspects of a situation stand to the fore, others are merely background, and still others are not adverted to at all.

In addition, not only does our imagination affect the way we *describe* a situation, it shapes the way we *evaluate* it as well. Within a given situation, we are drawn by certain values and repulsed by others. This is the starting point of our decision-making. The more profound and the richer our sensitivity is, the better grounded will be our decisions.

But I hasten to emphasize that our imagination and our story are not composed in a vacuum. They are constructed out of the language, images, and role models offered us by our society. Consequently, my story is inevitably and inextricably interwoven with the civil and ecclesial societies of which I am a part, with the stories these societies tell. This is not to say we are totally determined by our society. But we are conditioned by society both with regard to which of our potentialities are realized and with regard to the specific form this realization takes.[57] Thus, the types and qualities of a society's sensitivities are deeply significant. Or to put it another way, prudence is a social justice issue.

Described so neutrally, conscientiousness as sensitivity, as imagination based on narrative or story, applies to everyone without taking into account the quality of their sensitivity. If we leave the description of this cardinal virtue here, we have to conclude that both thief and economic reformer, both murderer and social worker are equally prudent. Such is not the case.

[57]This point will be discussed further in chapter 5.

Prudence or conscientiousness is the primary cardinal virtue because through it temperance, justice and courage are actualized. But if prudence or conscientiousness is the vehicle for the other cardinal virtues, they in turn are its substance. In other words, the truly virtuous person is so sensitized that he or she attends to the world in a way that brings justice to society and integration to the self, and is emboldened to do so despite the presence of evil and the opposition of friends and neighbors. The virtuous person has or is a distinctive story, but one that allows that person to interact with his or her environment in a manner that is temperate, just and courageous.

Here again the social qualification must be included. It is not a matter simply of determining substantively what the sensitivities of the virtuous person are in the abstract; they are developed in light of the realistic possibilities offered by a specific society. As James Sellers remarks, "we are shaped by our Americanness whether we like it or not, and the sound thing to do is to identify with those aspects of the American heritage that hold promise for the human prospect."[58]

Not only, therefore, are the general parameters of the moral life—the focus on virtue and, specifically, on the cardinal virtues—determined in reference to the configurations of a particular society, but the specific sensitivities essential to appropriate interaction with the environment likewise are shaped within that society. Given the perspective taken in this book, the virtuous person in the U.S. at present is especially sensitized to those values, images, role identities, and structures needed to overcome the destructive impact of individualism.

## Thoughtfulness

There is a second dimension to prudence or conscientiousness: thoughtfulness. Thoughtfulness is a dimension both of the moral life and of moral decision-making.

Who we are as persons—our character and accordingly

[58]Sellers, p. 168.

our imagination—has its foundation and basic components established in childhood, during our so-called "formative years." But it is only as we move toward adulthood that our ability—as well as our responsibility—to take charge of our character gradually develops. And the primary tool for doing so is our power of reflection. We reflect on the basic aspects of our person and how they have been shaped so that we can own and give direction to who we are. Thoughtfulness, then, is an important factor in the development of the moral life.[59]

But, given the problems raised by the use of reason in U.S. individualism, it is also important to keep in mind the limits of this thoughtfulness. Thoughtfulness is ancillary to sensitiveness. It is not the source of our character and the images that guide our life. Rather it is the means to reflect critically on these so that we can understand our options, make proper choices, and bring flourishing to life—in short, so that we can have an appropriate sensitiveness.

Even so, the scope of thoughtfulness is circumscribed. We cannot call the totality of our being into the court of our conscious, critical reason. And even in the case of those aspects we reflect on, we cannot always completely reverse their direction or even substantially modify them. Such reflection may simply make us aware of our fatedness. This is not to argue for a passive acquiescence, only for a realism. We have to work as strongly as we can to move our life toward greater flourishing; but we have to do so with a humble acceptance of the fact we will never totally change, we will never totally overcome all our deficiencies and weaknesses.

The thoughtfulness connected with conscientiousness is also involved in our concrete moral decisions. In making decisions, the prudent or conscientious person is first of all sensitized to those values which are of special import within

[59]John Dewey explains thoughtfulness in this way: "While the possession of . . . an immediate, unreflective responsiveness to elements of good and bad must be the mainstay of moral wisdom, the character which lies back of these intuitive apprehensions must be thoughtful and serious-minded. There is no individual who, however morally sensitive, can dispense with cool, calm reflection, or whose intuitive judgments, if reliable, are not largely the funded outcome of prior thinking." Dewey and Tufts, p. 377.

the situation. In other words, because of the way we attend to our world based on our story, we understand or are sensitive to those values within that particular situation which bear on our commitments. As virtuous persons, therefore, we are able to home in on the most significant. Thoughtfulness assists us in moving in the direction where the most significant values receive their best expression. This process will be treated further in chapter eleven.

The Roman Catholic tradition is a strong asset in developing and maintaining the virtue of prudence or conscientiousness. Aquinas's legacy of interpreting ethics from the perspective of virtue and of understanding conscience as prudence is a powerful challenge to individualism's fragmentation of the self and its reduction of the moral life to isolated decisions.

But the church does not always draw upon this legacy in fashioning and stating its stance on ethical issues. The church explicitly distances itself from much of classical liberal thought that grounds individualism. Still, it tends to address ethical issues, particularly personal ethical issues, in a manner that isolates one aspect of the person from others, that focuses attention on individual moral decisions considered in isolation from one another, and that limits responsibility to what is knowingly and willingly done.

This is evident, in particular, in the traditional celebration of the sacrament of penance where the penitent's listing of individual wrongful acts done with knowledge and volition makes life appear to be a series of segmented events. As a result, the agent, in whom the matters confessed find meaning and unity, remains a vague shadow in the background. Thus, rather than challenging individualism, the church can end up implicitly supporting the underlying structures of individualism.

These, then, are the cardinal virtues—the qualities of character which should inform our interaction with our environment so that we can respond creatively to the problems caused by individualism. They are general and do not provide a foolproof recipe for correct action. But they are not so general as to offer no guidance. Their purpose is to establish a broad critical framework that orients our consideration of the concrete ways we interact with our environment in a specific culture and generation. The next step is to ask what guidance these virtues provide in considering the morality of sexuality, of business, of medical care, etc.[60] Such a discussion, however, is beyond the scope of this book and offers a challenge for future work.

## *The Theological Virtues*

To this point, the discussion of the virtues has been carried out on the philosophical plane. We have looked at the cardinal virtues without considering their relation to religion in general and to Christianity in particular. It is now time to explore that relationship. And I do so in the context of the theological virtues of faith, hope, and love.

The relation of the theological to the cardinal virtues is not abstract; it exists within a specific context. Thus, at issue here is how faith, hope, and love provide a religious dimension to our discussion of virtue within a culture of individualism—a religious dimension that responds creatively and redemptively to the problems raised by individualism.

We begin by establishing the negative boundaries. Religion is an ambiguous reality, capable of making life flourish, but also capable of being co-opted in the service of movements which are destructive.[61] From a negative perspective, then, how can the theological virtues be used to *promote rather than challenge* U.S. individualism?

This promoting of individualism occurs, first of all, when the theological virtues (or the cardinal virtues, for that matter) are seen as the object of human endeavor—a very likely possibility in U.S. culture which values individual effort and accomplishment so highly. Looking at the theological vir-

---

[60]For a discussion of what this might look like, see William F. May, "The Virtues in a Professional Setting," *The Annual of the Society of Christian Ethics: 1984*, ed Larry L. Rasmussen (Vancouver School of Theology: The Society of Christian Ethics, 1984), pp. 71-92.

[61]See Baum, chapters 1, 2, 4, and 5.

tues in this way distorts the fact that they are gifts; they cannot be earned or created through our efforts. To use Carney's language, it makes them into "acquiremental" rather than "relational" virtues: they are the result of good works rather than a response in faith to "the justifying relation God freely offers."[62]

This acquiremental perspective has implications for the problems caused by U.S. individualism. With its emphasis on freedom and independence, U.S. individualism—particularly in its utilitarian form—stresses the "pull-oneself-up-by-one's-own-bootstraps" spirit. When the ties of the individual to society are loosened, such a mentality, rather than strengthening us as individuals, leaves us with a profound sense of powerlessness since the world—even our own small piece of the world—is so intractable to isolated effort. And so, to make faith, hope, and love the objects of personal effort not only distorts them, it also deepens the alienation and despair already present. They become one more task we fail at: not only are we unable to affect out world, we feel powerless in our relation with God.

To guard against this "acquiremental" view of virtue, some would remove the theological virtues from any connection with this world, making them totally "spiritual" realities. Such an approach is no less problematic. As Gregory Baum points out, all religion "is a hidden political language." No religious statement or practice can isolate itself from the political realities of society.

> Even the great saints were often so identified with their culture that without knowing it, and despite their other-worldliness, they unconsciously sanctioned the injustices of their society. Reading, for instance, the letters of Thérèse of Lisieux and Père Charles de Foucauld, both remarkable religious figures and prophetic in the context of the ecclesiastical tradition, we discover that they provided religious legitimation for the colonial expansion of France and its claim of cultural superiority.[63]

[62]Carney, p. 14.
[63]Baum, p. 104.

Some think we in the U.S. are immune to this mixing of politics and religion because we hold strongly to the separation of church and state. But the fact is, even as we argue for this separation, we just as strongly infuse society with the religious through the presence of civil religion. Civil religion in the U.S., according to Robert Bellah,[64] is not tied to any particular denomination; drawing on Jewish and Christian symbols, it places the whole American experience in relation to the divine will. Within that context, "other-worldly" religion has a way of becoming very much "this-worldly." Religious concepts are shaped in ways amenable to, even mirroring, the culture.

Thus, the theological virtues can end up being defined in ways that support the basic tenets of individualism. A good example of this is to be found in George Gilder's *Wealth and Poverty*, a book promoting supply-side economics. Gilder is an economist, not a theologian. But he makes a strong case for the religious foundations of his theory; and, in so doing, he sets forth an interpretation of the theological virtues clearly supportive of U.S. individualism. It is not difficult to imagine faith, hope, and charity as defined by Gilder being preached from the pulpit on Sunday—without, of course, the explicit economic references.

Gilder elides faith and hope. For him, "Faith in man, faith in the future, faith in the rising returns of giving, faith in the mutual benefits of trade, faith in the providence of God are all essential to successful capitalism." In our "fallen world," we are not always rewarded by our efforts. In fact, at times our effort is for naught and our future goes up in smoke. Thus, to keep up our work ethic, we need "confidence in a higher morality."[65]

But faith, according to Gilder, also disciplines our temptation to exceed our human capacities by reminding us we cannot separate ourselves "from chance and fortune in a

[64]Robert N. Bellah, *Beyond Belief* (New York: Harper and Row 1976), pp. 168-189. See also, John A. Coleman, *An American Strategic Theology* (New York: Paulist Press, 1982), pp. 108-130.

[65]George Gilder, *Wealth and Poverty* (New York: Basic Books, Inc., 1981), p. 73.

hubristic siege of rational resource management, income distribution, and futuristic planning."[66] In other words, faith keeps us god-fearing capitalists and saves us from atheistic socialism. It makes sure we do not stray beyond technological rationality.

Love also has a place in Gilder's system, for love as altruism is essential to capitalism. ("Capitalism begins with giving."[67]) A gift responding to another's need implicitly places the recipient in debt to the giver. That is to say, "the demand was inherent in the supply" since the initial offer started the process. Through the repayment and the consequent "contest of gifts," there results "an expansion of human sympathies."[68]

Such an understanding of love and altruism strongly legitimates utilitarian individualism where life is seen as an interaction between autonomous entities. The veneer of sympathy covers over, but does not remove, the basic self-seeking and competition. Since this individualism, as we have seen, affects negatively both the individual and the community, we need more adequate reflection on these virtues.

How, then, should we interpret the theological virtues so as to preserve their gift quality and bring out their redemptive power within our culture? We can accomplish this by understanding the theological virtues to be the foundation which makes the cardinal virtues possible. Faith, hope, and charity are present within temperance, justice, fortitude, and prudence as their very soul.

Faith is the conviction that the fundamental power in the universe is a positive, life-giving, and life-seeking force. Within Christianity, this conviction is symbolized through the image of God as Creator of the world. In Genesis, God is pictured as the Breath of Life, hovering over chaos, bringing out of it an ordered universe teeming with life of all kinds, and acknowledging that this indeed is good. Throughout Scripture, God is active within history as a re-creative force,

[66]Ibid., p. 268.
[67]Ibid., p. 21.
[68]Ibid., p. 22.

working through the strengths and weaknesses of individuals and nations to establish a city, global in size, where all will live in peace and justice—a city that is truly the City of God.

In Christ who is the Logos (the Word of God), the creating and saving power underlying history is made evident in a distinctive way. He comes preaching the kingdom; "his exorcisms, healings, and miracles are signs of the breaking-in"[69] of its power.

Our response to the presence of this God revealed in Christ cannot be simply an intellectual assent or a fideistic passivity. To know this God, we must do as this God does, pursuing a new heaven and a new earth by doing justice for the poor and the oppressed, the alienated and the powerless.

Grounded in this faith, we are enabled and empowered to pursue the virtuous life. And in so doing, we are united with the divine effort in history as a member of a believing community. Thus, morality is at once divine gift and human response. Character, formed on the basis of the cardinal virtues as defined in response to the problems caused by U.S. individualism, is made possible through God's grace; and it becomes a creative, redemptive force because of God's activity.

Not only do we need the conviction that the ground of life is positive, we must have hope that our efforts will indeed make a difference, that all is not ultimately doomed to frustration and failure. This is not a "cheap" hope, based on a vague feeling that somehow everything will work out for the best. Nor is this hope a capitulation to chance or fortune, as Gilder would have it. As the U.S. bishops point out in their pastoral on war and peace, "Hope *sustains* one's capacity to live with danger without being overwhelmed by it; hope is the *will to struggle* against obstacles even when they appear insuperable."[70]

What is the source of that hope? The great symbol offered by Christianity is the resurrection: the sign that death is not

[69]Francis Schüssler Fiorenza, *Foundational Theology* (New York: Crossroads, 1985), p. 221.

[70]National Conference of Catholic Bishops, *The Challenge of Peace: God's Promise and Our Response*, p. 2, para. 2. Emphasis added.

the final victor. John Macquarrie sums this up well: "Perhaps the center of the hope is simply this: that man will never find himself in an absolute *cul-de-sac*: there will always be the possibility of an opening to a new future, always the possibility that grace will transmute folly and death into atonement and resurrection."[71]

Hope thus understood is the ground for the cardinal virtue of courage. As noted earlier, because of courage we have the strength to dare to stand guilty, to forego the drive for innocence and acknowledge our participation in the evil of the world. To have such courage, however, we must rely on more than our own strength. That strength is rooted in the God revealed through Jesus Christ, a God who accepts us not in our perfection but in our sinfulness. This hope frees us to accept broad responsibility for our world, to own up to our implication in the sin of the world, and to make our contribution toward overcoming that sinfulness through the power of God's saving presence with us.

Such hope is at once gift and response. It comes to us unearned and unwarranted. Yet it does not render us passive, leaving us with the smug feeling that everything is going to turn out just fine without our lifting a finger. To quote Macquarrie once more: ". . . as far as the eschatological hope is concerned, we have to remember the dialectic of grace and endeavor. The hope is not fulfilled automatically, but only as men give themselves up in hope for its realization."[72]

Again, this hope is never a purely private gift. Not only does it direct us out toward others, it also is first and foremost present within the church. Because we have been formed and fashioned by a hope-filled community and because we continue to join with that community in action and reflection, we as individuals are grounded in that hope.

Hope thus understood makes our efforts possible; and our efforts are essential if the goal toward which hope points is to be actualized. Hope, then, is the sustainer of the cardinal

---

[71]John Macquarrie, *Three Issues in Ethics* (New York: Harper and Row, 1970), p. 143.

[72]Ibid.

virtues. At the same time, the type of character formed through the cardinal virtues is the creative force needed for the new future to become the real present.

Finally, love establishes the basis for meeting the challenges faith and hope set before us. Convinced of the fundamental goodness of the source of life and of the ultimate openness of the future, we are confronted by the need to overcome the personal, interpersonal, and social alienation blocking the realization of the City of God. By our own efforts alone, that is impossible. How can we, who stand in need of healing, be physicians to others?

Love is the great reconciling power, bringing into harmony and unity distant or warring elements. Such a love reaches much more deeply than a sympathy which fuels supply and demand, and keeps competition within bounds. It also reaches much more broadly, for it includes not only those who do good to us or give us gifts, but even those whom we hold as enemies. And it drives us not merely to establish strong interpersonal relationships, but to build up political, economic, legal, and cultural structures that will promote harmony and unity. Love then, is the school for prudence, focusing and sharpening our sensitivity and thoughtfulness.

Love comes first of all as a gift. "In this is love, not that we loved God but that he loved us and sent his Son to be the expiation for our sins. Beloved, if God so loved us, we also ought to love one another."[73] It is a gift mediated to us through the church, a community of love, which surrounds us with love so that we as individuals can reach out to others.

Because we have been loved, we are enabled but also challenged to respond: to become in turn a reconciling and harmonizing force within the world. We are empowered and inspired to work courageously and conscientiously for integration and the common good. In responding to God's love, we bring a healing power to the divisive forces of alienation. In short, love which grounds prudence is the ground of all the virtues.

---

[73] I John 4:10-11. All translations are from *The Jerusalem Bible*, ed. Alexander Jones (Garden City, NY: Doubleday and Company, Inc., 1966).

Thus, the theological virtues are the soul of the cardinal virtues. They make the cardinal virtues possible, showing clearly the giftedness of all of life; and through the cardinal virtues, their own goal of the City of God is being realized.

In that we have the goal of morality.

# 5

# Sin: Participation and Responsibility

With sin we seem to be back on more familiar, even if less comfortable, ground. Virtue may have been mentioned here and there in the past. We may even recall having had to reproduce the names of the cardinal and the theological virtues on some religion exam along the way. But our greatest experience, certainly educationally if not existentially, has been with sin.

Within the Roman Catholic community, that experience has been focused for us primarily through "going to Confession." We examine and evaluate our lives morally in light of what we believe we have to declare to the priest in the confessional. That defines for us the reality of sin.

As I pointed out in the third chapter, morality interpreted through the experience of confession (particularly through its more traditional aspects) appears to go along with U.S. individualism in a number of ways. This is the case, first of all, when sin is understood as a *single action*. As a result, our lives take on the appearance of a series of discrete actions lacking any underlying coherence or pattern—staccato notes struck one after the other without any basic melody. We can find that we have used vulgar language six times, but never face the question of whether we might be a truly vulgar person.

The experience of sin is also easily read in a way amenable to individualism when it is limited to the evil that we *knowingly* and *willingly* do. This adds to the difficulty of considering our individual lives in their totality since the percentage of what we do deliberately is very small. Most of our life is guided by attitudes and habits operating at the subconscious and unconscious level. (And, as I have pointed out, these attitudes and habits impact our conscious decisions as well.)

Limiting the evaluation of our lives to what is knowingly and willingly done also restricts the scope of our responsibility. In particular it allows us to avoid responsibility for the social dimensions of life. To be sure, we are never told we bear no responsibility for the world's problems. But that responsibility remains rather abstract and of secondary importance. Since we did not intentionally contribute to social evil, we are not personally implicated in it; and our main energies are directed toward those areas where we are guilty of sin.

This divorcing of the personal from the social also occurs when confession is experienced in a way that promotes the *pursuit of innocence*.[1] Because confession has been understood in a juridical framework, sin can easily be interpreted as the breaking of a law. God, then, is pictured as the Enforcer and the Punisher. And our goal is to keep our souls free of the stain of sin lest we suddenly be called before the judgment seat of who is too often seen as an angry and vengeful God.

In such a framework we want to limit our responsibility as much as possible. The less we can be judged on, the better chance we have of avoiding punishment. The circle of limitation has been drawn so that personal and interpersonal issues fall within it, while social issues (unless they are the result of deliberate action on our part) are outside it. This circle congrues easily with U.S. individualism.

To interpret sin in a way that challenges this individualism,

---

[1] The theology of the traditional rite of confession did not urge us to seek innocence. This was more a result of the juridical perspective used to interpret the sacrament. This juridical perspective placed the priest as judge; and it spoke of penance as satisfaction—satisfying an offended God for the *poena*, or temporal pains of purgatory, after the *culpa*, or sin, had been forgiven. Thus penance takes the form of a sentence repaying an offended God. For a discussion of the development of the concept of satisfaction, see Henry Charles Lea, *A History of Auricular Confession and Indulgences in the Latin Church* (Philadelphia: Lea Brothers and Co., 1896), vol. 2, pp. 169-284.

I will build upon some elements set out in the chapter on virtue. Sin will be seen not primarily as a single act but as a definition of the general orientation of our character and the general status of society. Responsibility will be determined mainly in terms of the future rather than the past, looking not at what we have done but at how we can change our way of interacting with our environment. And, in doing so, the scope of responsibility will be broadened to include social as well as personal sin. Our indeliberate, unconscious actions will be held as important as our deliberate, conscious behavior.

I will reverse the usual way of considering sin and make an addition to boot. Traditionally, sin has been divided into original sin and actual or personal sin, with the latter receiving first and much more extensive treatment. Here I will begin with a discussion of original sin (for reasons which will soon become apparent). Next I will make use of the insights of some present-day theologians who have introduced a new category—but by no means a new reality: social sin. Only then will I turn to the issue of actual or personal sin.

## Original Sin

Original sin has been more than a bit of a puzzlement for people. It is not just that original sin cannot be totally grasped (that is never a possibility since we are dealing with mystery); original sin seems to elude our efforts at making even a little sense of it. How is it possible to understand something that we are told we are born with, that in the view of many disappears after a ritual involving the pouring of water over the head of an infant, and yet that seems to leave the baptized not discernibly different from the unbaptized?

The problem, in part at least, stems from the fact that the reality to which the term original sin points has been conceptualized in privatized and otherworldly categories. It evokes the image of an unbaptized individual standing distanced from God through no personal fault. Social and this-worldly (but nonetheless transcendent) categories, I believe, offer better insight into the mystery that is original sin.[2]

While emphasizing that original sin is a this-worldly rather than an otherworldly reality, I do not mean that it can be empirically verified in an easy and direct manner. To be sure, there is no lack of evil around us; the morning paper and the evening news make that abundantly clear. But original sin is not just a factual report; it is a religious statement about the world as interpreted through the eyes of faith. We who believe in Christ and who understand, at least to some degree, the mission of Christ to establish the Reign of God, evaluate the present world from that perspective.

The word "perspective" is very important. We see nothing in its totality or as it is in itself. Our perception is from a particular angle of vision and out of a certain set of presuppositions, all of which influence our way of understanding.

This was brought home to me a number of years ago by a television advertisement which sought to motivate people to keep the physical environment clean. Pictures of a landscape cluttered with debris and of a polluted stream were shown, raising feelings of disgust—at least they did so in me. But then a Native American, with headband and feathers and dressed in buckskin, walked on the scene and stopped to survey the ravaged environment. The ad ended with the camera full on the Native American as a tear ran down his cheek. Suddenly I was pulled out of my normal perspective into that of the Native American with his great respect for the holiness, even the sacramentality, of the earth. This was no longer a scene calling forth merely feelings of disgust. It was desecration; it was the type of violation associated with rape.

In a similar way, we see original sin because of our angle of vision. We who have been baptized into Christ, who have been sensitized to what Christ stands for, look on our world from the perspective of a believer. With that perspective, the morning paper and the evening news show us more than just a world with some problems of hunger that call for greater

---

[2]For a discussion on the need to translate the dogma of original sin into present-day categories, see Christian Duquoc, "New Approaches to Original Sin," *Cross Currents* 28/2 (Summer 1978): 189-200.

relief efforts, more than just a world with some problems of unrest between nations that require a better balance of power. Seen in light of Christ's vision of the Reign of God where all will enjoy a life grounded in justice understood in its deepest meaning, and where all peoples will live together in true peace, our sensitivity to the length and breadth and depth of the evil present in the world is qualitatively different. Original sin, then, is a secret of faith, revealing the deep tragedy that pervades the human condition.

We cannot hold ourselves aloof from this tragedy that is original sin, claiming to be unaffected by it. It qualifies our very being, despite the fact that at birth we do not opt to be a part of it and have done nothing to contribute to this condition of the world. It is present in us from the beginning, at the pre-personal and involuntary level. It exists within us prior to any decisions on our part and qualifies them when they occur. As a result of it, we are passive and powerless in the face of the evil; and even more disturbingly, we experience a positive attraction toward that evil—what has been termed "an involuntary connivance with the sins of others."[3] Original sin indicates that from our earliest days we are in solidarity with the evil of humanity.

This, no doubt, has a strange, almost medieval sound to it. It does not ring true with a perception of evil as that which is deliberately done and with a desire to find the high ground of innocence. To be sure, this unrelieved discussion of evil and its rootedness in the human heart is neither the full nor the primary story of Christianity. But to understand the meaning of Christianity, we have to recognize the reality which original sin symbolizes. It is a faith statement indicating the state of the world but also the condition of our hearts, a condition that exists in spite of ourselves.

Not only does original sin point to the pervasiveness of evil in the world and within us, it also indicates that we cannot do away with this evil through our own efforts. William Van Der Marck, a Dutch theologian, brings this out well:

---

[3]Brian O. McDermott, S.J., "The Theology of Original Sin: Recent Development," *Theological Studies* 38/3 (September 1977): 510.

Thus, original sin is, as it were, diametrically opposed to *virtus infusa* [infused or theological virtue]. Original sin is a *vitium naturae*; it is the impotence of a dead man to come to life again. For he cannot, unless the God who has become man stretches out his hand to him and commands him, "Arise!"[4]

But we do not remain in our impotence. The secret of faith—the perception and evaluation of the world and of human life from the perspective of faith—involves more than just the length and breadth and depth of evil present. Even more powerful and even more central than that evil is God's saving presence in our midst. "When law came, it was to multiply the opportunities of falling, but however great the number of sins committed, grace was even greater;...."[5]

This saving presence is, if you will, the other side of the coin: original sin cannot be understood apart from redemption. That image, however, can be misleading. It is not as though there first was original sin, and then God came to rescue us. We began in a state of "original blessing."[6] God's saving presence has been active and effective from the very beginning. Original sin brings home the significance of that presence. As we ponder the radicalness and the power of sin and consider what the world and humanity would be like without the presence of God as revealed through Christ, we understand better the meaning and power of God's redemption. At the same time, because we know that the evil symbolized by original sin is only part of the truth—and not the primary or strongest part of it at that—we can dare to look at the full extent of evil in the world and in our own hearts. And so we are empowered to continue the mission of Christ by working toward the Reign of God.

Thus, in acknowledging original sin, we are making a

---

[4]W.H.M. Van Der Marck, O.P., *Toward a Christian Ethic* (Westminster, MD: Newman Press, 1967), p. 107. See also, idem, "Toward a Renewal of the Theology of Marriage," *The Thomist* 30/4 (October 1966): 307-342.

[5]Romans 5:20.

[6]Matthew Fox, *Original Blessing* (Santa Fe, NM: Bear and Co., Inc., 1983), p. 44.

confession as members of a community through whom the presence of God is mediated to us. We confess first and most importantly that God is with us; that the saving power of God, revealed through Christ, is more fundamental and more powerful than the evil we experience around us and within us. At the same time, we confess who we are. We acknowledge our most basic need for God's saving grace, both individually and corporately; we give thanks for the ways in which the power of sin over us has been broken; and we declare our obligation and willingness, as a people empowered by God, to work to eradicate that evil and so prepare a fitting milieu in which God's people—all of humanity—can live together in harmony and respect, and God can once more walk with us in the cool of the evening.

Interpreting original sin, then, in social and this-worldly categories helps us see sin as a pervasive reality in our lives and not just a single action; as a reality which precedes and affects our conscious choices; as a reality linking us closely with society; and as a reality giving the lie to any presumptions of innocence on our part. In short, it speaks a critical and constructive word to U.S. individualism.

This interpretation of original sin, however, can still remain abstract. For, even though it is located solidly in this world, it is removed from a particular historical setting. Unless that is addressed, the mystical aura with which the traditional popular understanding surrounds original sin continues. And that can undercut the challenge original sin represents for U.S. individualism. To place original sin concretely within the social and historical world, we turn to "social sin."

## Social Sin

While social sin is an important concept for addressing the problems of U.S. individualism, it raises a number of problems of its own. In fact, it has become something of a theological pariah. After an initial time in the sun following the publication of *Justice in the World*[7] by the 1971 Synod,

---

[7] See Gremillion, pp. 445–476; especially, pp. 446, 455, 472–473.

the popularity of social sin has given way to questions and challenges—questions and challenges that bear directly on individualism.

The reason for this waning popularity cannot be laid to a lack of awareness about social evil among Roman Catholics. We have become well-versed of late in biblical references to social evil, especially as found in the prophets of the Hebrew scriptures. Modern Roman Catholic social thought, dating from Pope Leo XIII's 1891 encyclical, *Rerum Novarum*, has provided us with an analysis and moral evaluation of social structures. The pastoral letters of the U.S. Catholic bishops on war and peace and on the U.S. economy follow in this tradition.

Nor have we Roman Catholics been blind to the social consequences of sin. We have spoken of social sin from what might be called a *subjective* perspective, pointing out the social evils that result from personal sin. Thus, adultery is shown to have destructive effects reaching beyond the life of the person and the family involved; it unravels to some degree the fabric of the community. Even so-called "bad thoughts," despite the fact that they occur in an inner realm, are shown to affect the way we look at and relate to the world around us and as such have social consequences.

The difficulty arises when the word sin is used to qualify social structures; when, for instance, a political or economic system is called sinful. Why the problem? First, as James Hug points out, two different currents in contemporary Catholic moral theology run at cross-purposes on the subject of social sin. On the one hand, there are liberation theologians for whom the morality of social institutions is a primary concern. They speak about sinful social structures and attempt to raise people's consciousness and broaden their sense of moral responsibility about working for social justice. On the other hand, there are theologians who are anxious to moderate "the exaggerated burdens of moral responsibility and the correlative fears of divine judgment which characterized the Catholic community in the U.S. before Vatican II."[8] They want to limit the scope of moral responsibility in

---

[8]James Hug, S.J., "Social Sin, Cultural Healing," *Chicago Studies* 23/3 (Novem-

order to free people from an exaggerated sense of duty and guilt. At present, the latter group appears to have the upper hand.

Second, serious reservations are expressed in official Roman Catholic statements about the term social sin. Pope John Paul II acknowledges here is a social dimension to every sin inasmuch as "each individual's sin in some way affects others"; inasmuch as "some sins . . . by their very matter constitute a direct attack on one's neighbor."[9] But when social sin refers to "the relationships between the various human communities," the term sin is being used *only analogously*. The word sin applies primarily to personal sin.

To speak of social sin in anything other than an analogous sense, according to John Paul II, creates problems. For then, personal and social sin are contrasted "in a way that leads more or less unconsciously to the watering down and almost the abolition of personal sin, with the recognition only of social guilt and responsibilities.[10] As a result, blame is "placed not so much on the moral conscience of an individual, but rather on some vague entity or anonymous collectivity such as the situation, the system, society, structures of institutions."[11] What must be upheld is the "truth of faith, also confirmed by our experience and reason, that the human person is free. This truth cannot be disregarded in order to place the blame for individual's sins on external factors such as structures, systems or other people."[12]

It certainly is important to lift overblown and unwarranted moral responsibilities from people's shoulders. And it is essential that individuals not duck their moral duties. Such concerns, however, cannot be addressed in the abstract. They have to be worked out in light of the specific issues raised within a particular culture. Therefore, the question that faces

ber 1984): 335. Emphasis in original.

[9]Pope John Paul II, "Apostolic Exhortation on Reconciliation and Penance," *Origins* 14/27 (December 20, 1984): 441.

[10]Pope John Paul II, "Closing address of Pope John Paul II to Synod," *Origins* 13/22 (November 10, 1983). 378.

[11]Pope John Paul II, "Apostolic Exhortation," p. 441.

[12]Ibid.

us is this: how are we to develop a proper sense of moral responsibility in a way that responds constructively to the problems caused by U.S. individualism?

I suggest that, while the difficulties with understatements and overstatements of moral responsibility exercising Pope John Paul II and some Roman Catholic theologians are very real, the solutions they offer can too easily be interpreted in a manner that supports rather than challenges individualism. While exaggerated burdens of guilt have indeed been laid on Catholics in the past, and while social sin may allow individuals to avoid moral responsibility, it is not adequate in the U.S. context to place emphasis primarily on personal sin. The stances taken by the pope and the theologians, when read in light of U.S. individualism, can be seen as supporting the dichotomy between the individual and the social, and as valuing the individual over the social.

In order to insure a correct sense of moral responsibility while at the same time taking into account the issues raised by U.S. individualism, we should keep in mind the following. First, calling social structures sinful does not necessarily or automatically mean that we as individuals are absolved of responsibility. Social structures do not come into existence through some mysterious, foreign power. They are a human construct; we are their authors. Thus, while we are indeed *formed* by society, we also *form* society.[13] Accordingly, to remove either the human person or social structures from the equation, or to make one secondary to the other, is to falsify reality.

Human freedom and responsibility, then, are not destroyed by social sin. Just the opposite is true: they can be protected and promoted *only* as the social dimension of life (and social sin) is taken seriously. The social dimension shows the scope of human creativity and freedom: the world we build is broader than just that of our individual identity. And, because of the inextricable involvement of the world in our lives and vice versa, our moral responsibility extends beyond our personal lives. In speaking about social sin, then, we are

---

[13]See Peter Berger and Thomas Luckmann. *The Social Construction of Reality* (New York: Doubleday, 1967).

simply reminding ourselves of that responsibility. Moreover, because our involvement in the world extends far beyond our intentional acts, our responsibility cannot be limited to those actions that are knowingly and willingly done. In short, by taking social sin seriously, we are addressing some of the principal issues of U.S. individualism.

Second, Roman Catholics indeed have been weighted down in the past by an excessive burden of moral responsibility and guilt. The problem however, stems not from the presence of guilt but from the types of actions with which that guilt has been associated.

Guilt in and of itself is not bad. It is the moral equivalent of our bodily response to heat. If we put our hand on a hot object, we pull back in a hurry, warned by a built-in sensor. Guilt provides the same type of warning system, alerting us to a potentially destructive situation and preparing us to respond properly.

The difference, of course, is that while our warning against heat is inborn, our guilt is a learned response. And as history shows, our sense of guilt can be—and often has been—misshaped. Within the Roman Catholic community, sexuality has been emphasized to the point that, at times, it seems to be the only moral issue. The necessity of physical presence at church on Sundays has been so stressed that some believe it a matter of serious sin to be absent even for dire reasons of health. At the same time, racism, chauvinistic nationalism, or contempt for the poor often raises no feelings of guilt at all. The issue, then, is not that we feel guilty, but that we feel guilty about the wrong things.

We need to be formed and educated, therefore, in a right sense of guilt. A right sense of guilt is one that alerts us to our real and realistic responsibilities based on our understanding in faith of what God is doing in our midst. Social sin is essential if our guilt is to be properly educated.

(It goes without saying, of course, that we can have no proper sense of guilt without the virtue of courage rooted in the virtue of hope. To live with guilt, we have to be able to overcome our need to be innocent. We can do so only as we believe in the forgiving and liberating God revealed to us in Christ.)

Social sin, as presented here, is indeed an analogical concept; but so too are original and personal sin. No concept totally captures the mystery that is sin. None symbolizes that mystery better than the others. Here I am differing with the position taken by Pope John Paul II that "social sin . . . obviously has an analogical meaning," that "sin, in the proper sense, is always a personal act, since it is an act of freedom on the part of an individual person and not properly of a group or community."[14]

To make personal sin (that is, the deliberate wrongful act of an individual) the primary analogue or referent of sin too easily feeds into the individualism of U.S. culture. Rather than protecting our full freedom as individuals, however, it actually endangers our freedom by blinding us to our participation in, and thus our responsibility for, the social dimensions of life. When that happens, John Paul II's great efforts at raising people's consciousness about the terrible injustices existing around the world are undermined.

The point of continuity uniting original, social, and personal sin is the reality of sin itself. Sin is a theological term pointing to the quality of human reality in relation to God. Since the God we believe in is a God of history who seeks to renew the face of the earth in order to establish the promised Reign, we analyze and evaluate all aspects of history from the perspective of what that God is doing among us. Original sin points to the universality of the opposition to God's Reign. Social sin designates the social and historical forms that opposition takes. And personal sin, as I shall argue shortly, indicates the ways in which we as individuals actively participate in that opposition.

My main reason for including here a discussion of social sin has yet to be addressed. Social sin was needed, I claimed, in order to make concrete the realities pointed to by original sin. Up to now, I have argued about the importance of social sin, especially within the context of U.S. individualism. But I have said nothing about what specifically and concretely social sin means in our culture.

[14]Pope John Paul II, "Apostolic Exhortation," p. 441.

This is easy to remedy. I simply have to refer back to chapters two and three where I detailed the problems caused by U.S. individualism in the ways we relate to ourselves, our society, our physical environment, and in the ways we understand and practice religion. That is the concrete reality of social sin in our society—the historical manifestations of how the realization of God's Reign in our midst is being blocked.

Before concluding, however, it is important to note the significance of identifying the problems of U.S. individualism with social sin. This identification brings out well the broad meaning of the word "social" when we speak of social sin. The social refers to all those impersonal (or maybe better, superpersonal) dimensions of human reality that make our common existence possible and that provide an ordered world by which we establish our personal identities and carry on our lives.

These dimensions include, first of all, *formal social structures*, the officially sanctioned institutions and policies by which we organize our lives at the public and private level. These formal structures involve the *political* by which we order power within our common life, determining how decisions are made and carried out; the *economic* by which we establish how goods are produced and distributed; and the *legal* by which we specify and adjudicate rights and duties.

There are also *informal social structures* such as language, customs, social roles, ways of associating, values, etc. These are called *informal* because they do not have the same official sanction as the formal structures. But they are *structures* nonetheless: they are the taken-for-granted part of everyday life that influence and condition in a thousand different ways the interaction between us and our world and the manner in which we shape our individual identities. Their power comes from our general acceptance that this is "the way things are."

Finally, the "social" takes in religion as well. Religion is not primarily a personal matter; no matter how private it may seem, religion, as I have pointed out, bears at least an implicit connection with the society in which it exists. And, as part of society, it cannot remain neutral: it either blesses or challenges what is happening there. Insofar as religion is a part of the social structures that deform us and our environment as judged from the perspective of faith, it is socially sinful.

Original sin and social sin, thus understood, stand in dialectical relation one to another. Social sin is the specific, concrete form that original sin takes in a particular culture and a particular generation. Through it we become inheritors of the human sinful condition. In line with the discussion of this book, individualism is the symbol by which original sin is historicized for us in the U.S.

At the same time, original sin shows the depth of social sin. Social sin is part of a much broader and deeper mystery. It reaches back and down to the very foundations of human existence and is the universal experience of all people. To be more specific, original sin indicates for us the depth of the issues raised by individualism. And since original sin cannot be understood except in light of Christ's redemption, it also makes clear that social sin (individualism in our case) is not the final word.

## Personal Sin

The term "personal sin" can be misleading, especially with the connotations it bears from the past. To take it to mean something distinct from or opposite to social sin, or to see it as referring only to those sins for which we as individuals are personally accountable (i.e., those we have knowingly and willingly done), is not sufficient. When that happens, personal sin is placed in conflict rather than in continuity with original-social sin. And that implicitly supports individualism.

Personal sin as used here refers to our participation in, and thus our responsibility for, original-social sin. Both "participation" and "responsibility" are key here. In the past, the social implications of sin have been seen more as secondary consequences. Such and such is a sin because it breaks a law of God and/or because it affects negatively who I am as a person; and somehow as a by-product of that, it is also destructive of society.

Personal sin, in my judgment, is not something that *also* happens to affect society; it is a way in which we participate in the sinfulness of society. Through it, we are acting in consort with the sinfulness of our environment, abiding by its spirit and not that of the God who is acting in our midst.

This participation sets the context for our responsibility. As I have indicated, the primary referent of responsibility is not what we have done in the past. It is not a matter of determining the degree of freedom with which we deliberated, decided, and acted. Past actions are over and done with; we cannot erase their effects either in the world around us or within ourselves. What remains open to us, however, is the future: how we will act when faced with a similar situation; what type of world will exist because of how we act. To take responsibility is to declare that next time things can and will be different, that next time we will respond to these as a different person.

Participation and responsibility, then, clearly broaden the meaning of personal sin. Personal sin includes the conscious *and* unconscious, the deliberate *and* indeliberate ways by which we participate in and contribute to original-social sin.

Consider first the unconscious and the indeliberate. This no doubt causes the greatest difficulty; for, even when we become comfortable with using the word sin to describe destructive social structures, we are hesitant to lay accountability for these social sins at our own doorstep. Our individualism makes it seem unreasonable to do so. The drive for innocence raises anxiety at the prospect.

But we pay a great price both individually and communally for limiting our moral responsibility. To do so, we have to hold ourselves personally untouched by the evil of the world around us. Since in fact that is not the case, however, we end up denying a part of ourselves—and indeed a sizable part. We put out of our minds the ways in which society in all its dimensions and in any of its goodness or evil has been woven into the fabric of our being. Such a denial is destructive of life. It does not halt the negative effects of society on our life; but it does hinder our ability to interact with our environment in a life-giving way.

Communally, limiting moral responsibility means no one

is held accountable for some of the greatest evils within the world. On the basis of that limited notion of responsibility, who is answerable for the 800 million people in the world who are absolutely poor? Or who is answerable for the millions of people who die from hunger each day? Or who is answerable for the atomic bombing of Hiroshima and Nagasaki; for the arms race in which we are now engaged? If we absolve ourselves of responsibility for these great evils, we are condemning the world to destruction by its unredeemed powers. And that world in turn deforms us.

The necessity of taking responsibility for our indeliberate actions is brought out well in a statement of the U.S. bishops on racism:

> The structures of our society are subtly racist, for these structures reflect the values which society upholds. They are geared to the success of the majority and the failure of the minority; and members of both groups give unwitting approval by accepting things as they are. Perhaps no single individual is to blame. The sinfulness is often anonymous but nonetheless real. The sin is social in nature in that each of us, in varying degrees, is responsible. All of us in some measure are accomplices. As our recent pastoral letter [*To Live in Christ Jesus*] on moral values states: "The absence of personal fault for an evil does not absolve one of all responsibility. We must seek to resist and undo injustices we have not caused, lest we become bystanders who tacitly endorse evil and so share in guilt for it."[15]

The issue, however, goes deeper than the final sentence of the U.S. Catholic bishops' statement indicates. In a society that is still in so many ways and so profoundly racist, racism has become part of who we are even as we are part of the society in which it exists. Therefore, if we do not "resist and undo injustices we have not caused," it is not simply a case of our becoming "bystanders who tacitly endorse evil." Since it

---

[15]National Conference of Catholic Bishops, "Brothers and Sisters to Us: A Pastoral Letter on Racism," in *Quest for Justice*, eds. J. Brian Benestad and Francis J. Butler (Washington, DC: United States Catholic Conference, 1981), pp. 475-476.

is impossible not to be enmeshed and actively involved in the formal and informal structures of society, we are more than just bystanders. We are participants. We cannot claim the high ground of innocence even when we are working to overcome injustice; for we can no more remove ourselves from our society with all that entails than a fish can remove itself from water.

What has been said about racism holds true as well, of course, for all the other destructive factors within society. We cannot hold ourselves aloof or absolve ourselves of responsibility simply because we did not knowingly and willingly involve ourselves in them. Our responsibility arises not from some abstract sense of duty but from an actual participation in sin.[16]

We turn next to deliberate sins. While it may seem that we are once again back on familiar turf, this category cannot help but be colored by the discussion thus far. First of all, the very nature of deliberation must be qualified. We never know the world "just as it is"; we never view it free of any bias or prejudice. We cannot will to do or avoid something with the dispassion of a computer, especially when it comes to matters of vital interest to us. The deliberate actions we perform are deeply affected by the impersonal or superpersonal dimensions of society as well as by the subconscious and unconscious dimensions of our own person. These form the realm of our destiny which is the ground of our freedom.[17] They necessarily condition our deliberations and

---

[16]While the concept of *simul justus et peccator* is usually identified with the lutheran tradition, it is by no means foreign to Roman Catholicism when properly defined. As Hans Kung points out, it is unacceptable within the catholic tradition "first, when the idea is mixed up through an exaggerated eschatological attitude so that justice is consigned to man only as hope and not also as present reality; or second, when due to a legalistic nominalism the idea is twisted to mean that justice can never become man's possession as an intrinsic reality." Hans Kung, *Justification*, trans. by Thomas Collins, Edmund E. Tolk, and David Granskou (New York: Thomas Nelson and Sons, 1964), pp. 247-248. My point here is that while we have been justified, we (both individually and socially) are still awaiting its fulness. We wait as a people justified by the life, death, and resurrection of Christ, but still suffering under that sinfulness. If we had not already been justified, we would not have the power to work with God for the realization of the Kingdom.

[17]On this point, see below, p. 265ff.

decisions.

Second, deliberate sin is not automatically more important than sin which results from unconscious and indeliberate action. The criterion of seriousness is the effect of our action, whether deliberate or indeliberate, on our environment and on our person. As an individual, for example, I may be very aware of inadequacies in my sexual behavior but very unaware of the destructive effects decisions made in a corporate board room have on millions of people. The mere fact that the former falls more within the category of the deliberate in no way determines automatically that it bears more significance.

This does not mean that guilt, sin, and responsibility do not admit of differing degrees. Take, for instance, the issue of racism which is clearly social sin. Given the way it is woven into all dimensions of U.S. society and culture, it is impossible for us in this country, especially for those of us who are white, to deny participation in this socially sinful situation. Not everyone, however, is equally sinful or bears the same degree of responsibility. The degree of sinfulness and of responsibility is determined by the depth to which racism has seeped into our soul, by the extent to which our state of being affects the sinful condition of society, and by the ability we have to redress this destructive situation.

Personal sin refers primarily to our state of being or the orientation of our life. It concerns the way we participate in and are responsible for the sinfulness of society because of who we are.

At the same time, we cannot overlook the relation of single actions to what we have discussed. Single actions are evaluated in light of their bearing on the orientation of our lives and the well-being of our social and physical environment. We do not redirect the patterns of our lives or the general status of the environment every hour or every day or even every week. But the actions we perform, both deliberate and indeliberate, are the means by which those patterns and that status are formed and reformed. To speak of sin in reference to single actions indicates that an action either further supports a destructive pattern or is part of a developing pattern that undermines an already existing positive trend. The weight or importance we give to an action is based on the degree to which it is involved in that support or undermining.

This sets the context for discussing mortal and venial sin. While these terms have at times been the source of more confusion than clarity, they offer insights that cannot be overlooked. For Roman Catholics in the United States, the Baltimore Catechism has been a primary means for understanding the terms mortal and venial. Before getting to the discussion on the particular commandments, the catechism indicated in the questions and answers on sin in general that a person is not guilty of either a mortal or venial sin simply for having performed a particular action. In addition to an action of serious import, there has to be knowledge and consent of the will. For some reason, however, the latter elements tended to be forgotten. People thought themselves guilty of mortal or venial sin simply because they performed an action labeled mortal or venial sin, regardless of any other considerations.

Some have criticized the Baltimore Catechism for burdening people with an exaggerated sense of guilt or laying on them a misplaced guilt. Their solution, as we saw in the discussion on social sin, is to reemphasize the knowledge and volition necessary for a human action.

While I agree that the effects of the Baltimore Catechism are at times less than desirable, my critique moves in a different direction. The problem, in my view, is one of abstraction: actions are evaluated in isolation from the general orientation of a person's life as well as from the general thrust of the environment, as seen in light of God's activity in history.

Despite the difficulties with past definitions and connotations, I believe the categories of mortal and venial in relation to personal sin should be retained. They alert us to the differing levels of import our actions have and so aid us in evaluating our lives in a nuanced way. To make sure they indeed are helpful, however, we should overcome the abstraction of these terms by seeing them within the context of our present historical situation.

In the past (and indeed still in the present) we have been very successful in communicating the serious import sexuality has for the individual and for society. We have failed, however, to point out adequately the serious negative consequences that can result from the ways we treat people because of race and gender or from the ways we set policy and make decisions for government, business, and church.

We cannot do justice to the reality of sin within our culture without rethinking the concrete references of mortal and venial sin. What are the general categories of action most apt to have a truly killing effect on life as viewed from the perspective of God's Reign? What general categories of action tend to affect life negatively in a lesser, although no less real, way? In this rethinking, we might give thought to the possibility that sexuality (or better, genitality) has been overemphasized and that the only way to call attention to the seriousness of other areas may be to play down its importance for a while. Or we might consider giving more time to issues of gender rather than genitality.

At the same time, the meaning of calling something a mortal or venial sin should also be addressed. These categories are tools for interpreting our lives, not pre-formed judgments upon us. Calling something a mortal or venial sin is a way to indicate its *potential* negative implications and import for ourselves and our environment. It puts us on notice that this particular action usually engages our person and the environment at levels that have a serious subversive effect on both. Whether or not that is the case, however, and the degree to which that is the case, must be judged in each particular instance.

Sin, then, is a faith judgment on human reality. It is a judgment not that a rule of God has been broken but that an aspect of reality is actively opposed to the realization of God's Reign. Sin refers to the universal bondedness we share with all humanity in opposing God's Reign. It indicates the impersonal or superpersonal dimensions of society that incarnate this opposition in a particular society or generation. It includes the ways we personally participate in that opposition, whether knowingly or unwittingly, whether deliberately or involuntarily.

But this faith-judgment of sin is not the last word. As we celebrate in baptism and reconciliation, the power of God's redemption is so much greater. And so we dare to pray that God "look not upon our sins but upon the faith of the church" in the liturgy prior to sharing a greeting of peace. For we truly believe that peace is a possibility—a reality, already among us, but yet to be made full.

*PART THREE:*

*The Sources of Moral Wisdom*

# 6

# Culture:
# The Source of Operative Morality

Now it's time to fill in the space between beginning and end. Part one set forth as the entry point for our inquiry into the moral life and moral decision-making the problems caused by U.S. individualism. Part two offered the conclusion to the inquiry by way of a discussion of virtue and sin. In this section and the next, we examine how the move from problem to solution was made.

We begin by considering in section three what I term "sources of moral wisdom": culture, natural law, scripture, and church. In discussing these topics, I will show how each provides insight for carrying out the moral enterprise in a way that responds to the difficulties caused by individualism; and how each helps establish the concrete particulars of the moral life and moral decision-making. And, as the opportunity presents itself, I will explain and justify some of the positions I took in the first two parts of the book.

The various subjects considered in the four chapters of this section are commonplace in any discussion of Roman Catholic ethics, with the exception of the first. Culture is usually given no more than passing reference, if even that. The presumption seems to be that whatever is said about morality is transcultural, applicable in each and every society in substantially the same way.

Such a presumption can have negative consequences. In any culture, if we do not consciously advert to the problems it raises, we may adopt a moral stance that promotes rather than challenges its destructive factors. Without critical insight into a culture, we simply take its accepted way of thinking and acting for granted.

Within the context of U.S. individualism, failure to take culture seriously can easily go along with, and even further, its loosening of the individual's ties to society. Since emphasis falls primarily on the individual in this country, the various aspects of society, including culture, are seen as having merely instrumental value. They are convenient; but they are not absolutely necessary. Images of the cowboy, the long-distance truck driver, and the loner leave us with the impression that we can go it on our own, that our personal resources are all we need. Downplaying culture does nothing to challenge this; in fact, it can easily promote it.

Moreover, not attending critically to culture increases its power over us. This is especially problematic in an individualistic culture due to the conformity it promotes. As I pointed out in the second chapter, when we as individuals find ourselves on our own, we are beset by feelings of powerlessness; and, because of that, we are more apt to comply with generally accepted attitudes and behavior rather than to call them into question. In spite of our strong belief in freedom, we acquiesce in the opinion of the majority.

Thus, the category of culture, which U.S. individualism tends to overlook, is a crucial tool in examining the culture of individualism. Our task here, then, is to consider what it means to take culture seriously in looking at the moral life and moral decision-making.

## Culture, Morality, and Identity

The world in which we live is a moral world—not moral in the sense that the demands of morality are always met, but in the sense that morality is an intrinsic, objective dimension of reality.[1] In the ongoing transaction between ourselves and

---

[1]This point will be discussed further in the next chapter.

our world, we find there not only facts such as a physicist or a chemist deals with but also values. Values are those aspects of our world we prize and hold precious, aspects we are attracted by and feel compelled to respond to. These values are moral inasmuch as they bear upon the flourishing of life.

This experience of morality is mediated for us by society. We have an initial sense or "gut feeling" about what is necessary to make life flourish, but society gives us the language and the ways of thinking we need so we can explain these values to ourselves and to others. It describes this experience of values at two different levels: the generalized or universal, and the specific or operative.

In presenting the moral dimension of our world to us, society offers us certain ways of understanding values that make us aware we share them in common with people across the world and across history. We have, for instance, an experience of expecting certain things from others and of owing them the same. We term this justice. All people have had a similar experience. Again, we have an experience—which we share with others—that there is a proper and an improper way to live out our sexuality; and the experience of this value we call chastity. Values described in this general, inclusive way I call *universal values*.

While justice and chastity understood at the universal level point to real aspects of our world, they are not the values by which we carry on our daily existence. They are much too general for that. Each culture and each generation has a particular interpretation and a particular working definition for justice and chastity and all the other moral values that give direction to personal and social existence. These I call *operative values*.

A couple of examples are in order. As I noted above, justice seeks to give each person his or her due. But how that "due" is interpreted differs. In the thirteenth century, for instance, Thomas Aquinas asked whether it is lawful to steal when one is in need. His answer:

> Since, however, there are many who are in need, while it is impossible for all to be succoured by means of the same thing, each one is entrusted with the stewardship of his

own things, so that out of them he may come to the aid of those who are in need. Nevertheless, if the need be so manifest and urgent, that it is evident that the present need must be remedied by whatever means be at hand (for instance when a person is in some imminent danger, and there is no other possible remedy), then *it is lawful for a man to succour his own need by means of another's property, by taking it either openly or secretly*; nor is this properly speaking theft or robbery.[2]

Five centuries later, Adam Smith defined the demands of justice in a very different way. He cautioned that one person should never bring harm to another, even though the benefit to oneself would be greater than the injury to the other. He explicitly mentions the poor in this regard, warning them that they "must neither defraud nor steal from the rich."

[F]or one man to deprive another unjustly of any thing, or unjustly to promote his own advantage by the loss or disadvantage of another, is more contrary to nature than death, than poverty, than pain, than all the misfortunes which can affect him, either in his body, or in his external circumstances.[3]

According to both Aquinas and Smith, then, justice must be practiced, and it requires giving to each one's due. But the two authors differ dramatically when they lay out the concrete, operative demands of justice.

For an example in the area of sexuality, we can compare our society's attitudes about appropriate physical distance between men with the accepted values of other cultures. In some European and African countries, it is not untoward for one man to kiss another or for two men to walk down the street hand in hand. In this country, all two men have to do to insure clear passage through a crowded room is to hold hands.

These operative values—justice defined concretely in terms

[2]Aquinas, II-II, 66, 7. Emphasis added.
[3]Smith, *Theory of Moral Sentiments*, p. 195.

of what one person can and cannot do with the property of another; chastity defined specifically as to its demands for the relationship between individuals of the same gender—are what we live by. Where do these originate? Culture is their source.

Culture is one of those words that is easily used but not so easily defined. A 1952 survey of its use among social scientists revealed 167 different definitions.[4] For my purposes here, the one offered by Clifford Geertz is helpful. Culture is "an ordered system of meaning and of symbols, in terms of which social interaction takes place"; it is "the framework of beliefs, expressive symbols, and values in terms of which individuals define their world, express their feelings, and make their judgments."[5]

Morality, then, is a part of culture; and culture is an essential part of morality. Through culture, moral values are concretely defined and made concretely available to us as individuals. This enables us to carry out the uniquely human task of engaging the world in a meaning-filled, symbolic and evaluative way. As such, culture is our first source of moral wisdom: *first* because it is our point of departure in considering what morality actually, concretely means in our society.

But, the impact of culture on morality—and the significance culture has for addressing the individual-society connection for U.S. individualism—goes further yet. To get at that, we have to consider the effect culture has on our very identity as individuals. As I shall argue, culture is much more than just the context within which we live out our lives and carry on the moral enterprise.

We human beings do not come equipped at birth with a specific identity already realized or only waiting to blossom

---

[4]A.L. Kroeber and Clyde Kluckhohn, *Culture: A Critical Review of Concepts and Definitions* (Cambridge: Papers of the Peabody Museum of American Archeology and Ethnology, 1952), pp. 43-79.

[5]Clifford Geertz, *The Interpretation of Cultures* (New York: Basic Books, Inc., 1973), pp. 144-145. See also, ibid., p. 89: Culture "denotes an historically transmitted pattern of meanings embodied in symbols, a system of inherited conceptions expressed in symbolic forms by means of which men communicate, perpetuate, and develop their knowledge about and attitudes toward life."

forth. In fact, what distinguishes us from non-human off-spring at birth is our low degree of specificity. The wildebeest, for example—admittedly a not overly gracious example, given its less than gracious appearance—must be able to run with the herd within fifteen minutes of birth or else it becomes an afternoon snack for some predator. For us human beings, the ability to move under our own power takes a few years; the ability to take our place as a contributing member of society many more than that. We have to fashion our skills. But more importantly, we have to integrate the various dimensions of our person into an identity.

In emphasizing the low degree of specificity that is ours at birth, I do not mean we are all born alike, simple blobs of modeling clay that can be molded any which way. Our possibilities are limited by human possibilities. For example, we never expect to be able to propel ourselves to the top of a tree merely by flapping our arms. And for our humanity and personality to develop, we pass through certain stages in a certain order, as psychologists have shown. These are but a couple of the restrictions we all share as part of the human condition.

Individually our physical, emotional, and psychological possibilities are limited and distinguished from those of others by our inherited genetic make-up. The potential combinations among our 46 chromosomes open the door to a wide range of unique results—unique in the sense of distinctive. At the same time, while this unique combination is the foundation for our distinctiveness as individuals, it also limits the possibilities open to each one of us.

But at birth these possibilities remain just that—possibilities. The newly born infant finds itself suddenly thrust into the world. That world is a particular world, a world of people united with one another through their common participation in—or, better, their common immersion in—a particular culture. The infant becomes an instant heir to this world mediated through those with whom the infant interacts. Thus, the infant's potentiality for speech becomes a reality through contact with parents communicating through speech. And so, not surprisingly, a child grows up using the parents' particular dialect. Likewise, the parents' taste for food, their attitude toward clothing, their understanding of what it means to be male or female and the implications this has for relating with others and taking one's place within society will mold the potentialities present at birth, giving them a particular form and definition in the child's life.

The effects of this enculturation reach down much more deeply than individualism usually leads us to understand. It is not just that I am this individual who *happens* to speak the U.S. brand of English, who *happens* to live out this particular male identity, who *happens* to prefer the meat of a cow to that of a cat. I am not just an individual who *happens* to make use of this culture; this particular culture has, in a very real way, created the type of individual I am.

Culture cannot make me into anything that it wants; for, to repeat, at birth I am not merely a piece of modeling clay that can be manipulated into any shape whatever. I have certain potentialities and not others. But when these particular potentialities begin to interact with a particular culture, certain of them are developed and certain others are not. And out of this process our distinctive individuality emerges.

Culture, then, has the power of selection as well as of actualization. It in a very real way selects which of our potentialities will be realized. Certainly, nothing can be actualized unless its potentiality exists. But not every potentiality we have necessarily becomes a reality in our life. And the particular form and orientation that potentiality assumes depend upon the specific configurations of the culture.

Consider, for instance, the way culture affects our ability to see. We usually do not advert to this, since we take the sense of sight for granted. But, as one anthropologist points out, "the sharp vision of the Indians on the plains is not the result of any superiority in actual visual acuity. It stems from their learned ability to read meaning in the way an animal or rider moves, the kind of dust he raises, and the lay of the land."[6]

The same author presents a counter example, showing how culture can also lessen a people's ability to see—lessen, that is to say from *our* perspective.

[6]Hoebel, p. 216.

Trobriand Islanders cannot recognize any physiological similarity between father and sons. We look for and often see similarities that are doubtful at best. We feel that similarities should exist. Trobrianders feel that there should be no similarities, because theirs is a matrilineal society in which the mother's brother rather than the father has the important social position with respect to boys; and in denial of the father's significance the Trobrianders hold to a belief in spirit conception of offspring.[7]

Culture, therefore, is an essential ingredient in the development of our individuality. The fact that I have been born in the United States in the middle of this century has resulted, for both better and worse, in the emergence of a particular identity. But what would have happened if I had been born with the same possibilities in a different culture or a different time? It would not be just a matter of this same self's using different language and enjoying different types of food. The self would be different.

Or what would have happened if a person like Ludwig van Beethoven had been born a thousand years earlier? Even if the potentiality for musical genius had been present, he could not have come up with the Ninth Symphony. For the potentiality to become the reality we know, he had to fall heir to a culture which enjoyed the legacy left by composers such as Haydn and Mozart.

More specific to our purposes here, culture actuates our potentiality for responding to our moral world. Among the elements to which we fall heir at birth are the particular operative values of our culture. These give form and substance to our sense of value.

But these values are not given to us as separate, discrete entities. They are grouped around role-identities and organized into an integrated "design for living."[8] Therefore, we are not only presented with operative values by which to guide

[7]Ibid.

[8]Louis J. Luzbetak, *The Church and Cultures* (Pasadena, CA: William Carey Library, 1976), p. 60.

the living out of our sexuality; these values are "wrapped up" in culturally-based descriptions of what it means to be a male or female, a spouse, a parent, a single person. Rather than simply taking these descriptions and donning them as we would a costume for a Mardi Gras party, we work out our own specific identity through them. Thus, for example, though I may not be a male just like any other male, my own identity in that role can only be comprehensible to myself and to others if it maintains definite and substantial continuities with that culturally-based description. That identity is achieved only as I use the materials culture presents me to actualize the specific possibilities that are mine.

Thus the meanings, symbols, and values of the society of which we are a part are more than something we have and make use of. They are content out of which our self-identity and our way of being a part of the social and physical world are formed. Individuality, then, involves *both* participation *and* distinctivenes. We share in a common heritage; at the same time, we participate in that heritage in a distinctive way. We are not merely clones of society, mere replications of the standard U.S. model. Our uniqueness, however, rests not on the discontinuities that separate us from others but on the distinctive ways we participate in and are a part of our culture.

Thus, it is not a choice of either being related to culture or being distinct; it is both. We can be blinded to this by U.S. individualism much the way the Trobrianders are unable to see any similarities between father and child. We are very aware of the ways in which we differ from one another, but we fail to note the similarities and continuities.

A number of conclusions follow from this understanding of the relation of morality in general and of the individual's moral life in particular to culture. First, this gives foundation to and makes clear the necessary connection between personal and social morality. It is not just that what we do has broader social consequences. We cannot know ourselves unless we also know our culture. We cannot examine our conscience in any depth unless we first bring to consciousness the specific values our culture holds. For, like it or not, our culture is a part of us; and the more we deny that fact or refuse to take it into consideration, the more we fail to see who we are and what we are about.

Second, because of the relation of morality and culture, we bear a deep—indeed a fundamental—responsibility for the world in which we live. In a very real way, that world is at once creature and creator. It is a human product; at the same time, it plays an indispensable role in the realization of human identity. This is not a once-for-all event, occurring just at one point in our lives (namely, our childhood). Culture continues to shape us; and we, by living out who we are, shape culture. We truly take responsibility for our lives, therefore, only as we also take responsibility for our culture, for the world within which we live. Despite the contrary attitude that individualism can leave us with, we continue to be affected by our environment even if we do not take note of that fact.

Third, this connection between morality and culture points up the importance of emphasizing justice in discussing and pursuing the virtuous self. We have to evaluate all we do in light of the demands of the common good. A virtue approach to ethics need not, and indeed must not, result in a concern simply for a personalistic morality. The virtuous individual needs a virtuous environment; and, to be virtuous, an individual must pursue a virtuous environment.

Culture, then, is a primary factor in morality. It provides the operative values giving concrete direction to our lives. Even more importantly, it presents these values to us in a "design for living." This is the material, the substance out of which we fashion our individual identity—an identity that is at once distinctive and participative.

As such, culture profits from individualism's insight into the importance of the individual; but it challenges individualism by showing that culture has more than just instrumental value. Culture, which is woven into the fabric of our being, cannot be under valued without undervaluing our own humanity.

## Conformity and Critique

Thus far, I have underscored our essential participation in culture as a constructive response to the way U.S. individualism loosens the ties of the individual to society. We now have to consider another problem individualism entails, namely, conformity to cultural expectations.

Our previous discussion, however, has made this more difficult. For, the more we emphasize the impact of culture on our lives, the harder it is for us to explain how we can stand back and take a critical look at society. A critical stance requires that we be able to transcend our culture. For obviously if we are no more able to ask significant questions about our culture than a fish can wonder about water, it makes no sense whatever to talk about a critical spirit. We have no point from which to get some purchase.

At the same time, the transcendence necessary to get such purchase cannot be conceived in a way that places us outside the ambit of culture. Because of the depths to which we are affected by culture, we cannot simply walk beyond its boundaries and seat ourselves on a distant hill, from which to view it with the cold, dispassionate eye of the scientist.

The key to overcoming these difficulties is to understand that *transcending culture means breaking it open to discover its further possibilities*. This *does not mean* finding something completely unrelated to the present; it *does mean* not being limited to its present configuration. To transcend a culture is to look through its present operative values to its further and fuller possibilities. It is, if you will, a transcendence *within* rather than a transcendence *beyond*—a transcendence, that is to say, allowing us to challenge the conformity of U.S. individualism while at the same time overcoming the problems that individualism raises for the relation of the individual to society.

The history of our nation offers examples of this type of transcendence. In framing the Declaration of Independence, the authors proclaimed it to be "self-evident" that "all men are created equal." For many decades afterward, that equality was staunchly upheld by society even as it permitted slavery and denied the franchise to women and to those who did not own property.

But that self-evident principle prepared the way for something different. On the basis of those principles, for example, civil rights legislation has been passed, committing this society to refuse any longer to feel comfortable with segregation. This is by no means to say that all the problems in this area have been solved. We are still faced with the painful and painfully slow process of weaving this sentiment into the fabric of culture and of its individual members. But the transcendence of the status quo and the new direction which this critique made possible were accomplished not by leaving this society and culture totally, but by breaking it open to its further possibilities.

A primary resource for insight into culture's potential are a society's subcultures—communities within society which are informed by the main culture but which integrate into themselves elements from other cultures as well. This is the other side of my argument in the introduction[9] that we can sensibly talk about a national identity for the U.S. because individualism has qualified the ways of thinking and acting of all groups in this country. There I quoted the historian Arthur Mann to show that Irish-Americans, for example, when visiting Ireland, discover there is much they do *not* share in common with Irish nationals. The "American" in their hyphenated identity has had a deeply formative effect.

Here I want to make the point that the front of that hyphenated identity is equally important. While the Irish-Americans—to continue the example—may indeed be Americans, the Irish subculture introduces factors and perspectives that are not always easily wedded to U.S. individualism. This holds true of any subculture, whether it be based on nationality, on religious affiliation, on sexual orientation, or on any other grouping that involves a "design for living." Consequently, these subcultures can provide a distinct angle from which to view U.S. culture in terms of both what it is and what it might be. In other words, these subcultures can

[9]See above, p. 25.

be in a very real way a transcendence-within.[10]

In carrying out a cultural critique of the operative moral values which fashion our society and our identity in order to break them open to their further possibilities, we do so in a manner keeping with the very nature of culture. This involves the following four steps: knowledge; respect; critique; action.

(1) First, we have to bring to consciousness our culture's operative values. To accomplish this, we need to attend to two characteristics of culture: its unity and its uniqueness. As a humanly created "design for living," culture applies to the totality of life, providing members of a society with a means to interpret and evaluate all parts of their world, both internal and external. Culture is not, however, akin to a huge bank of mailboxes with each aspect separate from the next. Rather, culture offers an overarching vision of the meaning and value of life within which the various components are interrelated. Thus, no one aspect of culture can be understood in isolation.

> A culture consists of elements or single traits, but the significance of a culture is less in its inventory of traits than the manner of integration of the traits. It is theoretically possible for two societies to possess identical inventories of culture elements, and yet so to arrange the relationships of these elements to each other that the complexes within the two cultures and the total forms of the two cultures will be quite unlike. By simple analogy, a mason may take two identical piles of bricks and equal quantities of mortar. Yet according to the manner in which he lays his bricks, he may produce a fireplace or a garden wall.[11]

Accordingly, the simple fact that female virginity, for example, is valued within a particular culture does not immediately explain the significance it holds for that people. As Luzbetak points out, it might have religious import, but

---

[10]I am indebted to Jim Hug for bringing this point to my attention.

[11]Hoebel, pp. 217-218.

it could as well be a matter of economics: a virgin daughter brings her father a better bride-price.[12] Closer to home, the so-called sexual revolution in this country may not necessarily be the result of a growing moral bankruptcy among our young people. Gibson Winter offers the following as a possible alternative interpretation.

> My hypothesis about the sexual revolution, therefore, is that sexuality is a major locus for the struggle for personal values in this organizational society because sexuality is a sphere in which the powerless still have some voice. Sexuality often becomes a way of compensating for personal impoverishment; and compensatory sexuality can endanger the sexual maturity of many adults. However, I am also suggesting that sexuality is an alternative way of working at authentic human values in that society—the achievement of consent, freedom and participation.[13]

The distinctiveness of a particular culture comes not from its unique elements but from the unique ways these elements are interrelated within that culture's overall vision. The description of the main problem facing us in the U.S., which I set forth in part one, exemplifies this. I mentioned there, you will recall, that while I see a great deal of truth in Timothy O'Connell's and Daniel Maguire's analyses of the present situation, I believe the determinism and ideologism and nihilism they detect should be situated in U.S. culture to determine their specific meaning and import within this context. According to my interpretation, their significance is defined by the fact that they are a part of, and are shaped by, U.S. individualism.

Given the unity and the uniqueness of a culture, the first step in critiquing culture is by no means easy. We have to determine precisely what is meant, for example, by justice

---

[12]Luzbetak, p. 68.

[13]Gibson Winter, "The Outlook for an Adequate Ethic," in *Sexual Ethics and Christian Responsibility*, ed. John Charles Wynn (New York: Association Press, 1970), pp. 42, 43.

and truth-telling and chastity and charity in the U.S. But we cannot deal with these values in isolation. Their full operative meaning becomes apparent only as we see how they are connected with other values and what particular connotations they bear in light of culture's overall vision.

(2) Once these operative values have been identified, our initial response must be one of deep reverence and respect. This is not to say that in bringing them to consciousness we find only that which is good and true and beautiful. By no means. But, despite all the imperfections and deficiencies we see (and the more reflective we are, the more we become aware of), these values, woven together in the fabric of ourselves and of our culture, are the substance of human life. As such, we cannot take them lightly, nor can we deal fast and loose with them. Because they are the building blocks of human life, they must be treated as something sacred.

Beginning with this attitude makes all the difference where we end after criticizing an aspect or the overall orientation of our culture. It is similar to the difference between an operation carried out by a doctor with a deep and abiding respect for the human body and the human person, and an operation performed by a doctor for whom the human body is little different from the cadaver used during the first year of medical school. The possibility of coming out of the operation not only alive but able to look ahead to a productive future is much greater in the former instance than in the latter.

(3) This regard and respect for cultural values, however, cannot blind us to problems and defects. Nor can it commit us to a naive, uncritical acceptance—even though at times, especially during periods of national and international tension, this is demanded as a sign of loyalty and patriotism. Blind, uncritical allegiance makes the nation or the group an idol; and in worshipping at the altar of this false god, we sacrifice our humanity by abdicating our ability and our responsibility to ask of it challenging, critical questions. True love and true loyalty are grounded in the desire that any culture and any society rid itself of its evil and realize as fully as possible its moral potentialities.

But a critical stance toward culture must respect its unity and uniqueness. This means that a particular culture, like that of the United States, should be understood and critiqued from within, not from outside. That is to say, we cannot understand or pass judgment on a culture on the basis of certain of its dimensions taken by themselves in abstraction from its overall identity. Only as a culture is addressed from the inside, from its internal logic, from the ways in which its various meanings, values, and symbols are woven together, can it really be known and evaluated.

Thus, for example, the issue of abortion in U.S. culture must indeed be submitted to critical inquiry and evaluation. It cannot be understood, however, in the abstract, removed from its connection with the drive to overcome the effects of patriarchy, and with changing role-identities for women in general and for motherhood in particular;[14] it cannot be properly interpreted without taking into account its existence in a society defined by freedom as understood through individualism,[15] in a society which turns too easily to technological solutions. I am not saying that any or all of these are necessarily positive factors; but they have to be taken into account when discussing abortion in the U.S.

Likewise, the issue of U.S. participation in nuclear deterrence demands close scrutiny. This scrutiny should involve a study of the place and meaning of war in U.S. culture, an analysis of our national feeling of insecurity and powerlessness that makes us so ready to turn to military force, and a consideration of how all of this is interwoven in an individualistic culture.

This criticism from within no doubt raises concerns that it may actually result in unreflective acceptance of U.S. culture rather than in its judgment. This is always a danger and should be a matter of constant concern. But I believe this has to be risked to insure that the judgment be realistic and on-target—that is to say, that the judgment be made on a particular dimension of a culture in light of its actual meaning

---

[14]See Kristin Luker, *Abortion and the Politics of Motherhood* (Berkeley, CA: University of California Press, 1984).

[15]See Beverly Wildung Harrison, *Our Right to Choose* (Boston: Beacon Press, 1983).

within that culture and in light of its specific dehumanizing aspects.

Insistence on criticism from within, however, does not mean that no resources can be imported from outside a particular culture to aid in making evaluative judgments. Immersed as we are in our culture, we take it for granted and have a difficult time even bringing it to consciousness, much less critiquing it. Anything, therefore, that can help us break through our unconscious and uncritical acceptance of the meanings, symbols, and values that define our world and our life is important. Concretely, reading about or visiting a different culture as well as paying close attention to the distinctive characteristics of the subcultures to which we belong can be a great help. At a more general level, the other sources of moral wisdom which will be discussed in the next chapters— natural law, scripture, church—provide valuable assistance in getting a critical distance.

Still, these imports must be used in a way that respects the unity and uniqueness of our culture. We may be strongly taken by the different pace of life of the Italians; or we may be struck by an African tribe's strong sense of community. But we cannot, therefore, move to an immediate judgment on similar aspects of our culture taken in the abstract. We first have to understand what pace of life and sense of community mean *from within* our culture. Only then can we move to judgment. What that judgment involves will be explored in the following three chapters.

(4) Finally, this approach calling for transcendence-within rather than transcendence-beyond is likewise our guide in seeking solutions to the problems raised by our critique. To change a particular culture we have to look to its own possibilities.

In this, culture might be compared to a boat within which we make our passage through life. At no time can we sail the boat to shore in order to take on different resources. Its components and dynamics are the means—the sole means— at our disposal for responding to the difficulties we face.

Bearing this in mind helps us keep solutions proposed for the problems of society realistic. They are realistic because they are rooted in the true possibilities lying within the culture.

Few things are more debilitating and more enervating than unrealistic solutions. Anyone can spin out visions of great new worlds where want and death and anger and war are not known, and where "seldom is heard a discouraging word." Such visions are tailor-made for a summer's day when we are lying on the beach watching wisps of clouds chase one another across the sky at a snail's pace. But when those visions, totally out of touch with the real possibilities of the present, become the guiding visions by which we would re-form and refashion our society and our lives, the results are less than happy. They are impossible, since basically "we can't get there from here."

When impossible solutions are proposed and attempted, not only do we fail but we are frustrated. This frustration can be the breeding ground for a despair which asks, "What's the use? If no one is coming up with a realistic alternative to what we have, maybe such an alternative actually does not exist." And so we capitulate to the present state of things.

But, as history shows, impossible solutions can also be the breeding ground for totalitarianism. If the desired new society cannot be born out of the present, then an individual or a group becomes determined to make it happen regardless. Ideas, values, and people that stand in the way are ruthlessly eradicated; and those which are sufficiently pliable are fashioned by force into the proper form. Kampuchea (Cambodia), under the Pol Pot regime, is a recent example of this.

Another temptation in addressing the problems raised by culture is to seek piecemeal solutions. Now to be sure, we cannot solve all the difficulties at once. But, forgetting about the unity and uniqueness of culture, we can carry out the project the same way we take care of a burnt-out light bulb—we try to deal with the problematic piece in isolation, simply replacing it with something different. If there are too many people living together without benefit of clergy or magistrate, pass a law and put an end to it. If there are too many people on welfare, introduce "workfare" so that people will be "allowed" to earn what they get and so that the lazy deadbeats will be smoked out.

Here what appears simple is actually simplistic. The solutions do not arise out of an analysis of what the problem is in light of culture as a whole nor are they rooted in the realistic possibilities of society.

All of this can appear far removed from the issues of everyday life and personal morality. True, we cannot stop to work out a new plan for our culture based on its possibilities every time we run up against a moral problem. But that does not mean we can go about our daily lives as though they made no difference whatsoever for the type of world we live in. The mediating factor here is virtue.

As I pointed out in the fourth chapter, we consciously think out and decide only a small portion of what we do. By far the majority of what we do, including our deliberate actions, flow from the type of person we are. Given what I have said about culture to this point, our concern is gradually to develop the prudence, that is to say, the sensitivity and thoughtfulness that will habituate us to act in certain ways— ways which will build up the kind of person and the kind of society that best respond to the work of God in our midst, and thus that best contribute to the coming of God's Reign. Behind this lies a firm belief and a deep hope that from the smallest of all seeds will spring the largest shrub of all.[16]

## Culture and the Roman Catholic Church

To this point we have not factored in the Roman Catholic Church's role in the relation of culture and morality. In a very real way, this relation seems foreign to Roman Catholic custom and tradition. Official Roman Catholic statements about morality, especially those bearing on personal ethical issues, have had more of a universalist than a particularist cast to them. Pronouncements about birth control and homosexuality and premarital intercourse,[17] for example, are

[16]Matthew 13:32.

[17]See, for example, *Humanae Vitae* and the *Declaration on Certain Questions Concerning Sexual Ethics.*

addressed to the whole world and to each individual. No account is taken of cultural differences, nor is there place for such an account.

This can fit in well with U.S. individualism. Specific aspects of a particular culture are abstracted from the distinctive unity defining that culture; a judgment is made on them; then alternative forms of behavior are suggested or demanded without regard for their meaning within that particular "design for living." As a result, even though (as we shall see) the importance of culture is underlined by some official Roman Catholic statements, culture remains a shadowy entity which in its concrete forms seems to have little importance or value for the human project. Here once again, then, we have an instance where the way in which Roman Catholicism presents its position supports U.S. individualism, even though its fundamental stance is actually anything but individualistic.

But there is another dimension to Roman Catholic thought. The Second Vatican Council, particularly, though not exclusively, in the *Pastoral Constitution on the Church in the Modern World*, gives an important place to culture. "It is a fact bearing on the very person of man that he can come to an authentic and full humanity only through culture, that is, through the cultivation of natural goods and values."[18] The

---

[18] *The Pastoral Constitution on the Church in the Modern World*, para. 53. All citations from the Second Vatican Council are taken from Walter Abbott and Joseph Gallagher, eds., *The Documents of Vatican II* (New York: America Press, 1966). The importance of culture for humanity has been strongly emphasized by Pope John Paul II. In his 1980 address to UNESCO entitled "Man's Entire Humanity Is Expressed in Culture," he states: "Culture is a specific way of man's 'existing' and 'being.' Man always lives according to a culture which is specifically his, and which, in turn, creates among men a tie which is also specifically theirs, determining the inter-human and social character of human existence." In *The Church and Culture Since Vatican II*, ed. Joseph Gremillion (Notre Dame, IN: University of Notre Dame Press, 1985), p. 189. Linking the sovereignty of society to culture, he makes this impassioned plea: "With all the means at your disposal, watch over this fundamental sovereignty that every Nation possesses by virtue of its own culture. Cherish it like the apple of your eye for the future of the great human family. Protect it! Do not allow this fundamental sovereignty to become the prey of some political or economic interest. Do not allow it to become a victim of totalitarian and imperialistic systems or hegemonies, for which man counts only as an object of domination and not as the subject of his own human existence." Ibid.,

customs which are an integral part of culture are the "proper patrimony"[19] of each human community. And, while it is true that changes in our modern world are moving us toward "a more universal form of human culture,"[20] we must work to avoid "disturbing the life of communities, destroying ancestral wisdom, or jeopardizing the uniqueness of each people."[21]

Since the mission of the church does not lie in another world totally removed from this history, but is essentially tied up with the construction of a more human world—an endeavor in which it joins with all people—the dignity and integrity of specific cultures hold a place of special importance for it. The church "strengthens, perfects and restores them in Christ."[22] At the same time,

> Living in various circumstances during the course of time, the Church, too, has used in her preaching the discoveries of different cultures to spread and explain the message of Christ to all nations, to prove it and more deeply understand it, and to give it better expression in liturgical celebrations and in the life of the diversified community of the faithful.[23]

In noting this exchange and mutual enrichment between Roman Catholicism and particular cultures, the council is not naively pacific: "it is sometimes difficult to harmonize

---

p. 195. In 1982 John Paul II created the Pontifical Council for Culture, declaring: "Since the beginning of my pontificate, I have considered the Church's dialogue with the cultures of our time to be a vital area, one in which the destiny of the world at the end of the twentieth century is at stake." *L'Osservatore Romano* (English), June 28, 1982. Cited in Gremillion, *The Church and Culture*, p. 26.

[19] *The Pastoral Constitution on the Church in the Modern World*, para. 53.

[20] Ibid., para. 54.

[21] Ibid., para. 56.

[22] Ibid., para. 58. See also, the *Dogmatic Constitution on the Church*, para. 13.

[23] Ibid. See also, "The Address of John Paul II to First Meeting of the Pontifical Council for Culture, Vatican City, January 18, 1983," in Gremillion, *The Church and Culture*, p. 203; "One Church, Many Cultures," Pope John Paul II's 1984 Christmas address to the college of cardinals, ibid, p. 215; "Evangelization in Latin America's Present and Future," a section of the statement issued at Puebla, ibid., pp. 248-249.

culture with Christian teaching." But, in the view of the council, these differences are not to be overcome by a one-sided solution imposed by the church.

> These difficulties do not necessarily harm the life of faith. Indeed they can stimulate the mind to a more accurate and penetrating grasp of the faith. For recent studies and findings of science, history, and philosophy raise new questions which influence life and demand new theological investigations.[24]

In light of this attitude toward culture, the council in its document on the relationship of the church to non-Christian religions exhorts its members:

> prudently and lovingly, through dialogue and collaboration with the followers of other religions, and in witness of Christian faith and love, acknowledge, preserve, and promote the spiritual and moral goods found among these men, as well as the values in their society and culture.[25]

So, what I am arguing for here is not contrary to the official position of the church. In fact, it is very much in keeping with it. But it is necessary for Roman Catholicism to move from theoretical statements about the importance of culture to concrete deeds proving the seriousness of its intent. Particularly is this true in those instances where, in the words of Vatican II, it is "difficult to harmonize culture with Christian teaching."

Unfortunately, recent examples of this do not immediately jump to mind. In fact, it is easier to find instances where this has not occurred.[26] In a 1982 article in the english edition of

---

[24] *The Pastoral Constitution on the Church in the Modern World*, para. 62.

[25] *The Declaration on the Relationship of the Church to Non-Christian Religions*, para. 2.

[26] Bishop Peter Sarpong of the diocese of Kumasi, Ghana, is an exception. He speaks straightforwardly about the problems of responding to health issues while trying to respect a people's culture—in this case, the Ashanti tribe in central Ghana. He poses a number of questions, among them these: "A dying person must be given

*L'Osservatore Romano*, Rev. Diarmuid Martin of the Pontifical Council for the Family discussed the issue of inculturation in relation to *Familiaris Consortio*, Pope John Paul II's apostolic exhortation on the family. Martin reviews the Roman Catholic position on culture, pointing out the need for "a creative tension between the Gospel message and the culture of each believer,"[27] and offering principles for responding to that tension.

But when the discussion turns to specifics, particularly to instances where tension is more in the nature of a clash, there is no indication that this "can stimulate the mind to a more accurate and penetrating grasp of the faith," as Vatican II declares. Martin refers to difficulties encountered in trying to align Roman Catholic liturgical practice with the attitude toward marriage in some cultures where "it is often very difficult to identity (sic) a moment which can be considered as a decisive marriage."[28] In the ensuing discussion, Martin points out how some elements of culture can be introduced into the liturgical celebration; but he gives no indication that the difficulties raised by this tension might lead to a change in Roman Catholic understanding of marriage. The same approach is taken to the subject of polygamy.

In making this criticism, I am by no means saying that the Roman Catholic Church should adopt each culture in wholesale and uncritical fashion. To do so would undermine the church's integrity and place it in the position of legitimating destructive dimensions of culture. I am arguing, however, that the church should face the practical import of its own

---

water to drink to prepare him for the long hazardous journey ahead. Does a health worker agree to this cultural obligation?

"And what about the deformed baby? Does a health worker look after him until he grows and becomes a burden, the unmistakable evidence of sin, an object of shame? Or does he give the baby to his parents, knowing very well that they will sooner or later get rid of it in one way or another?

"What of the prolongation of life? Or what of a person accused of being a witch who would sooner die rather than live with the stigma of being regarded as a witch." Bishop Peter Sarpong, "Answering 'Why'—The Ghanaian Concept of Disease," *Contact* 84 (April 1985): 10.

[27]Rev. Diarmuid Martin, "The Question of Inculturation," *L'Osservatore Romano* (English), April 26, 1982, p. 10.

[28]Ibid., p. 11.

words. This is especially important in a culture defined by individualism where the social dimension of human life becomes problematic—a dimension which Roman Catholicism strongly insists cannot be overlooked without human life being devastated. Insofar as the church through its actions and statements undercuts or fails to promote the importance of culture, it can easily end up supporting rather than challenging the problems caused by U.S. individualism.

Culture, then, is the first source of moral wisdom, the first resource we turn to for insight into the specifics of the moral life and of moral decision-making. It is first because the operative values are in fact our starting point in any consideration of morality. They are the perspective out of which we approach any issue. Even more importantly, they are the material out of which we fashion the moral dimension of our own identity; that is to say, the distinctive way in which we participate in a particular culture.

This appreciation for the substantive role culture plays in morality offers a means for responding constructively to some of the problems arising from U.S. individualism. It highlights the social nature of morality and it brings out the social rootedness of our identity without denying our individual distinctiveness.

At the same time, the specific concrete values which culture presents are not to be accepted without question. But any criticism must be made "from within," that is, respecting the unity and uniqueness of culture. And any solutions offered for the problems raised by a particular culture must be in line with that culture's realistic possibilities. In this way, the conformity toward which U.S. individualism tends can be challenged without losing sight of our close, essential tie to culture.

While such an approach to morality at first glance appears foreign to Roman Catholicism, it is in fact in keeping with the attitudes toward culture expressed especially in the documents of Vatican II. The task now is to put those attitudes into practice.

# 7

# Natural Law: A Mosaic of Mosaics

We now turn to the other sources of moral wisdom to get some critical purchase on our culture and to crack it open to its further possibilities. Each of these other sources—natural law, scripture, church—contributes to this task in ways that are distinct yet interrelated. In brief, natural law and scripture provide the means to critique and raise up new possibilities, while the church mainly functions as the locus within which this is carried out.

I begin with natural law. Natural law, in contrast to the explicit revelation of scripture refers to our ability to get insight into the meaning of human well-being, and thus into morality, through reflection on human experience. This definition will be discussed more at length. Before doing so, however, it is important to explain why I am beginning with natural law and not scripture. After all, this book is an explicitly christian and an explicitly Roman Catholic undertaking.

There are a number of reasons for proceeding in this way, some of a more theoretic nature and some following upon the issues raised by U.S. individualism. I will discuss the latter first.

As I noted in part one, despite the emphasis on freedom and independence within individualism, there is also present a strong impetus toward conformity. Morality tends to fall in the area where conformity is demanded. This is especially evident in times of national unrest. During the Reagan administration, for example, individual freedom in the marketplace was regularly given strong support in both statement and policy. But along with this went attempts to return the country to the "old virtues" (presuming, of course, that these virtues did indeed once exist); and, to achieve this, those in power were not adverse to trying to pass legislation to make these virtues required of all.

This effort to return virtue to the land was bolstered by references to scripture. We must become a god-fearing people once again; and the substance of this faithfulness was supplied by people such as Jerry Falwell and the Moral Majority who became the palace prophets.

This citing of scripture to support and promote the "American way" is hardly new in the U.S. Despite the fact that we regularly invoke the principle of the separation of church and state, we as a nation have never seen ourselves as a purely secular people. We understand what we do in the U.S. as having a religious dimension, as explicitly related to the divine will. In fact, we have thought of ourselves as the New Israel, bearing salvation for the whole world.[1]

In light of the conformity which individualism attaches to morality, we have to find a means for critiquing and cracking open the operative values of U.S. culture that will address the authoritarian element implicit in the demand to conform. Scripture has a role to play in this; but, because of the ways in which it has been used to shore up a conformist national morality, scripture cannot be the principal actor.[2]

For this reason, I turn first to natural law. Not only does natural law enjoy a greater independence from the individualism of U.S. culture, but, by its very nature, natural law challenges an authoritarian approach to morality.[3] For na-

---

[1] See, for example, Sacvan Bercovitch, *The American Jeremiad* (Madison, WI: The University of Wisconsin Press, 1980).

[2] This is not to say that natural law cannot also become a legitimating factor within a culture. This happens especially when the precepts of natural law are kept at an abstract level, as I indicate later in this chapter. My argument is that, in the context of present U.S. culture, scripture is more apt to be co-opted into supporting the conformism of individualism, and that natural law as defined here is better able to counter it.

[3] This point is persuasively argued in Gerard J. Hughes, S.J., *Authority in Morals* (London: Heythrop Monographs, 1978), especially chapter 1.

tural law, something is right or wrong not because some authority has declared it to be so, but because it is in keeping or is out of step with the essence of our humanity. And convincing arguments have to be made showing how a particular moral demand is based on our essence. Thus, according to natural law, statements about justice or chastity or truth telling are not correct simply because they have been issued by someone in authority; they have to be in accord with the demand of our humanity. If we have a question about these statements, we can rightly request—and expect—a persuasive explanation.

In addition, the task of addressing the problems caused by U.S. individualism is not solely a Roman Catholic task. It requires the work of all—of all working together; and the Roman Catholic Church has acknowledged its willingness to join with others in this endeavor.[4] Within a pluralistic society, this cooperative effort is best achieved by appealing to natural law. For, unlike a morality based explicitly on a particular faith, which is not accepted by those not sharing that commitment, natural law is the result of reflections on the common human experience we share with all people.[5]

At a couple of steps removed from the specific issues raised by U.S. history and culture, natural law is addressed before

---

[4]*The Pastoral Constitution on the Church in the Modern World*, paras. 10, 40.

[5]In their pastoral on war and peace, the U.S. bishops state: "The conviction, rooted in Catholic ecclesiology, that both the community of the faithful and the civil community should be addressed on peace and war has produced two complementary but distinct styles of teaching. The religious community shares a specific perspective of faith and can be called to live out its implications. The wider civil community, although it does not share the same vision of faith, is equally bound by certain key moral principles. For all men and women find in the depth of their consciences a law written on the human heart by God. From this law reason draws moral norms." United States Catholic Conference, *The Challenge of Peace*, p. 7, para. 17. In their pastoral on the U.S. economy, the bishops write: "These biblical and theological themes shape the overall Christian perspective on economic ethics. This perspective is also subscribed to by many who do not share Christian religious convictions. Human understanding and religious belief are complementary, not contradictory. For human beings are created in God's image, and their dignity is manifest in the ability to reason and understand, in their freedom to shape their own lives and the life of their communities, and in the capacity for love and friendship." United States Catholic Conference, *Economic Justice for All*, p. 419, para. 61.

scripture because of the nature of these two sources of moral wisdom. Scripture, as I shall argue in the next chapter, is not primarily a moral textbook. Rather, it is our constitutional document as a people of faith. First and foremost, it describes authoritatively how our forebears in the faith came to understand through divine grace the saving presence of God in their midst. The moral demands and insights recorded in the scripture represent their response to this saving presence.

The biblical description guides us as we try to understand what God is doing in our own history and culture—how God is acting in ways that are related to the scriptural accounts, but that are also distinctive and new. Having come to this understanding, we then have to determine how most appropriately to respond in circumstances very different than those in biblical times. While we are guided by scripture in this, we cannot simply repeat what the Israelites and the early Christians did.

Moreover, scripture does not provide us with a principle of interpretation to determine exactly how its statements on morality are to be used. It does not indicate, for example, whether—or when—we should prefer Joel's "Hammer your ploughshares into swords, your sickles into spears"[6] over Micah's "They will hammer their swords into ploughshares, their spears into sickles."[7] Nor does it indicate why the statement in Matthew's gospel against divorce should be taken more literally than the command to tear out your right eye should it become a cause of sin.[8] We have to find some principle outside of scripture in order to interpret it correctly. As Hughes puts it, "an independent morality is an essential tool in interpreting the Christian tradition, since it enables us to distinguish the voice of God from the human voices through which he speaks to us in the tradition of the Church."[9] Natural law is that tool.[10]

---

[6] Joel 4:10.

[7] Micah 4:3.

[8] Matthew 5:29-32.

[9] Hughes, p. 24.

[10] In pointing out the dependence of scripture on natural law, I do not mean that

## Experience: The Basis of Natural Law

What then is natural law? Mostly, it seems, it is a puzzlement for us. Even though natural law is an integral part of Roman Catholic morality, many Roman Catholics have never heard of it; and of those who have, many have only a vague idea what it means. Part of the problem, no doubt, is the name itself: the word "law" seems to promise—or maybe threaten—a list spelling out specific moral do's and don'ts. In fact, however, natural law gives us no such list. It offers us, instead, a rather general insight into morality; and this is based on a type of common human experience. We will look at this experience first.

We have all confronted injustice. In our own lives or in the lives of people we know or have heard about, we can point to examples of unfair treatment. In some situations, the injustice can be corrected through legal procedures. But in others, even after a decision has been handed down by the highest court in the land, we still have a basic sense or gut feeling that the injustice has not been righted. In other words, the laws and the legal procedures of society do not have the final say; they themselves are subject to some higher forum. How else could we think them deficient?

A classical statement of this is found in Sophocles' *Antigone*, written in the fifth century B.C.E. In the play, king Creon orders Antigone, his niece, not to bury the body of her brother after he was killed in an unsuccessful coup. Antigone refuses to obey the decree. The dialogue in the play continues as follows:

Creon:        Now tell me, in as few words as you can,

---

natural law is totally independent of scripture. As I will point out in the next chapter, we do not attain the insights of natural law from some neutral point of view. We cannot step outside the human condition; we always know from a conditioned perspective. For Christians, scripture provides that perspective. Thus, natural law and scripture are dialectically related: natural law offers scripture a means of interpretation and scripture establishes the angle of vision from which we search out natural law. There is a certain—and indeed an inevitable—circularity here. That point will be addressed in the chapter on church.

Did you know the order forbidding such an act?
Antigone:    I knew it, naturally. It was plain enough.
Creon:    And yet you dared to contravene it?
Antigone:    Yes. That order did not come from God. Justice
That dwells with the gods below, knows no such law.
I did not think your edicts strong enough
To overrule the unwritten unalterable laws
Of God and heaven, you being only a man.
They are not of yesterday or today, but everlasting,
Though where they came from, none of us can tell.[11]

Our experience of injustice may not be as dramatic as Antigone's. We may not appeal to Zeus or the gods, or even to God. It is more likely just a basic feeling that in some way the proper order of things is not being respected. Many felt that way during the Viet Nam war, despite the fact that it was upheld by the president and not declared illegal by the Supreme Court. Some feel that way now about pornography: even though people appeal to the First Amendment of the Constitution for protection, there is still something about pornography that is fundamentally out-of-sync. Some feel that way, too, when companies suddenly move to another locale, giving their employees little if any warning: no law has been broken, but there is just something about it that is not right.

This experience that present events stand under the judgment of a higher order is not limited to legal and political matters. It is to be found as well in the cultural dimension of life. The meanings and values of everyday life that we take for granted can lead to detrimental, even destructive consequences.

A more recent play brings this out well. In *Equus*, written in 1974 by Peter Shaffer, psychiatrist Martin Dysert works with a 17-year-old boy, Alan Strang, who has blinded some racehorses with a pick. It is the psychiatrist's job to bring Alan from the tortured world he is inhabiting in his mind

---

[11]Sophocles, *The Theban Plays*, trans. E.F. Watling (Middlesex, England: Penguin Books, 1957), p. 138.

back to "normality." Martin Dysert is deeply troubled at the thought.

> My desire might be to make this boy an ardent husband—
> a caring citizen—a worshiper of abstract and unifying
> God. My achievement, however, is more likely to make a
> ghost!... Let me tell you exactly what I'm going to do to
> him! I'll heal the rash on his body. I'll erase the welts cut
> into his mind by flying manes. When that's done, I'll set
> him on a nice mini-scooter and send him puttering off
> into the Normal world where animals are treated *properly*:
> made extinct, or put into servitude, or tethered all their
> lives in dim light, just to feed it! I'll give him the good
> Normal world, where we're tethered beside them—blink-
> ing our nights away in a nonstop drench of cathodery
> over our shrivelling heads![12]

It is the normal world of everyday life that Martin Dysert finds demeaning and constricting. He bases his judgment on a fundamental sense that something more and better should exist.

Again, our own personal experience probably is not so arresting. Still, there may be a feeling that the way women are treated in our society, or the way in which our central city areas are left to decay, or the way people are accustomed to mind their own business and hurry past those in need, or the way people rush into court at the least provocation to "sue the bastard" is just not right.

This is the fundamental human experience that natural law seeks to express and explain. In the words of John Macquarrie:

> That most people do seem to believe in something like
> natural law may be seen from a simple consideration.
> There is no human law, not even that promulgated by the
> highest authority, about which someone may not complain
> that it is unjust. There seems to be found among most

---

[12]Peter Shaffer, *Equus* (New York: Avon Books, 1974), pp. 123-124.

people the conviction that there is a criterion, beyond the rules and conventions of human society, by which these may be judged.[13]

In explaining how natural law arrives at this criterion out of human experience, I will show that natural law theory itself presents a challenge to U.S. individualism as well as a critical and constructive perspective on our culture. Specifically, I will discuss (1) the commitment of natural law to a realism in morality; (2) the use of reason in natural law; (3) the content of natural law; and (4) the application of natural law to culture.

Finally, (5) I will indicate how this approach to natural law relates to the Roman Catholic tradition.

## Natural Law and Realism

Natural law theory as interpreted here is based on a belief that morality is grounded in reality, that the basic sense or gut feeling about fairness I have just discussed reflects reality. "Reality," according to Robert Johann, "far from being something behind or under direct experience, is precisely the ongoing, inclusive affair of everyday life, whose immediate quality, as something open to improvement, is the beginning and end of inquiry."[14]

One dimension of this "ongoing, inclusive affair of everyday life," of this ongoing interaction with our social and physical environment, is morality. Morality is not merely a personal, private matter based on an emotional reaction to something—"that is wrong because I don't like it." It is not just a human construct—another name for what is generally considered acceptable in society. Morality is an integral dimension of our interaction with the environment. Values are as real as facts.[15]

---

[13]Macquarrie, p. 98.

[14]Johann, p. 19.

[15]John Langan, "Values, Rules and Decisions," in *Personal Values in Public Policy*, ed. John C. Haughey (New York: Paulist Press, 1979), pp. 43-46.

This moral dimension is present to us initially at the affective, not the cognitive, level. Simply put, we feel it before we think about it. Thus, Aquinas speaks of our "natural inclinations" as the starting point for natural law.[16] Pope Paul VI in *A Call to Action* refers to these inclinations as "aspirations."[17] I prefer to call them our "natural affections," drawing us to that which is good in our interaction with the environment, and repulsing us from that which is evil.

The reason for taking our natural affections as the starting is that, as Johann points out, "[t]he good is not immediately the term of thought, but of feeling and sensibility. The good is what is experienced as congenial, healing, fulfilling, worth fighting and struggling for."[18] This does not mean that we merely assent to this affectively-presented sense of the good as is; it must be submitted to reason for further consideration. But our initial sense of morality, our native affection for the good, is trustworthy. We can trust our basic intuition because it puts us in touch with reality.

How do we know it is trustworthy? Well, that cannot be proved. To prove it, we would have to be able to get behind this experience and look at it from a vantage point outside our interaction with our environment. No such point is available to us. And so, ultimately, the trustworthiness of our moral experience is based on faith.

Grounding morality on faith, however, is not placing it on quicksand. As Maguire points out, "faith is a normal and basic way of knowing. Contrary to the common wisdom, seeing is not believing. Believing is *knowing* what you cannot see or provide, but what you still accept and hold with firmness."[19] Such belief is the basis for most of what we hold to be important and meaningful in our lives.

Belief in the reliableness of our moral experience does not mean it is never in error. It indicates only that our experiences are trustworthy, not that they are infallible. Nor does such

---

[16]Aquinas, *Summa Theologica*, I-II, 94, 2.

[17]Pope Paul VI, "A Call to Action," para. 22; Gremillion, p. 496.

[18]Johann, p. 29.

[19]Maguire, *The Moral Choice*, p. 87. Emphasis in original.

belief deny the existence of original sin either within ourselves or within our world. It presumes only that original sin has not totally destroyed the ability of our affections to be attuned to the demands God makes known to us through our basic human experience. To look at this from the positive side, natural law theory, as used in Roman Catholic tradition, holds that our basic sense or natural affection for value is an appropriate resource for understanding what the saving presence of God in our midst is asking of us.

For natural law, then, the starting point is our basic sense or natural affections about the correct order of things. It begins there because it holds that these affections provide a trustworthy access to reality; because it holds that reality is comprised as much of values as of facts; because it holds that, by getting in touch with this value dimension of reality, we can understand what God is asking of us, despite the effects of original sin.

Natural law theory, therefore, directly challenges U.S. individualism. Individualism, you will recall, tends to identify reality with the subject matter of natural science. Thus, the "really real" is what is scientifically measurable; and morality, dealing with values rather than facts, is confined to the private realm. Natural law presupposes a much richer and more complex world in which both facts and values are part of reality.

Moreover, natural law posits a more noble affective life in the human person. Like natural law, individualism holds that we are directed by our natural inclinations or aspirations. But for individualism, primary among these inclinations is self-interest. Even altruistic feelings get reduced to self-interest. Some people help those in need, it is argued, because that is what they happen to want to do; others would rather spend their resources on themselves. In either case, people are simply following out their personal preferences.

Natural law places no such restriction on our affectivity. For natural law, our affections alert and draw us to what brings integrity and flourishing to our person in its totality, to what produces justice and flourishing for our environment.

Finally, natural law believes these inclinations or aspirations provide us insights into our being that are a trustworthy basis for determining morality's demands. Individualism simply takes our inclinations as incontrovertible givens which we have a right to follow so long as they do not block another from doing likewise. They are neither good nor bad in and of themselves. Nor do they have anything to do with who we are as persons—fulfilling our interests makes no difference in our identity; we still remain the same type of individual.

Natural law, then, holds that values are indeed a part of reality; that these values are revealed to us, first of all, by our affections; and that these affections reveal to us not merely our personal interests but also the demands that life itself makes on us. In all of these, natural law offers a fundamental challenge to U.S. individualism.

## The Use of Reason in Natural Law

While our natural affections about the proper moral order are our starting point, they are not adequate by themselves. History shows only too clearly that at times these affections can lead us astray. We are encouraged, for example, by the moral sensitivity and instincts of Martin Luther King and Albert Schweitzer. But we must not forget that Hitler had a feeling about the Jews that we do not find morally acceptable. And Freud spoke of an instinct that, if uninhibited, would drive a male to have sexual relations with every female he encountered.[20] (For some reason, Freud did not believe women possessed that same drive.)

Thus, there is a second moment in natural law theory. While we begin with affective experience because it provides us trustworthy access to reality, we must submit that experience to rational critical reflection because it is not infallible. Maguire summarizes this nicely: "Ethics, which starts in awe, proceeds to reason."[21]

[20]Sigmund Freud, *The Future of an Illusion*, trans. W.D. Bobson-Scott (Garden City, NY: Doubleday and Company, Inc., 1964), p. 19.

[21]Maguire, *The Moral Choice*, p. 85.

Reason, in natural law theory, acts as midwife. Its role is not to be the source of morality, but to clarify and critique our moral experiences. For, as Johann notes, "Unless they are sorted out and integrated in a total quest, their separate tuggings can tear the heart apart."[22] Reason's task, then, is to weave the insights from our moral experiences into a unified whole that is internally consistent or logical, and that makes sense externally because it brings meaning and flourishing to life.

Reason, then, even though it is not the source of our morality, has a substantial role to play in determining our operative values. Through critical reflection on our affective experience of morality, we are able to work out a "design for living" that is truly a contribution to living.

We have engaged here in such a critical reflection on experience. At the beginning of this book, I described certain gut feelings I had that the present order of things in the United States is not quite right; and in the pages that have followed, I have sought to present a picture of what things should be like—a picture that, hopefully, is logically coherent and relevant to our world.

In carrying out this task of sorting out and integrating the input we have from our moral experience, reason does not act by itself, divorced from emotion. The affective has a strong part to play as well. We do not reason in a disinterested and dispassionate way about morality. We are naturally drawn to morality, to that which is good; and we have a tremendous stake in the outcome of moral reasoning since it determines the quality of our lives. If the affective is removed from moral reflection, we have seriously—if not fatally—undercut our ability to get to the truth.

Here some may complain that emotions and feelings get in the way of the clear, crisp thinking needed to achieve certainty. In my judgment, we can arrive at no truth without the affective. A scientist or mathematician working on a very abstract and abstruse problem does not solve it through an emotionless thinking process. Only reason accompanied by

22Johann, p. 30.

deep interest and vital concern—that is to say, by some very deep emotions—can accomplish that.

This cognitive-affective reflection on the moral dimension of our interaction with our environment is an ongoing process. Through reflection and judgment, we come to understand the demands our humanity makes on us. And as we work to respond to these demands, our experience leads us through reflection to further insights. To declare that a particular operative value—a particular concrete understanding, say, of justice or chastity—is henceforth normative for all people and all times is to stop this process. And doing so denies an essential dimension of the human person, namely, our continuous reflective interaction with our environment.

Our moral reasoning, then, is inductive, not deductive. We do not begin with general moral principles and from these deduce or reason out our concrete moral norms. Thus, for example, our point of departure is not some very general understanding of justice (what I termed a "universal" value in the previous chapter), from which we reason to what U.S. culture should be like. We start with our interaction with our environment as it occurs within a particular cultural and historical framework. To be more specific, we start with the types of experiences I pointed out at the beginning of this chapter: a basic sense that there is something amiss with the role women have in our culture, with pornography, with plant closings, etc. Through reflection on these experiences, we arrive at insights to guide our interaction, based on what is needed to make life flourish, on what is required to be true to our humanity.

As a result, there is a certain trial-and-error quality to morality. This is not to say that we tinker with moral norms like some inventor. But neither do we grasp totally *the* truth. And so, we cannot automatically condemn some behavior patterns simply because they run against the accustomed moral norms. We have to see how they play out. (The criterion for judging this will be discussed in the next section.)

To summarize, then, natural law theory begins with our basic experience of morality, based on the belief that our natural affection for values is trustworthy—although not infallibly correct. Reason is a second moment in natural law.

Its task is to reflect critically on our moral experiences to achieve an internally consistent and externally relevant view of morality. This reflection is at once cognitive and affective; it is an ongoing process which, while not grasping the total truth, gives us trustworthy knowledge to guide our interaction with our environment.

The task of reason in moral reflection set forth here contrasts sharply in a number of ways with the role reason plays in individualism. First, reason as defined here has a greater office in that it is allowed to address morality. Individualism tends to limit the scope of reason to the objects of the natural scientist's investigations. As a result, reason becomes technical rationality, focusing on how to do things but not asking if they should be done. It concentrates on means and simply accepts ends as given. I am arguing that reason is a significant factor in moral reflection, that it is an essential element in deciding not only what means we should use but also in choosing which ends are worthy of our attention.

But, second, greater limitations are placed on reason here than in individualism. Within its proper sphere, the reason of individualism is granted almost a carte blanche. According to Descartes, you will recall, the matter on which the mind works has extension but no intrinsic form. Thus, there are no restrictions on the way this matter can be shaped. The mind is guided by the self-interests of individuals and groups; and these self-interests have no intrinsic limits, merely the external demand that our pursuit not get in the way of others doing the same.

To be sure, the reason of natural law is a constructive force. It is not limited merely to discovering and informing us of moral laws. It helps us determine the operative values by which we live. The reason of natural law, however, does not empower us to make over the universe or ourselves in accord with any plan our imagination sets before us. Neither the human person nor the physical world nor indeed any part of life can be treated as modeling clay, to be shaped and fashioned to any form whatever.

As recent history has shown us only too graphically, simply because we can think up possibilities does not mean we should act on them. The human experimentations of the

Nazis, the political experimentations in Cambodia, the devastations resulting from nuclear accidents, chemical disposal, air pollution, and strip mining—to name but a few: all have been the product of human reason and all have left incredible devastation.

Who we are as human beings and what the world is has a fundamental structure that must be respected if life is to be fulfilled. This structure is not immediately evident to us; we grasp it only gradually and inductively. And we find that this grasping is not just a one-way movement of continual progress; for, as we are well aware, insights we once held with unquestioning acceptance at times have turned out to be unacceptable later. Still, the basic structures of our interaction with our environment as we come to know them must be honored, for it is in being true to ourselves and to the world that goodness and beauty are realized.

Natural law, in effect, insists that we be true artists. We are not paint-by-number hacks, simply placing in their proper place the specific contents ordained by God. But neither are we to treat life as a totally empty canvas. We are to cherish the goodness of life and explore all its possibilities so as to make real and to make full that goodness.

Third, reason as described here is more integral to the person. Individualism, influenced by Descartes, separates mind from body and emotion as well as from the world which it knows. I am arguing that, while mind and emotion are distinct, they must not be separated. Their interaction is necessary if we are to discover and respond to the truth available to us. Moreover, reason is not some power or faculty within us that looks out on a world from which it is detached. Reason is a dimension of our interaction with our environment. There is no separation between thinking and acting; it is simply a question of whether we are acting in a reflective or non-reflective way.[23]

Finally, reason as presented here does not enjoy the certitude that the reason of individualism does. The reason of

[23]See John MacMurray, *The Self as Agent* (Atlantic Highlands, NJ: Humanities Press, 1978), chapters 6 and 8.

individualism can discover the "laws" of economics, laws which parallel the laws of physics. No such power or certitude is available for the type of reason I have presented. It is grounded in reality but it cannot capture *truth*. Its conclusions are trustworthy. But they have to be reevaluated and may change.

## The Content of Natural Law

What do we have as a result of this critical reflection on our moral experience? In other words, what does natural law give us?

The name itself, as I have pointed out, can lead us to believe that natural law gives us laws. In one sense, that is true. The "law" associated with natural law, however, is not what we usually identify with the word "law" within our culture.

Natural law does not give us statutory laws or codified prescriptions such as those governing the flow of traffic on our highways. It is more like the "law of friendship" than "do not exceed 55 miles per hour" or "don't cross a double yellow line."[24] Now, if we think of law as a codified prescription, it seems absurd to speak of a law of friendship. For, it is of the very nature of friendship that what we do for another comes not from some externally imposed obligation but from the fullness of our heart.

If we offer to take a friend out to dinner, and our friend finds out that we did so because someone else demanded it of us, that friend will hardly see our offer as an expression of friendship. On the other hand, we cannot call someone our friend and then proceed to have nothing to do with this person. No one would say that is friendship. Why? Because it is of the very essence or nature of friendship that we take

[24]According to Macquarrie, "The Natural law is not another code or system of laws in addition to all the actual systems, but is simply our rather inaccurate way of referring to those most general moral principles against which particular rules or codes have to be measured." Macquarrie, p. 104. The only point where I take issue with Macquarrie is his identifying natural law with "general moral principles." The reason for my disagreement is spelled out later in this chapter.

time to be with someone we call a friend and that we be solicitous about his or her well-being. We have to do so, not because someone in the legislature has written a statute obligating us, but because otherwise our declarations of friendship are nonsense.

Like the "internal law of friendship" arising from the very nature of what friendship is and without which friendship would not exist, natural law is imposed on us by the very nature of our humanity. It is that which we must do to be true to our humanity, to make sense out of our life, to make life flourish.

Even so, while comparing natural law to the "law of friendship" is helpful in certain ways, it can leave us with other misperceptions. While this comparison alerts us that natural law does not give us a kind of moral statutory law, it should not leave the impression that we therefore get from natural law some very general principles such as "Be just" or "Respect life."

Identifying natural law with such general principles can distort this source of moral wisdom. First, principles so abstractly defined are shells needing content: what does it mean concretely to be just, to respect life? It is too easy to slip in the content of one's own culture and make that normative for everyone. For the people of Java, for example, "'To be human is to be Javanese.' Small children, boors, simpletons, the insane, the flagrantly immoral, are said to be *ndurung djawa*, 'not yet Javanese.'"[25] When we understand natural law as an abstract demand for justice, for instance, we can, without knowing it, equate "be just" with "act like us Americans." When the natural law gets identified with one's own culture, even implicitly, it is no longer able to critique that culture and break it open to its further possibilities.

Moreover, understanding natural law as providing a series of general principles can leave us with the impression that the main purpose of morality is to offer guidance for different aspects of our life, each considered separately. As a result, we end up with what Kohlberg calls "a bag of virtues."

[25]Geertz, p. 52.

But, as I pointed out in the chapter on virtue, our life is not lived in segments. We seek wholeness and integrity in our lives as we interact with our world; in other words, we seek to be virtuous persons. The content of natural law has to reflect this. Thus, I agree with Hauerwas that "natural morality is best understood not as a form of law, but rather as the cluster of roles, relations and actions the agent must order and form to have a character appropriate to the limits and possibilities of our existence."[26]

It is precisely through a "cluster of roles, relations and actions," that is to say, through an overall "design for living" that culture provides the means and milieu in which we can establish our identity. Therefore, we have to critique culture in its overall patterns, not in its isolated parts. To accomplish that, natural law holds up before culture an image of the human person interacting effectively with the environment within a social context, that is, interacting in a way to bring meaning and flourishing to life.

We have, then, the parameters for the content of natural law. This content is a general morality based on the essence of our humanity, that is, on what is demanded to be true to our humanity and to our interaction with the environment. But it cannot be too general, presenting merely abstract, universal moral principles. On the other hand, it is not merely a listing of concrete laws, setting forth do's and don'ts. Thus, the problem is to find a proper form of generalization about the essence of our humanity.

Key to the content of natural law is keeping in mind that there is no one single way of being human. History clearly shows the rich variety of ways in which our humanity has been shaped. To get at this multicolored portrait, it is necessary to take into account the social dimension of the person, especially the cultural dimension.[27]

---

[26]Stanley Hauerwas, *Truthfulness and Tragedy* (Notre Dame, IN: University of Notre Dame Press, 1977), p. 58.

[27]In this way, natural law does not legitimate individualism by presenting an asocial individual with certain qualities as the image of the human person—a problem which exists especially when psychological categories are used to define humanity.

The importance of including culture (not as an abstract category but in its concrete manifestations) in natural law is brought out well by Geertz. According to Geertz, culture is of more than secondary importance in understanding the human condition and the human project. In an article entitled "The Growth of Culture and the Evolution of Mind," Geertz addresses himself to the question of culture's place in the evolution of the human race. We normally assume that culture came after the evolutionary move from pre-human to human forms. Once the "great divide" had been crossed and the human species had made its appearance on the stage of history, then culture appeared.

But as Geertz points out, evidence does not support this assumption. There were, in fact, primitive forms of culture among the pre-humans. "In the Australopithecines we seem to have, therefore, an odd sort of 'man' who evidently was capable of acquiring some elements of culture—simple tool-making, sporadic 'hunting,' and perhaps some system of communication more advanced than that of contemporary apes and less advanced than that of true speech, but not others...."[28] The conclusions Geertz draws from this are important for the argument I am advancing.

> Though it is apparently true enough that the invention of the airplane led to no visible bodily changes, no alterations of (innate) mental capacity, this was not necessarily the case for the pebble tool or the crude chopper, in whose wake seems to have come not only more erect stature, reduced dentition, and a more thumb-dominated hand, but the expansion of the human brain to its present size. Because tool manufacture puts a premium on manual skill and foresight, its introduction must have acted to shift selection pressures so as to favor the rapid growth of the forebrain as, in all likelihood, did the advances in social organization, communication, and moral regulation which there is reason to believe also occurred during this period of overlap between cultural and biological change.

[28]Geertz, p. 64.

Nor were such nervous system changes merely quantitative; alterations in the interconnections among neurons and their manner of functioning may have been of even greater importance than the simple increase in their number. Details aside, however—and the bulk of them remain to be determined—the point is that *the innate, generic constitution of modern man (what used, in a simpler day, to be called "human nature") now appears to be both a cultural and a biological product* in that "it is probably more correct to think of much of our structure as a result of culture than to think of men anatomically like ourselves slowly discovering culture."[29]

If it is true, as Geertz argues, that culture was a central factor in human evolution, then we should not be looking for some human form that lies behind culture, the "really real human being" that appears once cultural accretions have been set aside. There simply is no such being, since culture has been essentially and inextricably present from the beginning. To quote Geertz one again:

A cultureless human being would probably turn out to be not an intrinsically talented though unfulfilled ape, but a wholly mindless and consequently unworkable monstrosity. Like the cabbage it so much resembles, the *Homo sapiens brain, having arisen within the framework of human culture, would not be viable without it.*[30]

Culture, then, has to be an essential part of any definition of the human project, of any discussion of human nature—culture, that is, not in the abstract, but in the concrete. And, since cultures are multiple and varied, it is precisely this multiform and multicolored portrait that provides our starting point.

This is not to say there are no commonalities among cul-

---

[29]Ibid., p. 67. Quotation is from S.L. Washburn, "Speculations on the Interrelations of Tools and Biological Evolution," in *The Evolution of Man's Capacity for Culture,* ed. J.M. Spuhler (Detroit, 1959). Emphasis added.

[30]Ibid., p. 68. Emphasis added.

tures and so among human beings. Rather, it is to argue that we have to look for the meaning of the human not in some universals that exist among people regardless of culture, but in the rich and varied picture presented by the various cultural realizations of human experience. As Geertz points out, "We must, in short, descend into detail, past the misleading tags, past the metaphysical types, past the empty similarities, to grasp firmly the essential character of not only the various cultures but the various sorts of individuals within each culture, if we wish to encounter humanity face to face."[31]

Finding the content of natural law in the concrete cultural realizations of humanity does not mean we accept each culture as it is. Only too clearly, all cultures include elements and dynamics that run contrary to human flourishing and proper interaction with the environment. We have to judge which aspects of culture should be included in natural law, which aspects reveal for us the demands and possibilities of our humanity.

Reaching such a judgment is not easy. To do so, we cannot retreat to some neutral site, unaffected by culture; nor can we turn to some fully-worked-out ideal portrait of humanity against which the various cultures can be measured. Making such a judgment is an ongoing task for a community. People draw upon their natural affections to see if things "feel right," and they use cross-cultural comparisons to see if they can discern any general patterns that give insight. Regardless, absolute certainty will never be reached. And, because that uncertainty is difficult to live with, there is always the danger that one's own culture will be made the paradigm of others, that the traditional will be clutched too strongly and new possibilities will be spurned.

Once judgment about specific cultures has been made, the resulting picture natural law presents us, showing the demands our humanity makes on us, is not done up stick-figure style with only an ability to think or to speak or to laugh penciled in. Nor is it, for that matter, a mere portrait

---

[31]Ibid., p. 53.

of an abstract individual entitled: Everyperson. Instead, it is more like a *mosaic of mosaics.* There is a mosaic of the human mind, showing not only that we should think properly but the varied ways this can be done; a mosaic of human communication, holding before us the demand that we carry this out correctly and depicting the multiple ways of doing so; a mosaic of human sexuality, challenging us to live this out appropriately and showing the many forms this can take. This mosaic of mosaics challenges us to live up to the demands of our humanity: it indicates the limits or boundaries we cannot exceed without betraying who we are as persons; but it also shows us the rich variety of possibilities for meeting that challenge.

Such a view of the content of natural law offers a strong challenge to individualism. Individualism, as I pointed out earlier, leaves the individual empty. It attributes to the self negative freedom protected by rights and the pursuit of self-interest. But these attributes, when realized, provide no substance to the person. Natural law takes just the opposite stand. When we pursue the challenges and possibilities natural law sets before us, we are striving for our true self-interest—that is to say, for that which truly brings flourishing to the self. But it is also "other-interested," for it brings flourishing to all of life. Insofar as these challenges are met and these possibilities actualized, our individuality has become richer and fuller; and so too our whole social and physical environment.

## The Application of Natural Law to Culture

To summarize the discussion to this point, natural law begins with our natural affections, with our being drawn to certain things and repulsed by others. These experiences are reflected upon critically to work out a unified view of morality that is relevant to our world. The content of natural law is a multiform picture, a mosaic of mosaics, that calls us to be true to our humanity and to all of life; and it presents us a rich variety of possibilities for meeting that call.

How, then, are we to use natural law? As I pointed out

earlier, natural law does not provide a ready-made paradigm of morality just waiting to be adopted in its totality. Its purpose is to give us some critical distance on our culture and to break it open to its further possibilities.

But, applying natural law to our culture is not a matter simply of inquiring whether or not our culture has a particular value or set of values. We do not run down a checklist to make sure it incorporates justice, truth-telling, honesty, chastity, respect for life, etc. Rather, the full image of the human offered by natural law, in all its challenges and possibilities, is brought to bear on our culture in its totality.

This does not mean that the complete "mosaic of mosaics" of natural law is applicable at any given time. Relevant elements are selected out through the interaction between natural law and culture. Our culture's specific configuration causes certain aspects of the vision of human nature presented by natural law to stand out sharply. Human freedom and individual rights, for example, are immediate, primary concerns for us in the U.S. when we look critically at our own culture or critique another nation. We check to see how these values are part of and integrated into all aspects of a society.

But natural law does more than just confirm our culture's primary value commitments. Natural law's rich texture opens up new dimensions of our culture to which we are blind because of too deep immersion in it. We are alerted to ways in which our culture has exceeded human limits and to areas we might explore for further realizations of meaning and flourishing. For example, natural law makes us aware that human rights are not limited to political rights. As the U.S. bishops point out in their pastoral on the U.S. economy,

> A number of human rights also concern human welfare and are of a specifically economic nature. First among these are the rights to life, food, clothing, shelter, rest, medical care and basic education. In order to ensure these necessities, all persons have a right to earn a living, which for most people in our economy is through remunerative employment. All persons also have a right to security in the event of sickness, unemployment and old age. Parti-

cipation in the life of the community calls for the protection of this same right to employment, as well as the
right to healthful working conditions, to wages and other
benefits sufficient to provide individuals and their families
with a standard of living in keeping with human dignity,
and to the possibility of property ownership.[32]

What happens when we use natural law to critique and
crack open U.S. culture? This book is just such an exercise.
Throughout it, we have been morally scrutinizing the image
of the human which lies at the base of our national identity.
History has helped us understand the various dimensions of
this ideology we call individualism; and images from other
cultures have put it into critical perspective. From that confrontation with a broader image of humanity, it has become
clear that a loosening of the ties binding the individual to
society and an emptying of the self are not adequate to
realize human well-being and flourishing.

In its place, I have suggested an image expressing the
experience of by far the majority of human societies down
through history: we as human beings require a close and
ongoing interchange between self and world. We are limited
by and fulfilled through our ties with our social and physical
world. And internally, we must maintain connections among
the various dimensions that comprise our self; i.e., between
the physical and the non-physical, however those are distinguished and labeled.

Only as this interconnectedness—between us as individuals
and society, between various societies, and between us and
our environment—is maintained, can we in general and as
individuals enjoy a meaningful and flourishing life. In other
words, this interconnectedness establishes a negative bounda-
ry beyond which we cannot venture without throwing into
question and into jeopardy our own humanity and indeed
the whole world.

This does not mean, however, that the U.S experience has
been for naught, that we have to see ourselves as a wrong

----

[32]United States Catholic Conference, *Economic Justice for All*, pp. 420-421,
para. 80.

road—indeed, as a dead-end road—in history. While we may have loosened too much the ties linking the individual to society and the physical world, we have made a major contribution to the growing awareness of the dignity of the individual person and the respect due the self.

Thus, the interaction between natural law and U.S. culture has been a two-way street. While natural law has helped bring out the negative impact of U.S. individualism, U.S. culture has made clear that, whatever form society takes, the dignity of the individual must be respected.

This interaction, then, between a particular culture and natural law is a creative process for natural law. The image of the normatively human offered by natural law is not an unchanging paradigm. As noted earlier, natural law is the result of insights into what is demanded of us morally through reflection on human experience. But human experience continues, and culture is the context within which this occurs. Therefore, as natural law judges a particular culture, so too is it judged. Its adequacy is constantly under question. And as new insights are generated through culture, natural law is enriched.

The application of natural law, then, is a dialogical process in which natural law and culture are the principal parties. There is give and take on both sides; and judgments have to be made where a particular culture should be challenged and where natural law should be broadened. Such judgments are always a human action: they cannot be carried out on a computer with the specifics of a culture entered on a floppy disk, then run against a program containing natural law's complete "mosaic of mosaics." This judgment is the task of society as a whole and of its subcommunities.

### Natural Law and the Roman Catholic Tradition

One question remains. Does the interpretation of natural law presented here square with the official stance of the Roman Catholic church? The answer is both yes and no. The ambiguity of the answer stems from the ambiguity of the Roman Catholic tradition itself.

This is evident if we compare the way natural law is used in two documents we have already considered: the 1976 Vatican statement entitled *Declaration on Certain Questions Concerning Sexual Ethics* and Pope Paul VI's 1971 *A Call to Action.*

In the *Declaration on Certain Questions Concerning Sexual Ethics,* the moral criterion is "the finality of the sexual act."[33] This is determined by an analysis of the purpose of the genital organs. As such, the criterion is ahistorical and acultural, holding for all societies and all generations; and it is presented like a statutory law backed by the authority of the church.

In *A Call to Action,* however, Pope Paul VI cites as criteria for evaluating social policy "the aspiration to equality and the aspiration to participation, two forms of a person's dignity and freedom." These aspirations are new, arising out of the changes caused by "scientific and technological progress."[34] The criteria here are not determined simply by considering the finality or purpose of a particular aspect of the person. They are arrived at through reflecting on human experience in changing times and coming to a judgment about what is required for the totality of a person in a specific historical era. The criteria are more general in nature; and in arguing for them, the pope refers to concrete experience rather than the authority of the church.

This ambiguity, needless to say, creates a great deal of difficulty and confusion. I am interested here in the effect it has within a culture marked by individualism. In my judgment, the type of natural law evident in the *Declaration on Certain Questions Concerning Sexual Ethics* (and in some other documents discussing personal morality) implicitly supports some of the negative consequences of U.S. individualism. I believe these consequences can be offset only as the church's ambiguous use of natural law is resolved to favor

---

[33]"Declaration on Sexual Ethics," sec. 5; in Liebard, p. 433.

[34]Pope Paul VI, "A Call to Action," para. 22; in Gremillion, *The Gospel of Peace and Justice,* p. 496.

the approach taken in *A Call to Action* (which is also found in other pronouncements on social justice).

Consider, first, the problem raised by the church's tendency to isolate on the physical and biological aspects of the human person in determining the norm for sexuality. As a result, the integrity of the human person and of human experience are lost to sight; and the specific meaning the various aspects of the human person and human experience have, precisely because of their place within the integral whole, is overlooked. Such an approach accommodates itself too easily and too uncritically with the piecemeal mindset of U.S. individualism where all aspects of life are dealt with as separate, distinct entities—like self-contained atoms. To respond creatively to individualism, natural law has to reflect on the experience of people precisely as human beings, taking into account the totality and integrity of their personhood.

Second, using physical nature as the basis for determining moral demand is problematic in another way. U.S. individualism denies reason's ability to address the course of history in a substantive way. Individualism, you will recall, has grave reservations about government's ability to provide positive social leadership. The most it can do is to act like a technician, adjusting this or that in accord with the "laws of nature" governing the economy.

By appealing to physical nature as the ground for moral criteria, the church's stance can implicitly support the approach taken by U.S. individualism. This is not to say that the church and U.S. individualism mean the same thing when they speak of nature. But the effect can be the same; for, in each case reason is left more passive than active. To challenge individualism, natural law has to emphasize more the active role of reason in interpreting how we should interact with our environment in changing historical circumstances.

Closely connected with this passive role of reason—and this is my third point—the use of natural law evident in the church's statements on sexual ethics tends to be static and ahistorical. A particular aspect of human experience is seen as pointing to an essential component of human well-being; and this becomes the basis for a moral demand. Because the mind is able to grasp "the authentic exigencies of human nature," the "immutable laws inscribed in the constitute elements of human nature,"[35] this moral demand always has been and ever will be the same.

In one sense, natural law is indeed unchanging. We cannot cease being human beings; and that fact places certain limitations on our future, whether we like it or not. But within those boundaries, which are broad indeed, the range of possibilities is great. It is through continuing reflection on human experience that we not only locate the boundaries but also discover the paths to human well-being and to the flourishing of all life that lie within them.

The static, ahistorical approach to natural law can (implicitly at least) support U.S. individualism. Individualism, especially in the economic sector, strongly promotes progress. New products are continually being introduced. The prospect is held out to all that each person with hard work and a little luck can "make it." But the overall social structure itself cannot change because it is rooted in the laws of nature—the same type of laws discovered by the physical sciences.

To challenge this, a dynamic understanding of natural law has to be set forth—an understanding that takes history seriously. History helps us recognize the developments that occur in our human nature as we interact with our changing environment. It helps us see the rich "mosaic of mosaics" that results as this interaction takes place within different cultures.

Finally, the ambiguities in Roman Catholic use of natural law morality feed into the separation of the personal from the social that marks U.S. individualism. In the two Roman Catholic documents we are considering, natural law is used to make some moral judgments about certain sexual and economic matters. These conclusions, however, seem to bear different weight. With regard to economic issues, there is greater latitude for differences of opinion—indeed, there is room for a pluralism of opinions.[36] But, in sexual issues, a

---

[35]"Declaration on Sexual Ethics," sec. 4; in Liebard, pp. 431-432.

[36]Pope Paul VI, "A Call to Action," para. 50; Gremillion, p. 510.

single position is set forth; and there is no indication there is a place for other views.

Given the authoritarian approach to Roman Catholic morality in the past, people can well end up taking the official Roman Catholic stance on sexual ethics very seriously; but they may see social ethics more as an optional matter, to be accepted "if that is one's thing." In fact, even if people totally disagree with the church's sexual morality, they still seem to see this as much more central to the church's teaching than social justice.

To overcome the personal-social dichotomy in morality, natural law has to be used in the same way when the private and the public sectors of life are discussed.

Can the Roman Catholic Church fashion its use of natural law so that in both its methodology and its conclusions it counters the difficulties raised by U.S. individualism? It can do so, I believe, if it resolves its ambiguous approach to natural law in favor of the way natural law is employed in social ethics. In other words, the church should use natural law in personal issues the same way it does in social issues.

If this happens, then certain aspects of its tradition will have priority: the person in his or her wholeness and integrity will be the subject of reflection; reason will be given a substantive role in history; the dynamism of history will be recognized. Adopting the approach taken to natural law in social ethics will also help challenge the dichotomy between personal and social morality. For, in modern Roman Catholic social teaching, the principle of the common good emphasizes the need to establish a society in which the value of both the social whole and its individual members is maintained.

The church, then, in its use of natural law, has the resources to counter some of the problems raised by U.S. individualism. But these resources can become a constructive force only as the church overcomes the ambiguity marking its moral teaching.

# 8

# Scripture: A Testimony of Faith

Scripture, the third source of moral wisdom, is, in many ways, unknown territory for Roman Catholics, at least as it relates to morality. Prior to the middle of this century, the principal use made of Scripture was proof-texting. A particular moral question was answered or a moral norm established on other grounds; then an appropriate biblical text was located to "prove" the point.

In *Rerum Novarum*, for instance, Pope Leo XIII first used natural law to argue the case for private property. Only then did he declare:

> The authority of the Divine Law *adds* its sanction, forbidding us in the gravest terms even to covet that which is another's: "Thou shalt not covet thy neighbor's wife; nor his house, nor his field, nor his man-servant, nor his maid-servant, nor his ox, nor his ass, nor anything which is his."[1]

Bernard Häring's *Law of Christ*,[2] published in the 1950's in Germany and translated into English beginning in 1961, was a turning point. Häring took the title of his work from

---

[1]Pope Leo XIII, *Rerum Novarum*, para. 11; in *The Papal Encyclicals*, ed. Claudia Carlen, I.H.M. (Wilmington, NC: McGrath Publishing Co., 1981), vol. 2, p. 243. Emphasis added.

[2]Bernard Häring, C.S.S.R., *The Law of Christ,* 3 vols. (Westminster, MD: Newman Press, 1961, 1963, 1966).

Romans 8:2, "You should carry each other's troubles and fulfill the law of Christ," and used this passage as the foundation for understanding the whole of morality. More recently, Pope John Paul II has made substantive use of Scripture in his encyclicals. In *Laborem Exercens*, for example, issued on the ninetieth anniversary of *Rerum Novarum,* his discussion of human work is grounded in the first creation account of Genesis.[3]

This "discovery" of scripture by Roman Catholics does not mean, however, that at long last we have found the answer to all our questions and problems in morality. It is one thing to discover Scripture; it is quite another to use it properly.

## Difficulties in Using Scripture

When we turn to Scripture as a source of moral wisdom, what should we look for? We tend to search for moral directives—more than that, for *revealed* moral directives. Naturally so, for scripture is the revealed word of God; and since how we act or fail to act is an important aspect of our relation with God, we expect to find in Scripture God's revealed word on such matters.

And, as we page through the Bible, our expectations are not disappointed. There are passages and themes ready at hand. The most obvious examples are the Ten Commandments in the Hebrew Scriptures and the demands set forth in the synoptic gospels such as "Love your enemies and pray for those who persecute you."[4]

But to draw upon Scripture when making a moral decision or trying to determine the moral life is not a matter of simply applying the right biblical dictate. In fact, the seeming forthrightness of some scriptural passages in giving direction for moral living can actually mask the difficulties that exist in using the Bible. And Scripture, used uncritically, can appear

[3]Pope John Paul II, *Laborem Exercens*, para. 13; Carlen, vol. 5, p. 302.
[4]Matthew 5:44.

consonant with U.S. individualism, thus contributing to the problem we are addressing in this book.

I pointed out in the previous chapter that Scripture does not have its own principle of interpretation. There is no indication in the Bible when we should follow Joel's command to "Hammer your ploughshares into swords, your sickles into spears"[5] rather than fulfill Micah's prophesy that "they will hammer their swords into ploughshares, their spears into sickles."[6] Nor do we find there any help in determining whether to obey Luke's or Matthew's statement about divorce. In Luke's gospel, Christ's words about divorce are absolute, admitting of no exception: "Everyone who divorces his wife and marries another is guilty of adultery, and the man who marries a woman divorced by her husband commits adultery."[7] In Matthew's account, however, a reservation is introduced: "But I say this to you: everyone who divorces his wife, *except for the case of fornication,* makes her an adultress."[8]

Moreover, Scripture does not always present us a unified picture. In some instances, a clear moral directive is laid down. But then an event is described in which (or so it seems) that directive is broken and the action is approved. The Ten Commandments, for instance, demand that we not kill. Yet the Israelites did not hesitate to kill men, women, and children—even the livestock—of some of the peoples they conquered. This killing is not condemned; but the Bible fails to explain why not.

Even though Scripture does not supply us with a principle of interpretation, we still have to decide how its various moral rules are to be understood and applied. If we do that unconsciously—that is, without critical reflection on what we are about—we more than likely will fall back on what we take for granted. In other words, the values of our culture will become the primary determining factor. Should that

---

[5]Joel 4:10.

[6]Micah 4:3.

[7]Luke 16:18.

[8]Matthew 5:32. Emphasis added. See also, Matthew 19:9.

happen, Scripture can easily be stripped of its ability to challenge culture and become simply a yea-sayer. In our individualistic culture, it can be made into a champion of individualism.

Some argue that there only *seem* to be ambiguities in scripture. In reality, they say, whatever was done was in response to God's command. And, since we cannot know or second-guess the mind of God, we have to accept it as proper. In fact, all morality is nothing more than the will of God: something is right or wrong because God has declared it to be so.

But, as Gerard Hughes points out, such an approach leaves us with no understanding of the relation between the demands of morality and what makes human existence flourish. And, "if we see no connection between our human fulfillment and the obligations under which God places us, then we would have no grounds for believing that our God was a moral God at all."[9] God appears to be arbitrary and autocratic, deciding morality on whim. That can fit in well with individualism's authoritarian element and its downplaying of morality.

Some hold that we should look to scripture for general ideals and values rather than specific moral directives. For them, the primary moral message of Scripture is not "Do this" or "Avoid that," but rather the demand that we strive to realize love or justice or peace in the world and in our personal lives. Such an approach does not seem burdened with the ambiguities of the Scripture's message about divorce and killing. General values like these are presented clearly in the Bible: the counter-values of hate, injustice, and war are not held up as patterns we should incorporate in our lives.

But here too difficulties are encountered. What, for example, are we to understand by "love" or "justice" or "peace"? We can, of course, believe their meaning is self-evident. But when we do that, we very easily end up defining them in terms of the operative values of our culture. Then Scripture simply bestows a blessing on U.S. individualism.

[9]Hughes, p. 5.

To guard against this, we may try to determine with the aid of Scripture scholars the exact meaning that love had for first-century Christians or that justice had for a sixth-century B.C.E. Jewish prophet. But then what? We cannot presuppose that the same concrete definition is automatically applicable and workable in twentieth-century North America. In fact, given the way specific values are integrated within that earlier culture as a whole, it is impossible to transplant them directly into our situation. And when we try to do so, we implicitly deny the essential role culture has in morality, thereby playing into the problems caused by U.S. individualism, as discussed in chapter six.

Despite its wealth of materials on morality, therefore, Scripture is not easy to use as a source of moral wisdom. And the difficulties it raises, unless carefully attended to, can be resolved in ways that support rather than challenge U.S. individualism.

The possibility that scripture will legitimate rather than challenge culture is by no means limited to the United States. This is an ever-present danger in any society. But it is especially so in this country because of the significant role the Bible has played here from the very founding of our nation. As Mark A. Noll notes,

> ... the Bible was woven into the warp and woof of American culture.... [I]n becoming common coinage a certain debasement of the Bible's message did take place .... The result was that although the Bible had worked itself into the foundation of national consciousness, it contributed little to the shape of the structures built upon that foundation—except for the conviction that *the structures were as sacrosanct as the biblical foundation itself.*[10]

Nathan O. Hatch links Scripture more specifically with U.S. individualism. He points out that, after 1800, the place

---

[10]Mark A. Noll, "The Image of the United States as a Biblical Nation, 1776-1865," in *The Bible in America, Essays in Cultural History*, eds. Nathan O. Hatch and Mark A. Noll (New York: Oxford University Press, 1982), pp. 45-46. Emphasis added.

given the individual in society on the one hand and the right to individual interpretation of the Bible on the other supported one another. "Both cultural values and hermeneutics ... addressed the common man without condescension and dismissed, out of hand, theories that would not square with common sense. *Both reinforced the importance of the individual as beholden to no one and master of one's own fate.*"[11]

## Using Scripture in Ethics

I draw attention to these difficulties and dangers of applying Scripture to the moral life and moral decision-making not to dismiss Scripture, but to make clear the issues at stake in determining how to use it as a source of moral wisdom. We cannot reject Scripture from the moral enterprise. If we were to do so, we would in effect say that Scripture is not central to Christianity. For, denying the Bible a crucial role in something as important as morality would consign it to the periphery.

But integrating Scripture into the discussion about morality, and doing so in a way that challenges rather than supports U.S. individualism, is not easy. We have to find a principle of interpretation that does not surreptitiously import individualism into Scripture, that values culture appropriately, and that does not make morality an authoritarian dictate of an arbitrary God.

The first step in this task is to change the way we look at Scripture in relation to morality. As I pointed out earlier, we have tended to think of scripture primarily as a moral textbook, that is, primarily as a source for specific and/or general moral norms. As a result, we have expected to find in the Bible *revealed morality*.[12] But that has contributed to the problems we just discussed.

[11]Nathan O. Hatch, "Sola Scriptura and Novus Ordo Seculorum," in *The Bible in America*, p. 74. Emphasis added.

[12]The differentiation between Scripture as revealed morality and scripture as revealed reality is found in James Gustafson, "The Place of Scripture in Christian Ethics: A Methodological Study," in *Readings in Moral Theology #4*, eds. Charles E. Curran and Richard A. McCormick, S.J. (New York: Paulist Press, 1984), pp. 159-168.

To get a different perspective on the use of Scripture in morality, it is instructive to consider how the biblical authors themselves arrived at statements on ethics. Did they receive their insights directly from God so that the moral directives and values they presented were unique, unknown to any other contemporary peoples? As Sean Freyne points out,

> Convinced that their behaviour must always reflect this God who had revealed himself in and through his dealings with them in history, [God's people] may use the *contemporary insights* into the good life with which they come into contact, refining them where necessary *in line with the particular stage of their awareness of God and their current understanding of his nature.*[13]

Thus, the biblical writers turned to their cultural environment for the specifics of morality. In the Christian Scriptures, for example, the authors drew upon "the sayings of the sages, the ethics of the Stoic philosophers, contemporary ethical standards, the teaching of the rabbis, the Jewish Catechism, the texts of the Bible, and the good sense of the New Testament authors."[14]

But, in using these sources, the biblical authors did not simply accept everything they found. They made choices; and they did so in light of their faith, interpreting the meaning of their choices in terms of the God in whom they believed.

Scripture, then, is the testimony by a faith-filled community of where they discerned God in their midst and what they perceived this God is about. It is a recounting of history, a recounting made from the perspective of faith. Within this reality, as seen through the eyes of faith, the various moral directives—whether specific commands or more general ideals—are the response demanded because of what God is doing. "In a word," Collins concludes, "it is *this theological*

---

[13]Sean Freyne, "The Bible and Christian Morality," in *Morals, Law and Authority*, ed. J.P. Mackey (Dayton, OH: Pflaum Press, 1969), p. 34.

[14]Raymond Collins, "Scripture and the Christian Ethic," *Proceedings of the Catholic Theological Society of America: 1974* (Manhattan College: The Catholic Theological Society of America, 1974), p. 20.

*context* that makes of the New Testament ethic a Christian ethic. *Its content is essentially secular,* but could we expect more of a God who has chosen to enter into our history and who sent his Son to be one of us."[15]

Thus, our focus in reading Scripture shifts. When we go to the Bible for insight and guidance in living out the moral life and finding solutions to the moral problems that beset us, an our purpose is not to find particular answers. It is to infuse our minds and hearts with the pathways of God as testified to by a people of faith. Not that this is going to give us an infallibly clear picture of how God is acting in our days; but it provides us with signposts that guide us in our search.

Once we recognize what God is doing, we act as our fore-bears in the faith did—not copying their specific forms of behavior, but becoming the human instruments of God's saving activity within a particular time and place. Morality, then, is understood not as obedience to the once-given and absolute demands of a stern God, but as the appropriate response to the gracious gift of God's presence and activity with and for us.

In short, Scripture is a source of moral wisdom for us, not as revealed *morality,* but as revealed *reality.*

But we still are not home free. Two further problems have to be addressed. First, the various books of the Bible do not present a single, unified vision of how God is acting in history. A pluralism of images, symbols, and theologies is used to show and explain the presence and activity of God. Thus, for example, "recent scholarship has shown how early Christians used diverse traditions to interpret Jesus: final eschatological prophet, crucified and Risen Lord, divine man, logos (John's prologue), and 'power and wisdom' (I Cor. 1:25)."[16] Since we cannot use all the various views offered by the Bible at the same time, how are we to determine which part of Scripture should guide us in any given situation?

Second, revelation is not finished. In saying this, I am by

---

[15]Ibid., p. 241.
[16]Fiorenza, p. 221.

no means denying that the canon of scripture is closed and that in Christ the fullness of God's message has been revealed. The meaning of this message, however, continues to overtake us in unexpected ways. Different cultures and different generations open up for us new dimensions of the Eternal Word of God.

How, then, are we to read reality with the eyes of faith in the midst of a changing world, guided by a Scripture that does not present a unitary view? Key here, I believe, is that we not see Scripture as *the* basis for judgment. Not that we deny the importance of Scripture for us Christians—after all, it is our constitutional document. But Scripture is not the sole place where we confront the God in whom we believe, nor the sole means by which we interpret that encounter.

God's saving presence is revealed to us not just by the Bible but also by the culture within which we live. In fact, the Bible and culture are revelatory for us not separately but through their dialogue with one another. Our reading of our culture, both in its deficits and in its strengths, leads us to focus on certain aspects of Scripture rather than others. At the same time, our reading of Scripture opens our eyes to new and different dimensions of our culture. Through this interaction of Scripture and culture—not simply through one or the other—we come to know what it means that God is with us.

In this dialogue, neither Scripture nor culture has priority as starting point or conclusion. We do not begin with one rather than the other. We cannot. Prior to any critical reflection on culture, we are inextricably immersed in Scripture through our Christianity; and, of course, we are inextricably immersed in our culture. We cannot rid ourselves of the influence of U.S. culture so that we can read Scripture with a mind unaffected by our culture, or so that we can judge our society from a pure and undiluted scriptural perspective. Nor can we lay aside Scripture and analyze our culture in a totally secular or scientific way. And we cannot presume before beginning our reflection that one rather than the other will have priority.

Through the dialogue between culture and Scripture, we have a principle of selection and interpretation which the

Bible, taken by itself, cannot provide. Culture raises up certain elements in the Bible and downplays or even dismisses others because they are not relevant at this point in history for helping us understand what God is doing in our midst.

This last statement may seem a bit strong. Even if culture offers us the needed interpretive principle for Scripture, can it actually downplay or dismiss part of the Word of God?

In fact, this is the way it happens. Consider the statement in I Peter 3:18: "Slaves must be respectful and obedient to their masters, not only when they are kind and gentle but also when they are unfair." This passage could easily be used to justify slavery—and it more than likely has been.[17] But we discount it. We do so because of the insights our culture gives us about the respect due each person and about the evil of using a human being as an object. At the same time, the reason we can believe these insights is that this antislavery stance represents to a community of faith, formed by the vision of Scripture, how God is acting in our midst.

Making culture the interpretive principle of Scripture does not mean that culture has ultimate priority. For, through the stories it tells of the differing ways God has acted within history, Scripture jogs our thinking and imagination to explore our own culture in new ways and break it open to its further possibilities. An example of the power Scripture has in this regard is the way it is presently sensitizing us to the priority of the poor. At a time when a calloused disregard for those in need has become an acceptable attitude in this country, the Bible utters a loud challenge and judgment.

We turn to Scripture then, not for immediate, specific solutions to our problems, but for perspective, insight, and motivation.[18] In doing so, we allow Scripture its own integrity

---

[17]James Michener, in his novel *Chesapeake* (New York: Fawcett Crest, 1978), has a white preacher try to convince black slaves not to run away from their owners. He bases his sermon on this passage from I Peter. While this is a fictionalized account, it is no flight of fancy to imagine just such an event in pre-civil war days in the U.S.

[18]This is the way the U.S. bishops use scripture in their 1983 pastoral on war and peace: "Even a brief examination of war and peace in the scriptures makes it clear that they do not provide us with detailed answers to the specifics of the question which we face today. They do not speak specifically of nuclear war or nuclear

as an account of a separate history and culture, as an account of how a people of faith deciphered God working in their midst *as a people.* And we maintain the integrity of our own culture, not attempting to replace aspects or elements of it with those of a different culture. In that way, the importance of culture is maintained.

At the same time, we do not allow U.S. culture to go unchallenged. And we are not so apt to use Scripture in a manner that legitimates the less than acceptable dimensions of who we are as a people. (There is, of course, no absolute certainty that this will not happen; and so, constant vigilance is required.)

Relating Scripture dialectically with culture in this way does not mean particular moral directives in the Scriptures are to be totally ignored. But they are not to be lifted out of context and directly applied to some very different culture and time. Their meaning comes from their context. It is this context as a whole—especially as it opens our eyes to who the God of history and salvation is—that is important for us. Keck summarizes this well; and what he says about the ethics of the Christian Scriptures applies as well to the ethics of the Hebrew Scriptures.

> In the long run, then, the significance of NT ethics may lie not so much in what it says should be done as in what it says about the doer and his or her community of faith. In this way, the NT may well be as great a disturber of our own ethos and ethics as it was originally. Should that happen, we would discover what its real authority is.[19]

weapons, for these were beyond the imagination of the communities in which the scriptures were formed. The sacred texts do, however, provide us with urgent direction when we look at today's concrete realities. The fullness of eschatological peace remains before us in hope and yet the gift of peace is already ours in the reconciliation effected in Jesus Christ. These two profoundly religious meanings of peace inform and influence all other meanings for Christians." United States Catholic Conference, *The Challenge of Peace,* p. 17, para. 55.

[19]Leander E. Keck, "Ethos and Ethics in the New Testament," in *Essays in Morality and Ethics,* ed. James Gaffney (New York: Paulist Press, 1980), p. 45.

Moreover, relating Scripture dialectically with culture in this way does not nullify the authority of Scripture. But, rather than locating that authority in specific moral directives—or, for that matter, in any specific aspect of the Bible—it emphasizes the authority of the encompassing vision of the Bible; that is to say, its vision of how God has acted in history. Lisa Sowle Cahill summarizes this well when she suggests that

> it may be most fruitful to see the "authority of the canon as a whole" primarily in terms of its overall forms and of the types of witness it includes. That is to say, in terms of the *patterns* of interaction, complementarity, and tension which characterize the religious heritage preserved in the canon and reappropriated in contact with it.[20]

In the search for moral wisdom, then, Scripture has an essential role to play. Through its dialogue with culture, it provides a perspective out of which to critique culture and break it open to its fuller possibilities.

In that dialogue, culture is valued; for it is seen both as the place where God continues to act in our midst and as a principle for interpreting Scripture. Moreover, culture's integrity is maintained; values are not simply lifted out of Scripture and placed within it.

At the same time, culture is not taken for granted. In the dialogue, it is critiqued through the view presented by Scripture and broken open to its further possibilities.

In all of this, Scripture remains an authoritative but not an authoritarian book. It presents us with a vision of God acting in history that we accept with gratefulness and humility. This helps us determine how we should respond to what God is doing in our midst at the present time. Thus, something is right not because God has declared it to be so,

[20]Lisa Sowle Cahill, *Between the Sexes* (Philadelphia/New York: Fortress and Paulist Press, 1985), p. 23. Emphasis added.

but because it is our proper response to the God in whom we believe.

## Culture, Scripture, and Natural Law

In this dialogue between culture and Scripture, there is a third party involved—natural law. The relationship between Scripture and natural law is akin to the relationship between Scripture and culture. Scripture is a source for natural law, not because Scripture presents moral insights not otherwise available, but because the biblical authors drew upon the insights and resources of so many different cultures and forged them into a distinctive pattern in light of Israel's history. As such, Scripture helps fill out the "mosaic" that is natural law.

Natural law, in turn, receives from Scripture a perspective for inquiring into the demands our human nature makes on us. As human beings, we do not see things the way a camera does, passively taking them in. We always view our world from a particular perspective; and that perspective affects what we see and fail to see, what we place in the foreground and what we relegate to the periphery.

Our inquiry into the meaning of our humanity, then, is guided by our perception of reality—*revealed* reality, that is. Our understanding of what God is doing in our midst directs our attention in certain ways, and so affects our way of seeing and contributing to the "mosaic" of natural law.

This is not to say that this particular perspective gives us the inside track on all knowledge or that it renders us infallible. As history shows only too clearly, we Christians have made our share of errors in morality. Nor is Christianity the only place within which the Spirit of Truth is to be found. The Spirit is present among all peoples, leading them to deeper moral insight as they seek to understand the meaning of life. Scripture does indeed guide us in our reflections on the meaning of our humanity. But, in addition, our insight into natural law is enriched through dialogue with others; and that enrichment, in turn, opens up for us in new ways the meaning of Scripture.

As sources of moral wisdom, therefore, culture, natural law, and Scripture are in dialogue with one another. None of them has *the* answer for the moral life and moral decision-making; but through their interaction we come to a deeper understanding. We see (at least dimly) what our humanity is demanding of us in a particular culture and at a particular time in history as we seek to respond to God's redemptive presence in our midst.

Culture is the starting point with its concrete values revealed in its patterned ways of living and its concrete possibilities. Through insights garnered from reflecting on our experience in light of the witness of Scripture, natural law provides a mosaic of mosaics that challenges and opens up culture—and is, in turn, enriched by it. Scripture instructs us in God's saving ways as revealed through the history and culture of a people. It provides perspective and content to natural law. Through dialogue with culture, it places a particular history within the drama of salvation; and, as a result, its own interpretation is broadened.

## Dialogue of Culture and Scripture: Examples

What I have laid out thus far is theoretical. It sets forth principles for using Scripture as a source of moral wisdom. But it does not pin down concretely what such a use actually looks like. In the remainder of this chapter, I will show how the dialogue between Scripture and culture I have presented in this chapter is exemplified in parts one and two of this book. Four topics will be discussed; social ethics, redemption, community, and moral responsibility.

(1) A major premise of this book is that social justice should be a primary concern for Roman Catholics and for the Roman Catholic Church, and that the dichotomy between personal and social ethics should be overcome by understanding the social dimension of the personal. What justification can be found for such a project in Scripture?

Certainly, concern for social justice is apparent in the Bible: it is understood as integral to God's activity within the world. But attention to social justice does not mean today what it meant during the centuries when the books of the Bible were being written. In the Hebrew Scriptures, the prophets, despite all their social concern, never addressed social issues in structural terms. For the prophets, "the problem is seen ... in volitional terms. Its basis is not a particular arrangement of social roles, but the personal qualities, commitments, and convictions of those who occupy the roles. If justice is finally to be realized, it will be achieved in a paternal social order."[21] Furthermore, while Jesus' death was that of a political criminal, we cannot recast his public life to resemble that of Gandhi or Martin Luther King, Jr.

On what basis, then, are we justified to work for structural change in the name of social justice? If we can be authorized by Scripture to do so only as we find specific instructions or parallel activities within the Bible, we will never have permission. The biblical authors had no awareness of this type of change.

But if we look to Scripture for a perspective on what we are doing, we find there some definite indications. The God of the exodus event, an event so central to the identity of the jewish people, was indeed a God of justice, a God who sought to establish equality among this people. This was not merely of passing concern. Israel was the sacrament, "the primary manifestation of Yahweh"; and, whenever injustice was present, the presence of Yahweh was concealed.[22]

In the Christian Scriptures, as Francis Fiorenza points out, one of the ways the authors explained Jesus was to link him with the wisdom tradition of the Hebrew Scriptures. "The meaning of the wisdom and logos underlying the universe now becomes manifest in the saving actions and proclamation of Jesus. *This linkage of the meaning of the historical Jesus with the meaning of the universe connects*

[21]Thomas W. Ogletree, *The Use of the Bible in Christian Ethics* (Philadelphia: Fortress Press, 1983), p. 68.

[22]Norman K. Gottwald, "Biblical Theology or Biblical Sociology? On Affirming and Defining the 'Uniqueness' of Israel," *Radical Religion* 2/2, 3 (1975): 50. See also, idem, *The Tribes of Yahweh; A Sociology of the Religion of Liberated Israel 1250-1050 B.C.E.* (Maryknoll, NY: Orbis Books, 1979), pp. 700-702.

*the Church's proclamation of Jesus with its political and social mission.*"[23]

Scripture, then, provides the perspective on what we are about in this book, revealing to us the significance of concern for social justice. But it is our culture that focuses our attention on this dimension of the Bible. Moreover, the meaning of the political and the social, the possibility of addressing these dimensions of human existence, and the tools to do so are all modern discoveries. These expand the possibilities we have of influencing our world far beyond anything the biblical authors could envision. And in doing so, they deepen our understanding of what it means to say that God is a God of justice.

(2) In the social analysis presented in the first part of this book, I argued that individualism has left us alienated. Within the Christian community, the term alienation invokes the image of its opposite: redemption. But what does redemption mean? Is it atonement, ransom, or expiation? All have christian/ scriptural roots. But all three have been interpreted in individualistic terms and leave human beings merely passive recipients of God's activity. How then claim that the orientation of this book has a scriptural basis?

Fiorenza, pointing out that all these ways of understanding redemption are socio-historically conditioned, argues that today we should think of redemption in terms of "emancipatory solidarity."

The basis of our redemption is God's presence in Jesus expressing his solidarity with us in and through Jesus. It underscores that Jesus' solidarity with the Father and with us even until death is the basis of our faith in him. But his solidarity was interwoven with an emancipatory praxis. He healed the sick, cast out demons, forgave sinners, and fed the hungry. In his actions, the kingdom that he proclaimed was already anticipated for his actions were signs of the future kingdom. Yet he was killed for the emancipa-

---

[23]Fiorenza, p. 222. Emphasis added.

tory solidarity expressed in his preaching and deed.[24]

This certainly rings true as an explanation of redemption in relation to individualism, emphasizing as it does a fundamental unity between God and us—an emphasis which implicitly demands a unity among us. But we do not find this spelled out specifically in Scripture.

Here again we have the result of a dialogue between Scripture and culture. By placing our concerns within the drama of sin and redemption, Scripture opens our eyes to the depths of the issues we face and to the significance of what we are about. But, to understand God's presence as emancipatory solidarity requires the tools of modern critical social theory. And this critical social theory itself is dependent upon a view of the relationship between humanity and its environment which is a product of reflection on modern human experience. It does not run counter to Scripture, but it cannot be located in any particular chapter or verse.

(3)The experience of alienation caused by individualism draws our attention to the strong emphasis on community in both the Hebrew and the Christian Scriptures. And that theme helps us understand more broadly and more deeply our alienation. Scripture makes apparent the social nature of God's saving presence: we are redeemed as a people, not as individuals. But the bible cannot solve our problem of how to relate the human person as individual to society.

The various cultures within which the Bible was written knew nothing of the modern self as a separate, discrete entity. To be sure, there were individuals around. But the interpretation given to the individual person was significantly different from ours since it was based on "dyadism."

> A dyadic personality is one that simply needs another continually in order to know who he or she is .... What this means is that *the person perceives himself or herself as always interrelated to other persons*, as occupying a

[24]Francis Schüssler Fiorenza, "Critical Social Theory and Christology," *Proceedings of the Catholic Theological Society of America: 1976* (Manhattan College: The Catholic Theological Society of America, 1976), p. 110.

distinct social position both horizontally (with others sharing the same status, ranging from center to periphery) and vertically (with others above and below in social rank).[25]

Thus, while we have from Scripture a clear indication that God's redemption is social, we are not clear on exactly what that means today. We can understand the value of the person from the creation accounts. But what it means to apply that to the self as presently understood and what it means to relate that self to a redeemed community, Scripture cannot answer. We cannot look to the authors of the Bible for any immediately applicable indications on how to respond to individualism.

Only as we interpret the results of individualism in light of the insights of natural law as guided by Scripture do we begin to understand that U.S. individualism stands under the judgment of that activity. That insight, in turn, helps us read the Bible in new light and to interpret in new ways God's working to bring salvation to us as a people.

(4) Closely related to the question of the relation of the individual to the community is the issue of moral responsibility. I argued earlier that just as we cannot define ourselves apart from others, so we cannot limit our accountability merely to what we knowingly and willingly do. Is that contention warranted on scriptural grounds?

Scripture clearly indicates that moral responsibility is to be assumed. But it cannot give us answers to the questions: by whom? for what? Or rather, it cannot give us answers that will satisfy our questions.

This is not to say there are no passages speaking to the subject. In Deuteronomy, for example, Yahweh declares that "I punish the fathers' fault in the sons, the grandsons and the great-grandsons of those who hate me."[26] Ezekiel states just the opposite, indicating that people should be held respon-

---

[25]Bruce Malina, "The Individual and the Community—Personality in the Social World of Early Christianity," *Biblical Theology Bulletin* IX (July 1979): 128-129. Emphasis added.

[26]Deuteronomy 5:9.

sible for what they personally do, not for their parents' actions.[27] And Jesus sets forth an ethic of the heart ("if a man looks at a woman lustfully, he has already committed adultery with her in his heart"[28])—although he also identifies sin with blindness.[29]

But the insights we have through depth psychology and social psychology were not available to the cultures out of which the Bible arose. Thus, our discussion of personal— and, of course, social—responsibility in light of God's presence is necessarily different; and, in its difference, it helps us understand in new ways our relation to God.

These examples hopefully shed some light on my contention that Scripture has a role in the moral enterprise as *revealed reality*; and that role is realized, not through Scripture by itself but through its dialogue with culture and natural law. This dialogue is the means by which we come to understand how God is acting in our midst. And from that, drawing upon the resources available to us through our culture, we determine our appropriate response.

[27]Ezekiel 18: 1-4.
[28]Matthew 5:28.
[29]Matthew 23:16-22.

# 9

# The Church: A Community of Moral Dialogue In the World

We consider now the church, the last of the sources of moral wisdom. The church plays a unique role in the search for insight into the moral life and moral decision-making. Unlike culture, which provides the operative values which are our starting point, and unlike natural law and Scripture which are tools for critiquing and breaking open culture to its further possibilities, the church is primarily the locus where this critical and constructive process takes place. In short, the church is a community of moral dialogue within the world.

Assigning the church this role does not mean that the church brings no specific content to the moral enterprise. It has, of course, its tradition, a funded history of moral teaching. Tradition, however, is not primarily a list of statements or a quantity of knowledge deposited in the church which it can draw upon like a bank account. It is indeed a source of wisdom: the result of the community's past response in light of Scripture and natural law to its perception of God's presence working in history. But tradition is a living source of wisdom: it not only continues to provide insight, but it continues to develop as it is used by new generations to confront new situations and new difficulties.

It is probably more correct to say that the church *is* its tradition rather than that the church *has* a tradition. The church's tradition is the church's identity; and that identity is what the church has become as it has struggled down through the centuries to be true to the Spirit of Jesus. Thus, it is precisely as a gathering of people in faith, as an event, that the church is a source of moral wisdom. And through the dialogue of this people about the meaning of God's presence within a particular culture, making use of Scripture, natural law, and past insights, the church remains true to itself and truly alive.

The church, in short, is a community of moral dialogue within the world.

And, by being this community, the church is not only true to itself; it counters as well some of the issues raised by U.S. individualism. More specifically, the church, acting in accord with its nature, models a way of strengthening the ties of the individual to society, provides a substantive insight into the meaning of truth, and establishes a proper use of authority.

To understand what it means to look at church as a community of moral dialogue within the world, we will look at each of the components of this definition-description. We will conclude with a discussion of truth and infallibility in morality.

## The Church as Community

There is an essential connection between church and morality: church needs morality just as morality needs church. The church is the community of those who bear explicit witness to God's saving presence in the world; as such, its behavior must be in line with its stated belief. Therefore, it has to be concerned about morality, and its morality is shaped by its understanding of God's activity.

At the same time, morality requires church. As I pointed out in the chapter on culture, the operative values we live by are social and historical products, the result of people as a group seeking to respond to their environment in ways that bring flourishing to life. Thus, morality needs a social setting. And so, if there is to be a Christian or a Roman Catholic morality, there has to be a church. As Gregory Baum points out,

> ... Christian morality demands the Church. In the first place we recognize that moral convictions are usually the creation of people who experience life together. The community discerns the values that protect and promote its well-being. Even when these convictions appear to us as highly personal and private, it is likely that their origin is more social than introspection is able to detect. What counts in detecting the genesis of values is not a psychological analysis of individuals but a sociological analysis of their lives.[1]

In speaking about the necessary connection between morality and society, however, we cannot forget we do so within a culture marked by individualism. Individualism does not deny that we as individuals live within a social setting— that would defy our everyday experience. But individualism interprets the social setting as a voluntary association and our participation in that setting as a matter of free choice. Individualism, as I pointed out in part one, draws on the social contract theory which argues that the individual precedes society and that society is formed through individuals freely joining together. Thus, society is seen as an aggregate of independent individuals; and social participation is understood along the lines of membership in the Elks or the Knights of Columbus. Membership and involvement are voluntary and can be withdrawn at will.

The voluntary association model cannot do justice to the type of individual participation in society and culture I have discussed to this point; nor can it adequately account for society as the matrix within which morality is shaped. The involvement of the individual in society whereby an identity is formed and a society shaped runs deeper—much deeper—

---

[1]Gregory Baum, "Does Morality Call for the Church?" *Proceedings of the Catholic Theological Society of America: 1976*, ed. Luke Salm (Manhattan College: The Catholic Theological Society of America, 1976), p. 163.

than is described by an approach that uses membership in the Elks as a paradigm.

It is society understood with this more profound level of participation that is the matrix shaping morality. This understanding is based more on the paradigm of the family. The family makes no sense as a voluntary association. Children clearly are not part of a particular family because of some choice on their part. And, parents and children are not individuals with a predetermined identity relating to one another within an already established organization. Through the multiple levels of interaction between family members, individuals (children and parents alike) are shaped and changed; and the specific identity of the family is established.[2]

Understanding social belonging and involvement through the paradigm of the family rather than the Elks makes sense when we are considering civil society; but does it hold with regard to the church? After all, in our culture we tend to see church membership as voluntary. We go to church if we so choose; and we go to the church of our choice.

True, no one within our society can be forced by law to belong to or participate in a church. But we do not do justice to the nature of a faith commitment by looking at church membership as a form of voluntary association. For, in faith we are chosen more than we choose. As the great accounts of faith in the Scripture show, it is God who selects us.[3] Moreover, faith is a social reality: it is rooted and fed and fulfilled within a community.

Faith, in short, requires church. To be a member of a church, then, is not so much a matter of choice as a recognition of where we must be. We are simply doing what we have to do to be true to ourself, to be true to this person who has been graced by God to recognize the depth and the breadth of the meaning of life.

---

[2]See Peter Berger and Hansfried Kellner, "Marriage and the Construction of Reality," in *Recent Sociology, No. 2*, ed. Hans Peter Dreitzel (New York: The Macmillan Company, 1972), pp. 50-72.

[3]See, for example, Yahweh's call of Abraham in Genesis, chapters 12 and 17; Yahweh's call of Jeremiah in Jeremiah, chapter 1; and Christ's reminder to his disciples in John's last supper narrative, chapter 15.

It is in this context that we can talk about morality needing church. Church is a community of faith within which we as individuals, interacting at multiple levels, are shaped in our identity in light of the nature of our belief; and we, in turn, shape the community. This is the reality I am referring to when I speak of church as the fourth source of moral insight; but, by its very identity and dynamics, it stands in contrast to U.S. individualism, rendering a critical and constructive judgment on it.

## The Church as a Community in the World

While morality needs a social setting like church or society, this does not mean that church and society play the same role in the development of morality. Each is not a separate and self-contained entity, fashioning a distinct morality of its own.

At issue here is the relation and the mission of the church to the world. In the past, the church has at times identified itself with the Reign of God, seeing itself as the source of salvation for humankind.[4] In such a view, secular society and secular history are of secondary import: they are the stage on which the redemptive work of the church takes place, but are not essentially involved in that work. The church is the source of true morality, teaching secular society but not learning from it.

By downplaying society, the church can be perceived as supporting U.S. individualism. For individualism, you will recall, loosens the ties between the individual and society, emphasizing the former and subordinating the latter.

Since the Second Vatican Council, a different understanding of the mission of the church and its relation to the world has developed.[5] A copernican revolution has occurred

---

[4]Richard P. McBrien, *Catholicism* (Oak Grove, MN: Winston Press, Inc., 1980), vol. 2, pp. 1113-1114.

[5]See Joseph Komonchak, "Clergy, Laity, and the Church's Mission in the World," *The Jurist* 41/2 (1981): 422 ff.

in which the world has replaced the church as the central focus of the drama of salvation. In the words of Gutierrez, the church's "center is outside itself; it is the work of Christ and his Spirit."[6] This work is not located simply in the hearts of individuals or in some dimension removed from history. ". . . [T]he Church must turn to the world, in which Christ and his Spirit are present and active; the Church must allow itself to be inhabited and evangelized by the world."[7]

This revolution, however, is not merely the flip side of the old coin, so that, where previously the church was everything and the world not a central factor, now just the reverse is true. Not at all. The world is not a totally autonomous reality; it is not a law and salvation unto itself. The world is humanity, the results of humanity's endeavors as it strives to find meaning and flourish. It is humanity caught up in the drama of sin and redemption. As such, the world needs the church; for, the church makes explicit the nature of this drama and plays an essential role in the world's salvation.

This does not mean, however, that the church pre-exists the world and brings it a preformed message of salvation. Rather, the church is born out of and continues to exist at the heart of humanity's own struggles. "The Church does not come to be except in the world, in reference to the world, and even in part because of the world."[8] Thus, the church exists in and with and through the world. Not that it simply blesses whatever the world is; the church must stand against the world. But it is essentially tied to the mission of the world; and in contributing to that mission, the church comes to its own self-realization.

In other words, to make use of biblical imagery, the church should mirror the Reign of God which "is like the yeast a woman took and mixed in with three measures of flour till it was leavened all through."[9] Like the yeast, the church does

---

[6]Gustavo Gutierrez, *A Theology of Liberation* (Maryknoll, NY: Orbis Books, 1973), p. 269.

[7]Ibid., p. 261.

[8]Komonchak, p. 442. See also, *The Pastoral Constitution on the Church in the Modern World*, para 40.

[9]Matthew 13:31

not eradicate or replace a culture with something totally different. Rather, it respects a culture with its distinctive configurations, working from within to expand and explode it to the full dimension of its possibilities; that is, to the full dimension of the Reign which God is incarnating in its midst.

This has definite implications for the relation of church to morality. The church at its deepest level does not bring to each culture and each generation a set moral agenda. It exists primarily as a companion traveler, seeking to be a part of, and to contribute to, society's project of self-realization. A major part of the church's contribution, to be sure, is its insights into the drama of sin and redemption, insights which it has developed through the centuries. These insights it uses to uncover the fuller and deeper meaning of what society is about. And in so doing, the church learns more about its own mission—or better, the church becomes more of what it is.

This relationship of mutuality and interdependence between church and society can be seen in the experience of the Roman Catholic Church in the United States. In the development of its stance on religious freedom, for example, the church has learned much from the American experience. At the same time, the Roman Catholic tradition (as I am arguing in this book) has much to contribute to the U.S. and its problem of individualism; and it can do so without bringing ready-made solutions.

The church, then, is a community of faith existing within society as a companion traveler. It joins with society in its project of self-realization, making clear the in-depth meaning of the struggle by relating it to the coming of God's Reign. And through its participation in society's struggle, the church further realizes itself.

## Church as a Community of Moral Dialogue

How is the church to carry out this mission in and to the world with regard to morality? I contend that the church—the locus within which the interaction between culture, natural law, and Scripture takes place—actualizes and facilitates this interaction through dialogue: dialogue within the church between its members; dialogue between the church and other groups within society.

Dialogue within the Church

Within the church, this dialogue is not simply therapeutic in nature,[10] responding to the personal, subjective feelings of individuals about a particular moral stance. Its subject is the concrete morality of a specific culture: What are its operative values? How are they interrelated and integrated into a whole? Are they proper? If not, specific possibilities, latent within society, can be drawn upon?

This moral dialogue is the responsibility of all members of the church. As the Second Vatican Council makes clear,[11] the whole People of God carries on the prophetic mission of Christ, discerning and calling attention to the saving presence of God in the world. Thus all members, clergy and laity alike, are to participate in serious and substantive discussion about the morality of their culture and their generation.

This sounds radical, both in the sense that it seems to be a dramatic departure from previous church practice and in the sense that there appears to be no basis in previous church experience upon which to establish such a procedure. In fact, however, Pope Paul VI, in his apostolic letter *A Call to Action*, calls for just this type of dialogue:

> In the face of such widely varying situations it is difficult for us to utter a unified message and to put forward a solution which has universal validity. Such is not our ambition, nor is it our mission. It is up to the Christian communities to analyze with objectivity the situation which is proper to their own country, to shed on it the light of the Gospel's unalterable words and to draw prin-

---

[10]James Gustafson, *The Church as Moral Decision-Maker* (Philadelphia: Pilgrim Press, 1970), p. 86.

[11] *The Constitution on the Church*, para. 12.

ciples of reflection, norms of judgment and directives for action from the social teaching of the Church. . . . It is up to these Christian communities, with the help of the Holy Spirit, in communion with the bishops who hold responsibility and in dialogue with other Christian brethren and all people of goodwill, to discern the options and commitments which are called for in order to bring about social, political and economic changes seen in many cases to be urgently needed.[12]

I am, of course, suggesting a step beyond what Paul VI is calling for. Not only should the local church seek to apply the principles of the gospel and the church; but, in doing so, it could well discover that previous principles or approaches no longer apply, and thus, could provide new insights. Nonetheless, the pope's statement does call for substantive involvement at the local level.

In addition to Paul VI's challenge, we should also call to mind the fact that the U.S. Roman Catholic bishops consulted broadly when developing their pastoral on war and peace and their pastoral on the U.S. economy. The consultation happened more by accident than plan.[13] But happen it did. A precedent has been set; and, along with it, expec-

---

[12]Pope Paul VI, "A Call to Action," para. 4; Gremillion, p. 487. This position has some unintended backing in some of the more recent Vatican statements on morality that seem to represent the exact opposite use of authority. For example, in *Humanae Vitae,* the encyclical on birth control, Pope Paul VI mentions a number of times that the principles on which he argues against the use of artificial contraceptives are based on God's purposes for the human powers of generation and that these principles can be confirmed by people through deep reflection (paras. 12, 13, 17). Likewise, in the *Declaration on Certain Questions Concerning Sexual Ethics,* issued with the approval of Pope Paul VI in 1975, the following statement is made: "Whatever the force of certain arguments of a biological and philosophical nature, which have sometimes been used by theologians, in fact both the magisterium of the Church—in the course of a constant tradition—and *the moral sense of the faithful* have declared without hesitation that masturbation is an intrinsically and seriously disordered act." (sec. 9; Liebard, p. 436. Emphasis added.)

[13]The first draft of the pastoral on war and peace was stamped "confidential"; but some bishops decided on their own to distribute the document widely to solicit reactions. The National Conference of Catholic Bishops released subsequent drafts to the public at large and made provisions for people to submit their critiques and suggestions.

tations have been raised to the point where it is difficult to see how the U.S. bishops can ever again issue an important document without first seeking a wide range of input and reaction.

In calling for all within the church to enter into this dialogue on morality, I am not implying there is no room for authority. Any society requires authority. The individualism of our culture finds this hard to accept: because of our emphasis on negative freedom, we have an automatic negative reaction to police, to politicians, to management. True, we do admit that authority and the force it entails are necessary so long as there are malcontents and miscreants among us. But the best society would seem to be anarchy. Anarchy, that is, in the true meaning of the term: not social chaos, but a society in which people live together in harmony and work out their lives through voluntary associations without any central authority.[14] In other words, presidents, police chiefs and mother superiors are all first-class relics of original sin.

In my mind, authority is not simply the result of our fallen condition. Any society by its very nature, no matter what its size, needs some form of authority. To continue to exist, a society must have some visible core around which to group itself—a core which holds before its members the values and meanings fundamental to their commonality; a core which declares these values and meanings to external publics. In addition, society needs some recognizable and accepted source which offers an official interpretation of its tradition, and which makes sure that tradition is passed on to succeeding generations.[15] Authority is that core and that source.

The church, like any society, requires authority. Authority in the church, however, cannot be exercised in just any way. The form authority takes in the church must not parallel the authoritarianism that individualism spawns, thereby under-

[14]See George Woodcock, "Anarchism," *The Encyclopedia of Philosophy*, ed. Paul Edwards (New York: Macmillan Publishing Co., Inc. & The Free Press, 1967), vol. 1, pp. 111-115.

[15]Tillich, vol. 3, pp. 308-313.

cutting substantive participation of the individual in the church.

Is it possible for the Roman Catholic Church to avoid authoritarianism? The answer is no, so long as the church continues to manifest elements of the juridical or legalistic model of authority that are part of its past.

But historically this model developed as the church sought to protect its internal unity in the face of threats from Protestantism, Gallicanism, and Modernism.[16] As T. Howland Sanks shows, however, we are in the midst of a "paradigm shift" in the church. The juridical model is giving way to a service model. The role of authority as service, which is collegial rather than pyramidal, is "to summarize and express the consensus that is discovered in the community as a whole."[17]

The service model of authority, as applied to the area of morality, means that those in authority have the responsibility of enabling and empowering people within the church. They are to provide the tools people need to enter substantively into a discussion about morality in a particular cultural context in light of the Roman Catholic tradition. These tools include (1) an awareness of the nature and dynamics of morality; (2) an appreciation of the church's tradition: how it developed; why it developed as it did; what its spirit is; (3) insight into the concrete morality of a particular culture; and (4) an understanding of the insights of Scripture and natural law and how to use them.

Most important of all, because people within the Roman Catholic church—especially the laity—have been taught either implicitly or explicitly to be passive recipients of moral teaching rather than active agents helping to determine the church's stance, those in authority need to encourage and support them in this unaccustomed role. An important step in this process is simply taking people seriously; for people are not going to join in dialogue about moral issues unless

---

[16]The church here was understood as the continuation of the Incarnation and therefore identified with the divine. Sanks, pp. 109-111.

[17]Ibid., p. 173.

they have a sense that their own experience, insights, and opinions are valued, and unless they are convinced the conclusions they come to will be given proper weight by the church at other levels.

People must be encouraged to speak up, not out of hostility, but out of a conviction that they have a responsibility to do so in discharging their role in the church's mission. And they must be heard, not just listened to with the polite but patronizing ear of a politician.

In carrying out this ministry of service within the church, a person in authority should not stand off to the side as a sort of expert witness who is called upon when needed, but who is not personally involved in the process. The minister is an integral part of this search for a proper response by the church to the world. He or she both teaches and learns. And, as leader of the community, the minister becomes the spokesperson for the community's insights.

Approaching the moral dialogue within the church in this way requires that this dialogue be decentralized. In the juridical model of authority, the church is seen as a pyramid with all power and all teaching moving from top to bottom. Those at the top are obligated to protect and proclaim the deposit of faith—and, of course, morals. This model presumes that morality primarily involves universal values and principles which are equally and immediately applicable to any and every culture. With the shift of focus from universal to operative values, as discussed in chapter six, and with the emphasis on the importance of culture for morality, a single source for determining the church's stance on morality is no longer adequate.

The pyramid should not so much be inverted as reconfigured; responsibility for morality within the church should not so much be put in different hands as in more hands. The principle of subsidiarity should be invoked: responses to the issues that beset us should be handled at the most local level possible. The Roman Catholic Church's responsibility to speak to morality in the U.S. should fall primarily on the U.S. Roman Catholic Church. And even then, this responsibility should not be carried out simply through committees and subcommittees of the National Conference of Catholic

Bishops, which issues statements and directives. Ways should be found to permit substantive involvement and input from dioceses, parishes, schools, religious orders, lay organizations, etc.—from the grassroots.

In calling for the Roman Catholic Church to decentralize its process for establishing stances on morality, I am not suggesting some form of congregationalism. In addition to the local church, the regional church, the national church, and the international church are all necessary; and each needs appropriate power and authority. But, the relationship between these various dimensions of the church should be marked by dialogue along with shared responsibility. It is a dialogue between the more concrete and the more general, between the more particular and the more universal, with each essential to enriching the other.

The more universal levels of the church have the responsibility of alerting the more local levels to the different needs in the church, watching and guarding against a provincialism; and they are to keep before the more local levels the traditions of the Roman Catholic Church, making sure these traditions—past and present—are responded to in fullest range. The more local levels of the church, on the other hand, bring to this dialogue a more concrete understanding of how God is perceived as working in history and a more specific designation of how a particular people can and should be responding.

Adoption of this dialogical approach does not, of course, ensure that this process will go smoothly. In fact, it seems most likely that just the opposite will be the case. Differences of opinion and competing concerns will undoubtedly arise. Rome, at times, will speak out strongly, questioning and challenging a local church—and rightly so; local churches will raise questions about, and even disagree with, Vatican statements—and rightly so.[18]

---

[18]The perspective from which present trends in the church are considered determines how they are interpreted. The juridical or legalistic view of the church tends to look at reactions to hierarchical statements within the categories of obedience or dissent, i.e., of acceptance or nonacceptance. The understanding of church set forth in this book does not rule out the possibility a particular stance can be heterodox.

But such a dialogue keeps the church's tradition—that is, the church itself—alive. It allows the church to speak with one voice to the world, while at the same time speaking in different tongues so that it can respond with relevance and force to disparate cultural situations. It allows the church to keep before its members the reality of what it has come to be, while at the same time remaining open to new and, at times, jarring insights that will deepen and broaden that reality.

In short, the church in the area of morality must be truly pluralistic—at once unified and diverse in its message—so that it can fulfill its mission in and to the world. In the words of Pope Paul VI, "The same Christian faith can lead to different commitments. The Church invites all Christians to take up a double task of inspiring and of innovating, in order to make structures evolve, so as to adapt them to the real needs of today."[19]

### Dialogue Between the Church and the World

This dialogue about the morality of a culture cannot be confined simply within the church. As I have already noted, the church is essentially related to the world. Therefore, the church must actively seek dialogue with others—with all others. Again, Paul VI: "It is up to ... Christian communities, with the help of the Holy Spirit, in communion with the bishops who hold responsibility and *in dialogue with other Christians and with all people of goodwill* to discern the options and commitments which are called for in order

---

But there must be room for substantive input from all levels of the church; and disagreements are seen as healthy and life-giving. The church today finds itself in the awkward position of calling for and setting up dialogue with a wide variety of groups outside the church, such as atheists and communist Marxists—groups with whom it has fundamental disagreements—while at the same time refusing such dialogue to some of its own members (e.g., Charles Curran, Leonardo Boff, members of the Women's Ordination Conference, people who hold a pro-choice position on abortion, married priests, signers of the famous *New York Times* ads—to name but a few).

[19]Pope Paul VI, "A Call to Action," para. 50; Gremillion, p. 510; Pope John XXIII, *Mater et Magistra*, para. 238; Gremillion, p. 193.

to bring about the social, political and economic changes seen in many cases to be urgently needed."[20]

No one is to be excluded from this dialogue, not even the atheist. "While rejecting atheism, root and branch, the Church sincerely professes that all people, believers and unbelievers alike, ought to work for the rightful betterment of this world in which all alike live. Such an ideal cannot be realized, however, apart from sincere and prudent dialogue."[21]

To have a true dialogue, all parties are presumed and allowed to have something substantive to contribute. This means, of course that truth—or, at least, the truth available to us human beings does not reside in one party. The church cannot enter into discussion with others presuming that it has *the* answer. The Spirit of Truth is not limited to the church.

Not only is no one to be automatically excluded from this dialogue, but likewise no *subject* is to be declared foreign to it. The church cannot withhold itself from dialogue about the grave issues besetting humankind. Some people objected, for example, when the U.S. Roman Catholic bishops began speaking out on nuclear war and nuclear deterrence. The bishops, they said, have no competence in these areas. As the bishops pointed out, however, such issues have a moral and a religious dimension—dimensions which must be discussed if the full measure of these issues is to be taken; and it is within the competence of the bishops to address such dimensions.[22] The same can be said for all the problems we now face. Therefore, not only do the bishops, and indeed the whole church, have a right to make their voice heard, they have a duty to do so.

[20]Pope Paul VI, "A Call to Action," para. 4; Gremillion, p. 487. Emphasis added.

[21]*The Pastoral Constitution on the Church in the Modern World*, para. 21. In their "Pastoral Letter on Marxist Communism," the U.S. Roman Catholic bishops state: "It is in these two perspectives—maintenance of world peace and eradication of global poverty—that North American Catholics are most immediately confronted with the task of cooperation with Marxist regimes." National Conference of Catholic Bishops, "Pastoral Letter on Marxist Communism," *Origins* 10/28 (December 25, 1980): 443.

[22]*The Challenge of Peace: God's Promise and Our Response*, p. 39, para. 123. See also, "Catholic Social Teaching and the U.S. Economy," p. 33, para. 1.

## Truth and Infallibility

Two further issues have to be considered before ending this chapter. In spelling out the meaning and significance of looking at the church as a community of moral dialogue in the world, I have not indicated where moral truth ultimately is to be found. And nowhere have I discussed the infallibility of the church.

First, the matter of truth in morality. Prior to Vatican II and in some official documents issued since (particularly those addressing matters of personal morality), much in church teaching has followed the *correspondence theory of truth* according to which an idea is true insofar as it corresponds to reality.

Thus, Pope Pius XI, in his 1931 encyclical on the condition of workers, states that God has committed to the church a "deposit of truth," thereby bringing under its jurisdiction "not only social order but economic activities themselves."[23] The church exercises its authority in these areas by proclaiming that truth and by judging everything in light of that deposit.

And the 1976 *Declaration on Certain Questions Concerning Sexual Ethics* chastises those "who today assert that one can find neither in human nature nor in the revealed law any absolute and immutable norm to serve for particular actions...." The document goes on to declare that the church, with the assistance of the Holy Spirit, "ceaselessly preserves and transmits without error the truths of the moral order, and she authentically interprets not only the revealed positive law but 'also ... those principles of the moral order which have their own origin in human nature itself'.... "[24]

What the church says is true, then, because it corresponds to a "deposit" God committed to it or to some "moral order."

Truth as interpreted within the correspondence theory is seen as (1) *propositional*, concerned primarily with the

---

[23] Pope Pius XI, *Quadragesimo Anno*, para 41; in Carlen, vol. 3, p. 421.

[24] "Declaration on Sexual Ethics," sec. 4; in Liebard, pp. 431-432. Quotation from Second Vatican Council, *Declaration on Religious Freedom*, para. 14.

veracity of statements; (2) *certain*, able to be stated clearly and reliably in propositions; (3) *immutable*, open to development in our ability to understand but not to any fundamental change; and, (4) located in the *church as its ultimate guarantor*, with the church here identified primarily with the hierarchy.

By accepting the correspondence theory of truth, the church can end up supporting individualism in a number of ways. First, truth, according to the correspondence theory, is unaffected by history and culture; that is to say, by the specifics of our situated social existence. Such a stance demotes the importance of society for our humanity. Second, like individualism, the correspondence theory of truth indicates a strongly authoritarian element, positing the church (i.e., the hierarchy) as the ultimate interpreter of moral reality. Finally, and maybe most importantly of all, this approach to truth is a powerful preserver of the status quo. It demands that our ideas replicate reality. And that reality is often simply the way things presently are.

How, then, should we approach truth? In my judgment, a transformative theory[25] should replace the correspondence theory. According to the transformative theory, something is true not because it corresponds to some reality, but because it brings about the necessary creative change within society. As Marx stated, "Our purpose is not to know the world but to change it."[26]

The transformative theory of truth does not dismiss the here-and-now as unacceptable simply because it exists. It takes a critical posture toward the present, affirming its positive elements, challenging its destructive aspects, and allowing new possibilities to emerge. Thus, the transformative theory, placed in a Christian perspective, holds that to be true which builds the just society revealed and demanded by the Reign of God.

[25]See Dermot Lane, *Foundations for a Social Theology* (Ramsey, NJ: Paulist Press, 1984), p. 73.

[26]Karl Marx, "Theses on Feuerbach," in Karl Marx and Frederick Engels, *Selected Works* (New York: International Publishers, 1970), p. 30.

Transformative truth is embodied primarily not in propositions but in action. This is not to say that we are unable to make any statements about morality or to judge their correctness. But, emphasis falls on active involvement in the world rather than on removed contemplation of it. Truth emerges from ongoing interaction with our environment: action, reflection leading to new action, etc. Propositions point to this truth, but they can never totally capture it. Their purpose is to direct the interchanges between ourselves and our world; and they do so by keeping before us the insights born of past experiences and by being open to correction and improvement from insights arising from new experiences.

As such, transformative truth is not immutable, a once-for-all perception valid for all times and places. It is specific to particular cultures and to particular historical periods within a given culture. This does not mean, however, that truth is totally subjective, malleable to the interests and idiosyncrasies of a generation. It is objective, responding to the demands of an objective reality. But the shape of that reality is conditioned by culture and history. The world we have to deal with is objectively not the same world our forebears of a century ago or the first-century Christians faced.

Transformative truth is not clear and certain. Since it is affected by experience in changing cultural and historical circumstances, it can hardly be so. According to this theory, we do not so much capture truth as *point toward it*. Moreover, truth here is not seen as located with one particular group within society: it is neither totally dependent upon nor the sole possession of the church. Truth is a communal effort, the somewhat hazy vision that arises out of the dialogue and cooperative effort of various groups within a society.

Not only is truth not dependent solely on the church, but within the church it is not solely the province of the hierarchy. This is not to say that the heirarchy has no authority in the area of morality. As I have already pointed out, Christian morality needs the church, and the church needs authority. But all truth about morality is not born, and does not come to fruition, solely within the hierarchical structure, which then declares it to the other church members. Transformative truth arises out of experience—the experience of the whole church. The Spirit, which is the Spirit of Truth, has been conferred on all.

While this approach to truth has not received official Vatican endorsement, it reflects what has actually occurred within the church. I have in mind, for example, the Second Vatican Council's acceptance of the principle of religious freedom. A century before the council, in December of 1864, Pius IX condemned this principle in no uncertain terms.[27] Prior to Vatican II, all the smart money was betting that the bishops would continue Pius IX's position. But the principle of religious liberty was affirmed.

This principle did not begin in the church; its roots are in the modern West, particularly in the American experience. It did not become true only when affirmed by the Roman Catholic Church. Rather, verification was made through the witness of many different sources: political, religious, cultural, philosophical. The church added an important voice to this witness, but truth was not dependent solely on the church's acceptance.

It is through dialogue, therefore, that the transformative truth of morality is kept alive and continues to be found—dialogue within the church and dialogue between the church and the world.

What, then, about the church's claim to infallibility in morality? If the church adopts a transformative theory of truth, will there be a place for infallibility? My intuition is to say no. Infallibility appears to be closely tied to the correspondence theory of truth's concern to enunciate statements about immutable truth and to guarantee their certitude. When a transformative theory of truth is adopted, not only is the possibility of making infallible statements thrown into question, but also the advisability of doing so. Particularly is the latter the case, I believe, in a church seeking to address U.S. individualism as a community of dialogue in the world.

---

[27]Pope Pius IX, *Quanta Cura*, para. 3; in Carlen, vol. 1, p. 382.

Regardless, a discussion of infallibility is still necessary, for infallibility in matters of faith and morals is a part of the Roman Catholic tradition, and it continues to raise questions for many people, both inside and outside the church. Moreover, there is a strong authoritarian dimension to infallibility that can easily play into the issues raised by U.S. individualism. Here I shall consider infallibility in light of present-day theological reflection; in doing so, I shall place in parentheses for the moment the transformative theory of truth's critique of infallibility. My purpose is to show that, even with the challenge from a transformative theory set to one side, infallibility in morality is a very narrowly circumscribed doctrine.

To begin, it is important to note that historically, according to the majority of theologians, there have been no infallible statements on specific moral questions issued in a solemn or extraordinary way. That is to say, no church stances on specific matters of morality have been infallibly declared either by an ecumenical council or by a pope speaking "ex cathedra." Whether, in fact, there could be *solemn infallible* moral pronouncements is a matter of ongoing discussion.

In addition, a lively debate has centered around the universal *ordinary* magisterium of the church, that is, around the far more numerous authoritative statements made by bishops, popes, and councils in the ordinary exercise of their teaching role where they clearly had no intention of issuing a solemn, definitive declaration. Can these statements in any way be considered infallible?[28]

To look at the issue of infallibility in both solemn and ordinary church teaching on morality, we start with the declaration of Vatican I,[29] endorsed by Vatican II,[30] that the

---

[28]This question has arisen particularly about the church's stance on birth control. Here, however, I shall limit myself to discussing the theoretic issues at stake. For a discussion of infallibility and contraception, see Joseph A. Komonchak, "Humanae Vitae and Its Reception," *Theological Studies* 39/2 (June 1978): 221-257; John C. Ford, S.J., and Germain Grisez, "Contraception and Infallibility," *ibid.*, pp. 258-312; Francis A. Sullivan, S.J., *Magisterium* (New York: Paulist Press, 1983), pp. 143-152.

[29]*The Church Teaches*, pp. 99-102.

[30]*Dogmatic Constitution on the Church*, para. 25.

church does indeed enjoy the charism of infallibility. But that declaration and its endorsement are carefully spelled out and narrowly defined. Not all matters are possible topics of infallible statements. Such statements are limited to matters of faith and morals: more specifically, they are limited to the truth that God has revealed to us for "the salvation of souls."[31] This is the primary subject of possible infallible pronouncements. Secondarily, however, such pronouncements can be made as well on those matters which are "so necessarily connected with revelation that the magisterium could not safeguard and expound revelation if it could not teach [them] with infallibility."[32]

Does morality fall within the parameters of the primary subject matter of infallible statements? Insofar as any of the basic principles of natural law are formally revealed (even if they are also available to us through rational reflection), and insofar as they are essential to our salvation, they can be the subject of a solemn, infallible declaration, just like aspects of faith—although, as I have mentioned, this has not in fact happened.[33]

Even so, as J.P. Mackey points out, morality raises difficulties not encountered when we are considering matters of faith.

> It appears (a) from the probable source of most of even the biblical moral teaching, (b) from the development that can be expected, and seen, in moral codes over the centuries, and (c) from the very nature of a truly moral decision or action, that morality is based on reason, and

[31]Second Vatican Council, *Dogmatic Constitution on Divine Revelation*, para. 10.

[32]Sullivan, p. 145. This is the interpretation of the last clause of the statement made in paragraph 25 of Vatican II's *Dogmatic Constitution on the Church*: "This infallibility with which the divine Redeemer willed the Church to be endowed in defining a doctrine of faith and morals extends as far as the deposit of divine revelation, which must be religiously guarded and faithfully expounded."

[33]For a discussion of the problems of language at stake in making such declarations, see Hughes, pp. 99-110.

must be based on reason, in a manner in which faith is not and cannot be; conversely, that the realm of faith is co-extensive with the content of special divine revelation in a manner in which the moral teaching of the church is not, and that faith is totally dependent on the revelation event in a manner in which morality of its nature cannot be.[34]

Can morality be included among the secondary subjects of infallible pronouncements? This category embraces the majority of morality. Social analysis, prudential judgments, and inductive reasoning play such an essential role in moral directives, particularly in the concrete specifications of the natural law, that they cannot be said to "follow with metaphysical certitude from revealed premises."[35] Nor are they "so necessary connected with revelation that the magisterium could not safeguard and expound revelation" without declaring them infallibly. Moreover, the more concrete the moral instruction, the more it is conditioned both historically and culturally. This, as Sullivan points out, renders it inappropriate as the subject of an infallible statement:

> ... [F]or a norm to be the proper object of infallible teaching, it must be a norm which, at some point in history, can be so irreversibly determined that no future development could possibly call for the substantial revision of this determination of what the natural law requires.[36]

Therefore, while it is possible for the church to make infallible pronouncements about morality, the possible subject matter of such pronouncements is very restricted.

There likewise are restrictions on the way in which the charism of infallibility is exercised. In the case of *solemn* official statements, it is not enough that a pope or a council simply make a declaration on some issue. They must speak

[34]J.P. Mackey, "Teaching Authority in Faith and Morals" in *Morals, Law and Authority*, ed. J.P. Mackey (Dayton, OH: Pflaum Press, 1969), p. 103. See also, Hughes, p. 108.

[35]Sullivan, p. 150.

[36]Ibid., pp. 150-151.

in a definitive way about a matter that is properly the subject of an infallible declaration.

In the case of the universal *ordinary* magisterium, the church's stance on a matter of faith or morals is not infallible simply because it has been held over an extended period of time. Church teaching of long-standing must indeed be respected; and the burden of proof rests on those who would change it. But it can change—as, for example, the history of the church's stance on interest and on religious freedom shows.

To be considered infallible, it is not sufficient merely that a particular moral norm has been set forth as a serious moral obligation. It has to be declared unanimously as a matter "which must be held conclusively."[37] In commenting on this phrase from paragraph 25 of Vatican II's *Dogmatic Constitution on the Church*, Karl Rahner states that

> there can be question of the infallible teaching of the ordinary magisterium ... only when the unanimous teaching of the whole episcopate proposes a matter of faith or morals 'to be held definitely' (*tamquam definitive tenendam*). An absolutely strict and irreformable assent must be explicitly called for. Hence not every doctrine taught unanimously by the whole episcopate is of itself infallible, even when it deals with faith or morals or intends to do so.[38]

Finally, who in the church enjoys the charism of infallibility? As is clear from the discussion to this point, infallibility is attributed to the pope and the body of bishops. But Vatican II's *Dogmatic Constitution on the Church* indicates that "the body of the faithful as a whole, anointed as they are by the Holy One (cf. Jn. 2:20, 27), cannot err in matters of belief."[39]

[37] *Dogmatic Constitution on the Church*, para. 25.

[38] In *Commentary on the Documents of Vatican II* (New York: 1955), vol. 1, pp. 210-211; quoted in Sullivan, p. 126.

[39] *Dogmatic Constitution on the Church*, para. 12; quotation from St. Augustine, "De praed. sanct.," 14, 27; PL 44, 980.

Infallibility, then, rests on the entire church. Within the church, its exercise takes different forms. The hierarchy has a distinctive role to play; but the laity are not merely passive recipients of teaching. The teaching itself arises out of the faith experience of the whole church—a point which highlights the importance of a more decentralized church, as discussed earlier in this chapter. And how the teaching is received is a significant, indeed an essential, element; for reception by the church members "is not a matter of blind obedience to formal authority, but of the divinely assisted recognition of the truth of what is taught."[40] If a teaching is not well received, that fact must be given serious consideration.

On the subject of reception, should only reactions within the Roman Catholic community be taken into account? As I pointed out earlier in this chapter, a copernican revolution has occurred, placing the church's center outside of itself and joining the church in dialogue and common effort with other groups to work for God's Reign. At least in the area of morality, therefore, I believe the church should *at a minimum* be highly sensitive to the experiences and reactions of all people of goodwill. This sensitivity should be apparent not only with regard to possible infallible statements but indeed with regard to all statements bearing on morality. (The U.S. bishops' pastorals on war and peace and on the U.S. economy have set a good example.)

Here we can close the parentheses in this review of recent theological discussion of the doctrine of infallibility and consider whether the church should make any infallible statements on morality at the present time. It seems to me the church has much to lose and little to gain by doing so.

First, making an infallible statement could draw attention away from the most significant issues of the day. As pointed out above, such statements necessarily focus on general principles, not on the concrete problems that beset us. And,

---

[40]Sullivan, p. 112. For a discussion of the implications of reception for authoritative, non-infallible church teaching, see John Coleman, "Development of Church Social Teaching," *Origins*, 11/3 (June 4, 1981): 40.

because discussions of concrete problems and their possible solutions are necessarily more uncertain than infallible pronouncements, the specific issues facing us could easily be taken less seriously and not given the time and energy they demand.

Second, an infallible pronouncement on morality could have a stifling effect on the dialogue and the common effort the Roman Catholic community is seeking with groups outside the church. It would raise fears and suspicions that the authoritarianism and triumphalism of the Roman Catholic church is only cloaked, not abandoned.

Third, an exercise of infallibility in an area of morality could have a deleterious effect on the laity within the church. Efforts to get the laity actively and responsibly involved in the social issues of the day as adult Christians could very easily be undercut; for more than likely, the laity would see such an exercise as portending the return of a paternalistic church where all power and importance rests with the hierarchy.

Finally, and more to the specific concern of this book, infallibility plays too easily into the problems of individualism. The alienation caused by individualism leaves the individual isolated and powerless, open to accepting answers and solutions presented with absolute assurance by an authoritarian source. Infallibility, as commonly understood, validates that attitude.

In short, it is difficult to see what would be gained through an infallible proclamation; what would be lost is too important.

Before ending this chapter, it is necessary to point out that questioning the use of *infallibility* in morality does not mean denying the use of *authority* in morality. As I indicated earlier in this chapter, morality needs community and community needs authority. Unfortunately, an overemphasis on infallibility has led some to equate infallibility with authority and so to believe that noninfallible church teaching is unimportant and nonbinding.

It is also necessary to point out that the most significant ecclesiological questions at the present time do not turn on the issue of infallibility. Much more important is how the church, as a community and not just an association, can respond to God's saving activity in the world; how the church in the United States can join in dialogue with all people of goodwill to search for ways to address individualism, and can join in common effort with them to overcome it.

# PART FOUR:

## Living Morally

# 10

## The Politics of Conscience

We return here once again to the concrete realities of the moral life and moral decision-making. In part one, we identified and analyzed a basic sense of uneasiness about the world in which we live. The problem, as I unfolded it, arises from U.S. individualism and the way the Roman Catholic Church, despite its non-individualistic tradition, implicitly supports that individualism. In part two, we discussed the goal of morality from a positive and negative angle, outlining what should be sought and what avoided in light of U.S. individualism. In part three, we considered how the sources of moral wisdom can be used so that they supply insight for pursuing this goal without themselves becoming part of the problem.

The final section of this book considers the implications of our discussion to this point: How does it affect the way we respond morally to our world? What difference does it make in the way we live out our lives? To get at this, we will first discuss conscience; then we will look at the moral life and moral decision-making.

For many years, psychology has been a primary source for insight into conscience. It has served us well, providing valuable knowledge about such areas as moral development and the impact of the unconscious on moral decision-making. Psychology by itself, however, offers only a partial picture. It does not help us see how conscience is linked with broader social realities—an important factor in responding to U.S.

individualism. And so, in addition to psychology, we turn to sociology to determine how social belonging affects both the content and the functioning of conscience.

Within sociology, we pay special attention to the ways in which conscience gets caught up in the political realities of the day. By politics, I do not mean simply what happens in the halls of government—although one would wish that conscience were more in evidence there. I am using the word politics more broadly to refer to the distribution and uses of power within society, with "power" signifying our ability to have a substantive voice in our destiny. Since human destiny includes the personal, interpersonal, and social dimensions of life, this substantive voice must lead to active participation in all aspects of the societies of which we as individuals are a part. Active participation is especially important in our culture, due to the tendency toward conformism caused by individualism.

Such an approach can leave us a bit uneasy. There is something intensely personal and private about conscience. While hopefully people will respond to their social duties out of their deepest and noblest convictions, we tend to believe conscience should be carefully protected from the types of influence we usually identify with politics and power.

But why do we associate conscience with the private and the personal? And what are the consequences of doing so, both for society at large and for our participation within society, particularly in an individualist culture?

## A History of Conscience

To answer these questions, a brief history of modern conscience is in order. It should come as no surprise, given our previous discussion, that conscience as we know it is closely linked with individualism. Conscience is commonly understood as the deeply personal response of an individual (that is, a separate, bounded self) made in freedom, independent of external influence and coercion. This understanding originated primarily in the search for religious freedom. "The idea of the individual conscience has been put forward mainly by religious non-conformists to combat both hostile communities and organized religions."[1] Thus, modern conscience from the beginning was identified with personal conviction and set over against opposing social forces.

As religious toleration became more and more the accepted order of the day, individual conscience was secularized and integrated into the new social institutions that were appearing. Following one's own convictions in the religious sphere was transformed into following one's own interests in politics and in the marketplace.

This transformation greatly affected the scope of conscience. Conscience was no longer rooted in the broader, shared world of one's basic religious beliefs; it now was identified with the internal world of self-interest. Moreover, these self-interests were held to be private matters, not subject to evaluation or challenge by another individual or group.

Despite this private quality, the new form of conscience was not anti-social or even asocial. As pointed out earlier, the classical liberal tradition holds that self-interest resolutely pursued redounds to the benefit of society as a whole through the magic of the "invisible hand." And, more specific to our situation, this conscience exists within a culture where there are ties binding the individual to society—ties which U.S. individualism has loosened but not totally broken.

In addition, this invisible hand and these loosened ties have been provided some powerful assistance through the internalization of social expectations. Adam Smith speaks of conscience in terms of an "Impartial Spectator." This "spectator" embodies the expectations of society and uses these to pass moral judgment on our behavior. Thus, although the so-called "voice of conscience" seems to speak a highly personal message, it actually presents us with the generally accepted obligations of society which we identify as our own. And, because of the aloneness and alienation caused by individualism, there is added incentive to "go with the flow": we are anxious about what "they" (our neighbors and friends, people in general) will think.

[1] Wolin, p. 338.

This history of the conscience of individualism helps us understand its distinctive responses. Within our society, we insist strongly—even religiously—on our right as individuals to make our own decisions of conscience in light of our own system of values. Nobody can tell us what to do. Even so, the decisions we reach closely conform to the general expectations of society at large, in both personal and social matters.

Understanding how conscience is formed in individualism also helps us interpret the politics of this conscience, i.e., the manner in which it participates in the social realm. At first glance—both from the outside and from within—this conscience can appear to be a very strong, even a dangerous, political entity. From the way it is described, it appears to be its own law-giver and judge, not subject to any external authority or code or morality.

But this conscience is much more the Freudian super-ego than the anarchistic revolutionary, for its moral criteria, as I pointed out, are internalized from culture. (In fact, individualism's ideology of freedom and self-sufficiency serves to hide this from view, denying conscience the critical tools needed to evaluate the impact of culture.) And the arena within which this conscience operates is narrowly circumscribed: the systems in which the individual lives are beyond its purview. Individuals are very mindful of the "rules of the road" within society—even if they do not always keep them; but they do not question the structures and dynamics of society itself. Herbert Marcuse refers to this as "Happy Consciousness—the belief that the real is rational and the the system delivers the goods."[2]

The self-sufficiency of this conscience is also its isolation. While the conscience of individualism can come to its own decisions about what is to be done or avoided, it has no easy way to enlist the support and cooperation of others since the basis for reaching the decision of conscience is so private and idiosyncratic. This results in further isolation and sense of powerlessness—which, in turn, increases the impetus for conforming to social expectations. Thus, the individualistic con-

[2]Marcuse, p. 84.

science offers the individual little basis for substantive voice in one's own destiny.

This, then, sets our agenda for discovering and determining conscience. What type of conscience, both as to its form and its content, should we look for in order to respond constructively to the problems created by U.S. individualism?

## Conscience in Roman Catholicism

The Roman Catholic tradition, I believe, has a strong contribution to make here. But, to do so, it has to overcome some serious obstacles. At present, there is a struggle in the Roman Catholic community over the meaning of conscience. This is not an academic struggle—an argument over a correct definition—but a political one, trying to determine where power lies in moral decision-making.

In this struggle, three different interpretations of conscience are in contention with one another: conscience as set forth in the traditional manuals of moral theology; conscience as born out of the reaction to *Humanae Vitae*, Pope Paul VI's 1968 encyclical on contraception; and conscience as described in the U.S. bishops' 1983 pastoral on war and peace.

It is my contention that the Roman Catholic Church has to settle its own understanding of conscience if it is going to address the problems of the individualistic conscience. But it cannot do so in a vacuum. The church has to carry out this process mindful of the culture within which it exists; for, only in that way can it understand what is at stake in choosing one form of conscience rather than another.

Within the *manualist tradition*, a major force in Roman Catholic moral thought from the Protestant Reformation up to the Second Vatican Council, morality is approached in an extrinsic and legalistic way. It is imposed from outside the person by an authority; and it takes the form of rules, detailing specific immoral actions and their degree of seriousness.

The authority in this case is, of course, the hierarchy which appeals to divine authorization for its power. All morality falls under the hierarchy's jurisdiction: morality as revealed through the scriptures, naturally enough; but also the morality of natural law.[3] Therefore, the proper interpretation of all moral obligation rests with the hierarchy.

Despite the strong emphasis on authority, conscience is not denied by the manualist tradition; but it does take on a particular form. When confronted with a moral issue, we as individuals have to reach a decision of conscience. But the decision we make is whether or not to obey a particular moral law; it is not a decision about what we as distinctive individuals should do to respond properly to these specific circumstances.

Formation of conscience here means receiving and retaining a certain body of information. This information focuses primarily on personal and interpersonal moral issues—especially sexual and medical matters. And, while judgment about whether or not we are guilty of sin takes into account the degree to which we know and choose what we do, that judgment ultimately is rendered by the confessor.

In sum, the manualist conscience involves a morality of law and a decision about obedience. Interpreted politically, it leaves power with the church hierarchy who appeal to God's authorization for the right to set forth both general and specific moral obligations and to judge whether or not we should be granted absolution. This type of conscience leaves us as individuals basically powerless in the moral enterprise: we have no voice in determining particular moral demands; our only decision may place us outside the system, it does not change our position within it.

This type of conscience, as I mentioned, was in ascendency between the Reformation in the sixteenth century and the Second Vatican Council. It has not, however, vanished from the Roman Catholic Church. At the popular level, it continues to exist among Catholics for a number of reasons: lack of education about new approaches to morality; people's desire for a strong authority component in morality; the

---

[3]See John Boyle, "The Natural Law and the Magisterium," in *Readings in Moral Theology No. 3: The Magisterium and Morality*, eds. Charles E. Curran and Richard A. McCormick, S.J. (New York: Paulist Press, 1982), pp. 431-441.

hierarchy's insistence on maintaining its traditional role—to name but three. It continues to be promoted through official church statements that set forth moral obligations in the form of a law or in a form that is easily interpreted by people as a law.

The manualist conscience has generated its own antithesis. Pope Paul VI's 1968 encyclical *Humanae Vitae*, while by no means the only factor, was a major event in the genesis of the *second form of conscience*.[4] In reacting against the pope's ban on artificial contraception, people not only disagreed with him on this particular matter, they began to seek another basis on which to reach moral decisions.

Morality now becomes internal and personal rather than extrinsic and legal. Individuals declare they are going to make their own decisions, not leave them to someone in authority. And the criteria for making these decisions is an intuitive sense of right and wrong. The word used most often is "feel": it is right because it feels right to me; it is wrong because it makes me feel uncomfortable.

There obviously is room for conscience in this approach to morality. In fact, conscience, understood as personal response, here seems to be the sum and substance of morality. This conscience does not merely decide whether or not to obey a moral law; it determines what is right and wrong in a particular situation. And the basis for this decision is something internal to conscience itself, with the result that conscience seems to be itself the source of morality.

Naturally enough, in this type of conscience, moral formation and judgment of one's actions become a highly personal matter. But, as was the case with the previous type of conscience, morality generally is restricted to the realm of the personal and the interpersonal.

Politically, this form of conscience has more power than

---

[4]Other factors which contributed to the formation of this conscience, at least in the United States, were the general attitude toward authority which existed in this country during the 1960s, as well as a sense of greater personal responsibility fostered by the Second Vatican Council. I have encountered this type of conscience primarily in discussions, comments, and questions within the Roman Catholic community rather than in the writing of Roman Catholic theologians.

the conscience of the moral manuals—or at least so it seems. It certainly is not beholden to authority either for moral decisions or for judgments on decisions. But, if power is understood as having a voice in one's destiny—both personal and social destiny—this type of conscience is still quite powerless. Its voice usually extends no farther than the personal and interpersonal sphere; it attends little, if any, to the social sphere. Moreover, it exists in isolation. Basing its judgments on intuitive feelings, and supposedly extending the same right to others, it has no solid ground on which to engage others in common dialogue or to invite them to join in a common effort. Such feelings are too personal and private.

The *third form of conscience* is set forth by the U.S. Roman Catholic bishops in their pastoral on war and peace. Toward the end of that document, they list six "specific steps to reduce the danger of war."[5] Among these is "the role of conscience." Paragraph 231 of the pastoral reads as follows:

> A dominant characteristic of the Second Vatican Council's evaluation of modern warfare was the stress it placed on the requirement for proper formation of conscience. Moral principles are effective restraints on power only when policies reflect them and individuals practice them. *The relationship of the authority of the state and the conscience of the individual on matters of war and peace takes a new urgency in the face of the destructive nature of modern war.*[6]

Morality here is understood in a significantly different way than in the previous two types of conscience. It is not legalistic and extrinsic; but neither is it intuitive and intrinsic. Morality is based on certain principles; and these principles, while set forth by those in authority, are based in moral reality available to all and open to rational discussion. The application of these principles is the responsibility of in-

[5] *The Challenge of Peace*, p. 63.
[6] Ibid., para. 231, p. 72. Emphasis added.

dividuals who must make prudential judgments in specific situations.

Conscience is the means by which these prudential judgments are reached. As such, conscience is charged with deciding how a particular person should act in a particular circumstance; it does not merely determine whether or not to obey a moral law. At the same time, it is not restricted to intuitive feelings in reaching that decision; it is guided by concrete moral principles.

Formation of conscience here involves instruction in moral principles. But it also requires that people be taught through word and example how to apply these principles to concrete situations, and that they be encouraged and challenged to make personal moral decisions. Moreover, the scope of personal moral responsibility is very broad. Individuals must not only be alert to personal and interpersonal matters, but as the pastoral points out, they must be ready to respond to social issues as well.

This form of conscience enjoys a great deal of power. Its decisions are not based on highly personal criteria, yet these decisions are its own. More than that, a basis exists for involving others in constructive dialogue and mutual effort. And this conscience has the right as well as the duty to address broader social issues and to stand up to the misuse of authority. In fact, it is held up as a means of restraining power—even the power of government.

When the bishops speak about conscience standing as a deterrent to the misuse of power, they refer only to the power of secular government—as is appropriate, given the context. But surely this conscience has the right and duty to resist the misuse of ecclesiastical authority as well. Moreover, earlier in the pastoral, the bishops indicate that the "universal moral principles and formal Church teaching"[7] they present

---

[7]"In this pastoral letter, too, we address many concrete questions concerning the arms race, contemporary warfare, weapons systems, and negotiating strategies. We do not intend that our treatment of each of these issues carry the same moral authority as our statement of universal moral principles and formal Church teaching. Indeed, we stress here at the beginning that not every statement in this letter has the same moral authority." Ibid., para. 9, p. 4.

are binding in conscience in a way that the specific applications they make of those principles and teaching are not.
While this is true, it does not mean that these principles and
teaching are therefore off limits to further consideration,
even challenge. Individual members of the church, whether
clergy or lay, have the right to enter into dialogue not only
about the application of moral principles but about the
principles themselves as well.

Therefore, the conscience proposed in the pastoral is from
a political perspective a conscience of great power. It does
not claim to determine its own criteria for moral judgments;
but it has a voice in the development of those criteria; and,
on the basis of those decisions, it can challenge those in
authority, whether that authority be civil or ecclesiastical.

## Conscience: Settling the Political Issues

Conscience, then, is a double issue: an issue in U.S. society
and an issue in the Roman Catholic community. How are
these issues to be addressed? It is my contention that they
have to be dealt with together. The discussion about the
three different types of conscience in the Roman Catholic
community cannot be brought to a satisfactory conclusion
unless we take into account the implications each of them
has within the U.S. culture. To decide without doing so is to
overlook the close ties existing between religion and culture
as well as the intrinsic relationship between the church and
the world.

We consider, first, which of the three types of conscience
under discussion within the Roman Catholic cummunity is
the most appropriate in the context of U.S. culture at the
present time. In my judgment, the first two types—the conscience of the manuals and the conscience arising out of
reaction to *Humanae Vitae*—are both inadequate. Each of
them ends up aiding and abetting individualism.

The conscience which developed in opposition to the encyclical on contraception is clearly individualistic in nature.
It is the conscience of a separate, bounded self, standing

against an overly intrusive authority, making its own decisions on its own moral criteria. Given the circumstances out of which this type of conscience developed, its configuration is readily understandable. But nonetheless, it supports rather than challenges individualism.

At the same time, the authoritarianism of the manualist conscience against which this revolt took place is itself no solution to the problem of individualism. As I pointed out earlier, the isolation and powerlessness caused by individualism lead people to turn to authoritarian figures. Unable to find any suitable resources within themselves and despairing of salvation from some Invisible Hand, they hand over their decisions to an individual or a group who can supply the correct solutions. Thus, it should come as no surprise to find people in U.S. society turning to a strong, authoritarian voice for answers—specific, direct answers—to the moral issues that beset us. The manualist tradition does nothing to offset this; in fact, it feeds it.

It is only the third type of conscience—the type suggested by the bishops in their pastoral on war and peace—that stands as a critical and constructive response to individualism. It places the individual within a community of moral dialogue, both secular and ecclesiastical. At the same time, it calls forth from the individual personal responses to the specific issues he or she faces both personally and as a member of society. These responses are made, not because of some law or out of some self-interest or personal intuition, but in order that the life of the individual and of society may flourish.

These dimensions of the third type of conscience allow it to make a significant contribution to U.S. culture. Because individualism includes a strong belief in a negative freedom that both emphasizes the separateness of the individual from society and moves people to hand matters over to a strong authority, it easily finds itself caught moving between the extremes of a pendulum swing. Overemphasis on freedom leads to calls for greater authority; and too much exercise of authority results in demands for greater freedom.

The third type of conscience offers not merely a third way, but, more importantly, a chance to get off the pendulum.

This is not to say it does away with all disagreement and conflict; but it offers a basis for adjudicating differences that respects both the individual and society, and that ties them together in a common effort.

Before ending this discussion of the third type of conscience, however, I have to add some further elements to the description offered thus far. First, this conscience is not some distinct and separate faculty operating within us. It is ourselves—who we are and what we stand for. In the exercise of conscience, it is who we are and what we stand for that make demands on us in concrete situations as we try to determine how we should act. Conscience is the demand that we be true to ourselves; it is the puzzling out of what that means here and now. Macquarrie describes this as the third "level" of conscience.

> At its most concrete, conscience wrestles with some particular occasion of choice and decides on the right course of action in the situation. We can also think of conscience in a broader way as a more generalized knowledge of right and wrong, good and bad.... There is, I believe, still another level of conscience. It can be understood as a special and very fundamental mode of self-awareness— the awareness of "how it is with oneself," if we may use the expression.[8]

Being true to self, of course, must not be understood individualistically. Self is a part of society, as a society is a part of self. Thus, to be true to myself I must be true to my environment as well.

Second, the person who has—or better, who is—the conscience is, first of all, an agent, not a knower. Our relationship to our world is not that of a spectator. We are actively involved in our world, and, through reflection on that involvement, we come to know.

Because of our action the world changes; and that action and change, in turn, changes us. Thus, conscience is formed

[8]Macquarrie, pp. 111-112.

primarily through our interaction with the environment, not by learning abstract moral principles. Through our conscience, we seek to act in ways that are true to who we are; and, in acting in those ways, we are changed—and so too our conscience. This does not mean that moral principles should not be taught. It does mean, though, that they should be presented in ways that enlighten us in our struggle for authenticity.[9] And we should be given an opportunity to speak about the insights we have come to through our own struggles, thereby having a voice in setting these principles.

Third, decisions of conscience are more a recognition of what must be done than a cognitive exercise. Decisions about how we should act, particularly in weighty situations, are in large part not made in the conscious chambers of our mind. They are reached more in the depths of our heart, below the conscious level, where the demands for authenticity gradually are sorted out and become clear. Thus, reaching decisions of conscience is primarily a coming to recognize and accept a growing sense of how we should act. (I shall discuss this further in the next chapter.)

Moreover, and this is the last point, these decisions are not so much conclusions as commitments. Since we are not present to our world as a spectator but as an agent, we are not merely deciding about some matter *out there*; we are placing who we are on the line and dedicating ourselves to developing a certain self and a certain world.

## Freedom and Conscience

In light of the description of conscience presented thus far, we can now consider two further issues: (1) what does it mean to speak about freedom in relation to conscience? (2) do we have a right and/or a duty to follow our conscience?

[9]For a discussion on the place of principles in ethics, see Richard Gula, *What Are They Saying About Principles in Ethics?* (New York: Paulist Press, 1982).

That freedom is an essential and intrinsic component of morality goes without saying. If we were totally determined, having no more control over our actions than a rolling stone has over its path down a hill, we could not be held responsible for them—at least not in ways that do justice to the term "responsibility." To judge our actions right or wrong, good or bad, we have to make a significant enough contribution to what has happened so it can meaningfully be termed *our* action. And so, to link freedom to conscience is almost redundant—there can be no conscience without freedom.

The problem comes when we try to define what that freedom is, particularly when we try to do so within an individualistic culture. Individualism grounds its definition of the individual—a separate, bounded self—in negative freedom. This freedom protects the individual against either external or internal coercion and influence.

The price of this freedom is great indeed. If we try to put aside all that influences us, we have to set aside our very selves. As we saw in the discussion on culture, we cannot cease being affected by the world outside us—both the personal and the impersonal world—without throwing out a vital aspect of our very person, viz., our interaction with our environment. And we cannot shut off the influences from within us without thereby denying our very selves.

As a result, linking conscience and freedom in an individualistic culture is dangerous. Conscience, you will recall, is nothing else than our very self; and that self is threatened by the freedom of individualism.

Our task, then, is to define freedom in a way that preserves the basis of morality, while at the same time avoiding the problems connected with individualism. To do so, we begin with an understanding of the self as essentially tied to the world. As should be apparent by now, this does not destroy the possibility of a separate identity for the individual. Rather, it locates it in the distinctive ways the individual participates within society. Accordingly, life flourishes for us not through independence but through interdependence.

In light of that, freedom is best understood as a qualification of our way of interacting with our world. To put it succinctly, freedom is not the opposite of necessity; freedom is built on, indeed depends upon, necessity. Thus, to be free means acting in a particular way in relation to what necessitates or conditions us, not doing away with those factors.

Tillich speaks about this in terms of the essential connection between freedom and destiny. We cannot escape our destiny since it is fundamentally who we are. "Destiny is not a strange power which determines what shall happen to me. It is myself as given, formed by nature, history, and myself."[10] Freedom is grounded in destiny; for, only in who we are do we have our power to act. Freedom is our power to direct our lives by determining which real possibilities will be acted upon—*real* possibilities grounded in our destiny.

We are free, then, because we can do something with the possibilities of our lives. We can move in one direction rather than another; and in so doing, we become a certain self, a certain character.

That means, of course, that our freedom does not allow us to do whatever we want: we cannot make ourselves into whatever we wish, as individualistic freedom would have us believe. The outcome of our choice is as important as the process leading to it. To make a decision that narrows or debases us as a person can only mean we are less free because we are less a person. In short, we have the freedom to direct our destiny; but we cannot direct it in just any direction. In fact, certain directions, even if pursued without coercion, lead to a lack of freedom, precisely because they undermine our personhood.

Freedom, then, is primarily freedom *to*—freedom to respond to the call of our humanity to make it flourish by being an instrument for the flourishing of all creation. Freedom *from* is important, because there are aspects of life that can obstruct this positive freedom. But freedom *from* is always secondary to, always in service of, a fuller and more flourishing life.

Freedom, thus interpreted, establishes a basis for understanding our right and duty as individuals to follow our own

[10]Tillich, vol. 1, p. 185.

conscience. The duty arises from the fact that we must take responsibility for our own lives. Responsibility here refers not merely to the obligation we have of doing this or that action correctly, morally speaking, or of avoiding this or that situation on the basis of moral considerations. It goes beyond the particular action and the particular situation to the person, the self who performs the action. Our responsibility is to see to the realization of our self in the fullest manner and to the fullest degree possible—a realization which requires us to work as well, of course, to make the entire environment, both human and nonhuman, flourish.

Such a responsibility cannot be fulfilled merely by relying on the orders of others, that is, by letting others determine our lives for us. The decisions we make form ourselves and, therefore, our world. But, since we have the responsibility of directing our own lives, the duty of conscience falls to us alone. This is not to say we should reach our decisions of conscience without any consultation or advice. To do so would be foolish. But the ultimate decision, that is, the commitment of ourselves to a certain course of action and the resulting integration and formation of ourselves, lies with us alone.

This duty of conscience in no way confers on us infallibility. As we are all too well aware, we can and do make mistakes. One of the gifts we fall heir to with age is a deep sense of humility arising from remembrance of past deeds which, though done with honest conviction, were such unbelievable mistakes. That is inevitable. Our humanity in no way allows us perfection; morality by its very nature admits of only a limited degree of certainty. In spite of that, we have to make our own decisions. We must come to as clear an understanding of our circumstances and of our own convictions as we can; we must reach as enlightened a decision as possible; and then we must act.

Coexistent with this duty of following our conscience is our right to do so. The right is grounded in our humanity. Insofar as we are human beings, we have a right to whatever is required for our development as a human person. Since such development can occur only as we make and carry through on our own decisions of conscience, we must be protected against whatever undermines this. Eric D'Arcy argues this point in the following syllogism:

> The individual has the right to receive from the State whatever of the goods committed to her is necessary for the attainment of his end; therefore, in so far as the State renders the attainment of his end impossible, he suffers a violation of natural justice. But it has been found that substantial fidelity to moral duty is a condition of attaining one's end; and a person is untrue to moral duty if he acts against his conscience. This now leads us to the conclusion that, if the State forces a man to act against his conscience, it renders impossible the attainment of his end; it will therefore be violating natural justice and acting *ultra vires*.[11]

What D'Arcy says, of course, applies not just to the State but to all of society, and to the church as well.

As the U.S. Roman Catholic bishops' pastoral on war and peace points out, we must stand behind our convictions. In doing so, we are but declaring who we are. We cannot arrive at our decisions in isolation: we need a community of moral dialogue to direct us. It must be our decision, however, based on our deepest belief and clearest thinking that what we do will further the Reign of God in our midst. This is our true freedom.

[11]Eric D'Arcy, *Conscience and Its Right to Freedom* (New York: Sheed and Ward, 1961), p. 222.

# 11

## The Moral Life and Moral Decision-Making

We are accustomed to think of morality as a dimension of life defined primarily by dilemmas and decisions. And naturally so, since morality comes to our attention in the form of questions about how we should act in particular situations. Should we be truthful with the boss? Should we blow the whistle about the water pollution caused by the company for which we work? Should we spend a weekend at a motel with a friend? Accordingly, any systematic presentation of morality worth its salt has to guide us toward a successful, or at least an acceptable, resolution of our moral dilemmas.

I do not deny such dilemmas exist. They are only too real a part of life. But I do question whether dilemmas are the heart and soul of morality. I go even further: in my opinion, moral dilemmas, and indeed the whole area of moral decision-making, are secondary to the moral life.

The majority of our lives does not revolve around decisions. We do not have to determine consciously how we are going to handle the greater part of our day—thank goodness! We set ourselves mostly on automatic pilot, following the usual patterns of everyday life. Only when these patterns prove inadequate in a particular situation, or when they lead to results contrary to what we expect or are comfortable with, do we consciously advert to the matter at hand and begin the decision-making process.

So too with morality. We are not constantly taking counsel

with ourselves about what is morally correct in certain circumstances. We do not have to decide each time, for example, whether or not to respond truthfully to questions put to us, whether or not to be courteous to the people we meet, whether or not to respect the property of others. We operate out of a certain moral automatic pilot based on the accepted patterns of our culture and the habits we have personally developed. This is the dimension of our lives I am referring to with the phrase "the moral life."

In distinguishing the moral life from moral decision-making, I am by no means dichotomizing them or opposing them one to another. They obviously are closely interrelated. But I want to argue that moral decision-making is not the totality of the moral life; that, in fact, to identify morality primarily with moral decision-making is to lose sight of aspects of our lives and ourselves that are crucially important for morality. For example, much time and ink have been spent discussing moral decisions about who should have genital relations with whom and under what circumstances. But we are only beginning (thanks largely to the feminist movement) to consider the moral implications of the gender identities propounded and promoted by our culture and our church. Obviously, questions and dilemmas about genital activity raise moral concerns that cannot be overlooked. But how we live out our maleness or femaleness has much more pervasive moral consequences. It affects everything we do; but the issues it entails cannot all be captured in questions about how to act in particular situations.

Further yet, I hold that moral decision-making is secondary to the moral life. This is not to say that our moral decisions are unimportant. These decisions, however, are not reached in isolation; they are grounded in the general tenor of our lives. Thus, defining morality in terms of decisions misconstrues reality; it omits an important aspect—the moral life; and it gives precedence to an aspect —moral decision-making—that should take a subsidiary role.

To overlook the patterns and habits of the moral life by focussing solely or primarily on moral decision-making has negative consequences for the moral enterprise in general, and it plays into the problems raised by individualism. We end up with what Edmund Pincoffs calls "quandary ethics" which holds

> that the business of ethics is with "problems," that is, situations in which it is difficult to know what one should do; that the ultimate beneficiary of ethical analysis is the person who, in one of these situations, seeks rational ground for the decision he must make; that ethics is therefore primarily concerned to find such grounds, often conceived of as moral rules and the principles from which they can be derived; and that meta-ethics consists in the analysis of the terms, claims, and arguments which come into play in moral disputation, deliberation, and justification in problematic contexts.[1]

Consequently, moral attitudes and actions found in culture as part of everyday life and in the habits of individuals are simply accepted without reflection and critique. Given the tremendous effect these have on our personal and social existence, such blind acceptance can lead to a deterioration of the moral enterprise; and it goes along with U.S. individualism's uncritical acceptance of the realm of everyday life, leaving unchallenged the conformity individualism tends to promote.

Second, quandary ethics supports the idea that the conscious, rational dimension of life carries the greatest importance and significance. The unconscious and the emotive may exist; but they are really an unfortunate part of the human condition, and, the more matters can be brought to the level of conscious, logical decision, the better. I agree that reason—conscious, rational decision—is an important aspect of our moral response to our environment. But, to play this up at the expense of the unconscious and the emotive is to demean the very dimensions which reason needs as ground and milieu to carry out its proper role. And it plays as well into the rationalism of individualism.

---

[1]Edmund Pincoffs, "Quandary Ethics," in *Revisions: Changing Perspectives in Moral Philosophy*, ed. Stanley Hauerwas and Alasdair MacIntyre (Notre Dame, IN: Notre Dame University Press, 1983), p. 93.

Third, identifying morality with response to moral dilemmas leaves the decison-making process isolated from the personal and social environment within which it occurs. We cannot abstract ourselves from our past and from our culture in making our decisions. They necessarily affect us—and rightly so, for without them there could be no continuity to our lives, no self who reaches the decisions.

The depth of the impact of the unconscious and the emotive, of our past and our culture on moral decision-making can be seen if we consider some of the important determinations we have made in life—determinations, for example, about following a particular way of life or about marrying a particular person. I purposefully am using the word "determination" here rather than "decision," for I wonder if they really should be called decisions at all. It is not as though we stand before a smorgasbord on which are set out all the possible directions our life could take or all the possible people we could marry; and then we calmly, cooly, and very rationally select one rather than another. In the case of our important determinations, it is, in the end, more a matter of recognizing what we have to do. Not that someone forces us to do this rather than that, to marry this person rather than another. Rather, the matter is mulled over below the conscious level, deeply influenced by the emotive and the habitual with some conscious, rational input. Only gradually do we come to realize what we have to do to be true to ourselves; and it takes the form more of recognition than decision.

To overlook the fact that our decisions are grounded in nonrational aspects of our lives severely limits our ability to prepare the groundwork for decisions. For, even though social patterns and personal habits can never be brought totally to consciousness, this does not mean they cannot be attended to. In fact, an important—better, an essential part— of moral life is cultivating a proper moral environment within ourselves and within our society. I shall speak more about this shortly.

And, to abstract moral decisions from other aspects of our social and personal life plays into the hand of individualism. It leaves us alienated by dividing our lives up into separate, isolated units.

Fourth, quandary ethics can give the impression that morality is primarily concerned with moral rules and principles. As Pincoffs points out, "to take the resolution of problems as central, and to conceive of problems on the collision-model is indefensibly reductivist. It reduces the topic of moral character to the topic of conscientiousness or rule-responsibility."[2] This can easily lead to a juridical and legalistic approach to morality. Such an approach harmonizes well with individualism, and it introduces a minimalism that is destructive of morality.

Finally, reducing morality to response to moral problems results in a loss of the agent, of the person who responds morally.

> Quandary ethics . . . conceives of a quandary which arises because I fall into a certain situation. *The situation is such that it can be described in perfectly general terms, without any reference to me as an individual,* including my personal conceptions of what are and are not worthy deeds and attitudes and feelings: worthy of me. I may, according to this conception, fall into the situation in virtue of my falling under a rule which would apply to any person, or in virtue of my falling under a rule which would apply to any person playing a particular role.[3]

Morality, accordingly, is thought of as a series of rational decisions made by persons who face difficult situations. But in analyzing the situation, the circumstances are discussed in abstraction from this particular person facing this particular situation. And the solution has to be universalizable—the proper response for Everyperson: a person without a face, without a past, and without an identity.

As a result, the human dimension of morality is lost since human beings always exist as individuals and cannot be reduced to Everyperson. The impersonal spectator of individualism is joined by the impersonal actor.

---

[2]Ibid., p. 111.
[3]Ibid., pp. 104-105. Emphasis added.

## The Moral Life

If the emphasis on moral decision-making in quandary ethics is so problematic and more attention should be paid to the moral life, what is meant by the moral life? I have already indicated that the moral life involves attitudes and habits found within a particular culture and in the lives of individuals. It is now time to flesh that out.

The moral life includes both the character of the individual and the moral ecology of church and society. First, the character of the individual. By this I mean the person as interacting with his or her environment. Through this interaction in which the individual both affects the environment and is affected by it, an identity is established so that it is this particular person who is actor and recipient. The various dimensions of the self are developed and integrated into a unity, into an intentionality interacting from a certain perspective, out of a certain belief system, and in terms of certain attitudes.

The self we are is neither totally our creation nor totally under our control. We do not begin life with a self standing behind what happens to us and what we do, directing the formation of our identity. Our self, our identity, our character arises from our interaction with the environment in light of the role-identities presented by society—again, not as some force standing apart from or behind this interaction, but as the form the interaction takes.

This understanding of the self is important for countering individualism. The position I am advancing holds that there truly is an "I," a distinct person who acts and takes responsibility for what happens. But it insists that this "I" develops through interaction with the social and physical environment, and so is essentially connected with the environment. Individualism posits an "I" that exists prior to any interaction and, therefore, bears no essential connection with the environment. Without that connection, the self is the separate, bounded entity who is subject to the alienation and powerlessness we discussed earlier.

The formation of our self or character begins within a particular social and historical framework immediately as we enter life. Thus, by the time we can respond to it consciously and effectively (that is, probably by our late teens at the earliest), it has been fundamentally established and worked out in many of its particulars.

This does not mean, however, that we bear no responsibility for who we are or that we can do nothing to change. But to take responsibility for our character, we first have to own ourselves. Who I am is a mixed bag: some good points, some bad points; some strengths, some weaknesses; but it is who I am. Only as that is owned, only as I begin to say, "This is me who is acting: this is me who is affected by my interaction with the environment in that way," can I begin to change and refine that interaction. The reason is that only as I own who I am can I have the power to do anything about myself. To refuse to accept myself is to leave myself powerless.

This self-ownership is every bit as much a social reality as the self that is being owned. I cannot just stand in front of a mirror and, through some great proclamation of the will, say: "I'm okay." I have to find that what I am about, that is, who I am, is significant for a community of people. If I do not have a sense that I am important in the eyes of others, I can say "I'm okay" till I am hoarse; but I cannot accept it as true.

Even when we are able to take responsibility for ourselves, the refinements and changes we can make in our character are never total. We cannot become a totally different person. To use an image from the chapter on culture, at birth we are like a ship launched on a body of water. During the course of our voyage we can make use of the materials from which the ship is made to change and refine it, but we can never pull over to shore and start over or take another ship.

But still we can and we must act; only in that way can we be truly human. For, as human beings our interaction with our environment is not the same as that of a rock. We can—and must—be active in that interaction. Not only can we affect the environment, we can (to a limited extent) also alter the form that interaction takes by changing our character.

Thus, part of the moral life involves bringing to awareness

and critiquing the ways we interact with our environment because of who we are. The basis for this critique is not some fully worked out vision of Everyperson against which we measure ourselves like Procrustes' bed. At issue rather is this: what qualities should mark the interaction between self and environment in this particular culture and in this particular generation to bring flourishing to life? I attempted to answer that in the fourth chapter when I discussed virtue. That interaction, I indicated, should be defined substantively by temperance and justice. This is to say, our actions should be such as to lead to integration of the self and to the common good.

These benchmarks, to be sure, are very general and their specific meaning has to be worked out for the various dimensions of our person and our interaction. They point in the direction I have in mind; yet, even when worked out further, they will not set forth detailed rules or even a particular pattern each person is to follow. No two persons will interact with the environment in exactly the same way. They cannot, for they are different selves. Morality's task is to provide individuals insight into the qualities essential for interaction with the environment at a particular time and place, and then encourage them to make those qualities a part of their life—but in their own distinctive way. The individual's uniqueness, then, is recognized; but it is a uniqueness based on the distinctive way the individual participates in society rather than the way the individual is different and separate from others.

One aspect of the moral life, then, is the character or self of the individual. The moral life here refers not to this or that particular action that we perform but rather to who we are as persons, how we interact with our environment. It includes our attitudes and prejudices, our roles within society, our ways of thinking and acting, of feeling and dreaming. In short, the moral life is concerned with the quality of our being, of our engaging our world. Is that quality such that it brings integrity to our self and justice to our environment, and allows us to pursue these goals with courage, with sensitivity and thoughtfulness?

The moral life, however, involves more than just our character as individuals, the quality of our interaction with the environment. This interaction is always carried out within a social context which is, in fact, part of the interaction and thus part of our character. As I have argued throughout this book, who we are as individuals cannot be understood without taking into account the society within which we live.

Thus, in considering the moral life, that is, the moral quality of all the various dimensions of the interaction between ourselves and our environment, we have to ask: what type of interaction is prompted and promoted by the society of which we are a part and which is part of us? What is the quality of our social milieu and what effect does it have on the character of its members?

The criteria by which we judge our society are the same we hold up before ourselves as individuals. We look critically at the attitudes and patterns of behavior promoted by society—attitudes and patterns which come to us primarily through the role-identities and role-models society presents to us, but as well through the various ways society structures our common life—and we ask: do they promote integration of the person and concern for the common good? Do they support courage and conscientiousness?

To the degree these questions can be answered affirmatively, the moral life of society is constructive and creative. To the degree the answer is no, destructive forces are operative and steps must be made to change them. (These steps, of course, have to be made in light of the concrete configuration of society and its realistic possibilities.)

Finally, we cannot overlook the church as part of the environment within which interaction takes place and thus as part of the moral life. In this interaction, the church does not function in the same way as society (as I pointed out in chapter nine). But it has an essential role to play, and this must be critiqued.

First, we consider whether the church either implicitly or explicitly supports the destructive forces within society. I have shown throughout this book how the Roman Catholic Church, although denouncing individualism, ends up at times supporting it. It is important, therefore, for the church to begin fostering role-identities with attitudes and types of behavior that introduce a creative alternative to individualism.

But the primary role for the church, as I have argued, is to be a community of moral dialogue within the world. This dialogue has the moral life as one of its topics—indeed, the foremost of its topics. The character of the person making the decisions rather than the decisions themselves should be one of the primary concerns.[4]

This is not to suggest that the subject of moral decision-making should be totally avoided. As Hauerwas points out, casuistry, or the discussion of specific cases requiring moral decisions, is important so that a community can understand and test the concrete implications of its moral vision and message. "Indeed the primary task of casuistry is to help us understand our interconnectedness so that we can better appreciate how what we do not only fits within the story of our lives, but also how it is determined by and determines the ongoing story of the Christian community."[5] Thus, casuistry's main purpose is to place specific situations in the context of the moral life, not to provide solutions to the moral problems people face. If the dialogue within the church moves too far in the latter direction, it can lead people to understand morality as primarily involving quandaries and to view the church as authoritarian. This fits in easily with individualism.

Finally, the church makes an important contribution to the moral life by mediating God's forgiveness. As I have pointed out, discussions about the moral life have to be personal in nature, helping us as individuals understand what our particular contribution to the common effort the moral life entails. But that understanding carries with it an awareness of per-

---

[4]This is acknowledged in the "Declaration on Sexual Ethics" which I have referred to many times in this book. In sec. 11 (Liebard, p. 439) we read: "... the purpose of this Declaration is to draw the attention of the faithful in present-day circumstances to certain errors and models of behavior which they must guard against. The virtue of chastity, however, is in no way confined solely to avoiding the faults already listed. It is aimed at attaining higher and more positive goals. It is a virtue which concerns the whole personality, as regards both interior and outward behavior." But, as I pointed out earlier (chapter 4, footnote 45), when the authors spell out what is required for living the chaste life, the means set forth are for the most part negative.

[5]Hauerwas, *The Peaceable Kingdom*, p. 130.

sonal failure and inadequacy. Perfection is not the human lot. While we may improve our lives, we simply have to accept the fact that some aspects will always be less than adequate, even deeply problematic.

If we are left with this awareness and nothing more, our personal involvement and contribution are easily hindered. A full effort comes only as we are assured of God's forgiveness. This is not a matter of cheap grace which merely relieves our anxiety and leaves us secure where we are. It is at once promise and challenge: calling us forward, but offering us the forgiving word of acceptance. That forgiving word allows us to accept ourselves as sinners and it empowers us to do what we can to bring flourishing to our life and to the world around us.

The moral life, then, is a rich and inclusive reality. It is the texture of life, the quality of our interaction with our environment as formed by the identities, patterns of living, and structures provided by the civil and ecclesial communities and by the distinctive ways we as individuals participate in these.

As such, the moral life is intrinsically both social and personal. To single out one without the other is to respond to an abstraction, and ultimately to falsify the moral enterprise.

## Moral Decision-Making

While the moral life is the main focus of this book, moral decision-making cannot be overlooked; for, it is a part of our lives. We all at times confront situations where we are in a real quandary about how to act.

But when moral decision-making is distinguished from, and assigned a role secondary to, the moral life, a new task presents itself. The category of moral decision-making was previously taken for granted; now it has to be described and analyzed.

### Quandaries

How often do we really make moral decisions? As we look over our lives, we certainly see that we have acted in certain ways rather than others, that we have walked certain paths and avoided others. But are these all the result of decisions? In each instance, did we find ourselves in circumstances where two or more real possibilities presented themselves; where we were in conflict about how to proceed; where we consciously weighed out the pros and cons, and finally determined how to act?

I believe we face few such quandaries. Most of what we do, as I pointed out before, is the result of our moral automatic pilot. We do not stop to think about how we should act; we just carry on according to our usual patterns of behavior— according to the usual patterns of our moral life. When we do advert to what is happening, it is more a matter of recognizing than deciding our responsibility. Recently, a friend and I had to pay for fixing a car after an accident. The person at the garage, knowing that we would recover the amount from an insurance company, offered to make the receipt out for $50 more than we were paying. Both of us said no immediately. We were both aware of what was going on and its implications; and, abstractly at least, we had an option how to act; but neither of us really decided (in the true meaning of the term) our response—we simply recognized it.

I go further yet. Not only do we usually recognize rather than decide how we should act, but that is the preferable state of affairs. This is by no means to say that we should duck our responsibilities. It is simply to recognize that we can meet our moral obligations as well through acting out of the general patterns of our life as through conscious decisions; that these patterns, because they are the foundation for our decision-making, take precedence; and that the more we can follow established patterns, the better founded is our character.

When we face a problematic situation, then, it is important that we carefully explore the circumstances to see if we really have to make a decision. By using our imagination and looking for other alternatives, we may very well find one that we simply recognize as the right thing to do; and so, we can act "in character" and do not have to undertake a decison-making process.[6]

---

[6]On the importance of using imagination to find further alternatives, see Daniel Maguire, *The Moral Choice*, pp. 170-178.

Nonetheless, it cannot be denied that quandaries do occur and decisions have to be made. But what are these quandaries? What causes them? They are not the result of the collision of two principles existing outside a situation that by some accident bump into each other at this time. It is not as though values somehow float free around us and suddenly come into conflict. Rather, quandaries happen when we are confronted by situations in which possible solutions run counter to the role-identities and accepted patterns of society and to the character we have developed, in which the usual responses for some reason no longer work or make sense.

Quandary situations, then, are neither isolated nor private. They are closely connected with the specific patterns of behavior within society and our individual lives. As such, they tell us a good deal about ourselves and about the communities to which we belong. They make us advert consciously to personal and social ways of interacting with the environment that we have taken for granted. They may indicate shifts in the environment and in the types of interaction that are taking place. Responses that used to be automatic may now raise questions or cause problems because things are changing.

Questions about the use of birth control, for example, grew out of a shift from an agricultural to an industrial and post-industrial society and out of the problems caused by a burgeoning world population. Kristin Luker has pointed out the relationship between the abortion issue and changing roles for doctors and women in U.S. society.[7]

Accordingly, we should not just take their existence for granted. Quandaries are important events both within the historical and cultural framework of a particular society and in the context of the character of a particular individual, requiring careful analysis and thoughtful consideration. They should be the subject of dialogue within the church, not simply as situations looking for solutions but as possible indications of a changing environment calling us to respond to God's saving presence among us in new ways.

In that dialogue, two questions ought to be considered: Should particular quandaries exist? Should other quandaries be raised?

[7]Luker, *The Politics of Motherhood.*

These questions may sound rather high-handed. They make it seem as though some quandaries are trivial. For someone confronting a difficult situation, however, they are anything but that. I agree that suffering through the perplexities of a moral quandary can be a painful experience. But I am also convinced that some quandaries are not worth our time and energy. They raise questions about issues which, viewed in terms of the problems of our day and what we see God to be doing in our midst, deserve much less attention than they get.

Consider the types of quandaries that seem to be exercising people within U.S. culture and within the Roman Catholic community at the present time. If titles appearing in the personal development sections of bookstores and if the topics discussed in personal advice columns (e.g., Ann Landers) are any indication, sexuality is an area where people are greatly perplexed. While some of this has to do with the definition of gender roles, mostly it centers on genital activity. An unofficial (and definitely unscientific) survey I made of people doing pastoral ministry reveals a similar focus.

In the United States, people in business are discussing issues such as affirmative action and truth in advertising, but accept the basic moral orientation of the economic and business system as a whole without question. Roman Catholics appear to be especially concerned about difficulties arising in the medical field, many of them having to do with women's reproductive capacity.

These are only some examples—by no means a comprehensive picture—of areas where people find themselves in a moral quandary about how to act. These should not be just taken for granted, but should be submitted to critical analysis and evaluation. What is there about the moral ecology of U.S. culture and the Roman Catholic community that makes these areas problematic at this time? Do they arise out of the individualism of our society? Are these areas where people indeed should experience so many quandaries? Are all the quandaries experienced of sufficient merit to warrant the time, thought, emotion, and energy they demand? The first two questions call for a social analysis; the third and fourth require an evaluation based on our perception in faith of what God is doing in our midst.

All four questions should be part of the ongoing moral

dialogue within the church. As a result of that dialogue, we may conclude that some of the quandaries we are experiencing are caused by moral directives or generally accepted attitudes out of step with our own era. Products of a different time, they create false problems at the present.

In addition, might there not be areas where people see no difficulties whatever but where in fact they should be plagued by quandaries? Viney Quayle, who heads up the St. Ambrose Housing Center in Baltimore, a non-profit corporation concerned with low-income housing, claims that Matthew's gospel is all wrong in its account of the last judgment. We are not going to be asked whether we fed the hungry or welcomed the stranger or clothed the naked. The questions instead will be these: Where did you work and why? Where did you live and why? Where did you bank and why?

These questions highlight areas where quandaries maybe should exist in our lives but more than likely do not. Bishop Leroy Matthiesen of Amarillo, Texas, made headlines in 1980 when he confronted people with the first question. He asked that those who worked at Pentax, a company assembling nuclear weapons, consider whether in conscience they should continue to work there.[8] A challenge like that could be directed to many corporations—and even the church is not immune.

Quandaries, then, despite their subordinate role in the moral life and my argument that they should be avoided as much as possible, do have an important place in the moral enterprise. While they cannot be taken simply at face value, they do provide an occasion for examining the general thrust of our individual lives and the accepted patterns of society. Their existence may indicate changes in the environment calling for new ways of interacting. On the other hand, their non-existence may be a problem; and we may well conclude that they should be precipitated to force a community to see the need for new ways of interacting.

---

[8]Bishop Leroy T. Matthiesen, "Amarillo Bishop Protests Nuclear Arms Buildup," *Origins* 11/12 (September 3, 1981): 180-181.

The "Subjective" Component

To this point, the discussion of quandaries has focused mainly on their roots within a particular historical and cultural environment, and only passing mention has been made of their relation to the character of individuals. It is now time to give more attention to the latter; and, in doing so, to consider briefly the general role of the individual in decision-making.

Quandaries for individuals are, of course, closely related to those existing within society; they are never merely private, personal affairs. As individuals, we participate in the larger social order in ways that integrate that order into our very identity. Therefore, quandaries existing in the historical and cultural context are present in our lives as well; and we cannot truly understand what is happening to us personally unless we see our situation in terms of the broader social context.

As individuals, however, we are not simply clones of society. We participate in it in a unique way, and the distinctiveness of that participation affects the way a quandary situation is interpreted and responded to. This may be referred to as the "subjective" component of morality.

The definition of any moral situation has to include the people involved; and their involvement is more than just a physical presence. How the people concerned put together and weight the various elements to describe what is going on is an essential aspect—essential to the point that there is no moral situation without it. Thus, the definition is always made from a particular perspective; and that perspective is determined by the character of the participants.

This does not mean we can define a situation in any way we wish. We are dealing with external realities that are not malleable to any description whatever. Moreover, we are responsible to communities of people; and, included in that responsibility is the demand that we give an intelligible and sensible account to others of what we are thinking and doing.

Nor does it mean that our description of a situation is infallibly correct or beyond challenge. We may have omitted certain factors; we may have downplayed some and overemphasized others. But if that is the case, we have to do more than just change the description and evaluation. For these are rooted in the perspective from which we view the situation; and that perspective arises out of who we are. Therefore, it is not a matter simply of exchanging one set of blueprints for another or of reprogramming a computer; it is an issue of conversion. To change our way of seeing things we have to change who we are. Thus, the importance of the virtuous person. The virtuous person is not just the one who acts rightly; he or she sees the world from a perspective that pinpoints the most important aspects and thus enables a proper response.

In a quandary situation, then, we as individuals face more than just a question of what to do in this situation. At issue is who we are and what we will be. Therefore, we have to analyze and evaluate the quandary in terms of what it says about our identity and what it implies for our distinctive place in, and our contribution to, the community of which we are a part.

There is as much a "subjective" dimension to the response we make as to the description we give to a moral situation. We have to respond to the full of our ability, that is, to the full of who we are, in a particular situation. We must do *what* we can and *all* that we can; but we cannot do what is beyond us. It may be that new ways of understanding and responding to a situation are beginning to dawn on us. We may see others involved in similar situations react in ways that seem—to us, at least—unbelievably heroic. We, however, recognize in all honesty that what we can do right now falls far short of that new vision and is by no means heroic. Still, it is what we can do and all we can do. Given hope by the presence of a forgiving God, we accept that fact. Buoyed and strengthened by this hope which allows us to accept our participation in sin,[9] we work so that we can respond in the future in ways to bring greater flourishing to life.

No doubt, this recognition of the "subjective" component of quandary situations can open the door to abuse. We can

[9]See above, pp. 126-127.

rationalize and alibi a great deal. But no way of understanding morality can totally head that off. It is not as though we are trying to construct a system of law that covers all possibilities and coerces people into being good. Morality depends upon people reflecting and acting in good faith.

In fact, the more we try to develop a system of morality that covers all the angles and keeps people in line, the more we end up with one that is legalistic and minimalistic. The more we try to find ways to make sure people are kept from evil, the more we fail to call people beyond themselves to great, even heroic actions. And without including the latter, we do not take into account the breadth of the moral experience.

A number of years ago a young woman, obviously disturbed, asked to speak to me. She had been hurrying somewhere and on the way had passed an old woman slowly making her way home burdened down with a bag of groceries. At this point in her story the young woman broke down and cried, for, as she made plain, she was guilty of a serious moral lapse for not stopping to help, even though she was late for an appointment. In my language, she had seriously failed to meet the demands of her character.

How are we to understand her experience? She had broken no moral rules—none, that is, except what she placed on herself. But I could not then—and still cannot—say to her: "Now, now. You are making too much of this. It would have been nice to help that woman. But let's not get carried away." What she felt obliged to do may not be felt by all—and maybe need not be felt by all.[10] That made it no less a moral demand on her. That type of demand, however, makes little sense in a system of morality that is legalistic and minimalistic. It makes little sense in an individualist culture.

The distinctive way we as individuals are attuned to and describe the world in which we live is important for any society, but particularly for the church as a community of moral dialogue. By providing a forum in which individuals

---

[10]For a discussion of whether or not moral judgments have to be universalizable, see Alasdair MacIntyre, "What Morality Is Not," in *Against the Self-Images of the Age* (Notre Dame, IN: University of Notre Dame Press, 1978), pp. 96-108.

can share their different perspectives and insights, the church enriches the lives of its members. But the church also benefits itself, for it thus has access to a great resource out of which it can continue to develop a rich and nuanced picture of the world in which it exists and to work out proper responses.


## Reaching Decisions

With quandaries thus understood, how are they to be addressed? What is the process of making decisions about problematic moral situations? This is an area of great debate these days. Some hold for a deontological approach, declaring that certain actions are right or wrong, regardless of their consequences. Others, holding to a utilitarian approach, argue that consequences are the only basis on which to determine the morality of an act. Still others—especially some Roman Catholic theologians—opt for a position called a "mixed teleology" or a "mixed consequentialism" or a "moderate teleology" which borrows elements from the other two systems. Definitions of the different positions vary depending on a given author's perspective, and depending too on whether an author is promoting or opposing a particular system. Here I will look at them in light of the issues raised by individualism.

The founders of *utilitarianism* were "primarily practical reformers."[11] They rejected the social contract theory as an explanation for the origins of society. People, they held, are bound to a ruler, not because of some original agreement made by an earlier generation, but on the basis of the ruler's ability to provide for their happiness; and on this basis, a ruler's competence is judged and society shaped.[12] This criterion is founded on the utilitarian's presumption that people act for their own benefit: they seek pleasure and try to avoid pain. Since these pleasures and pains can be measured, a

---

[11] Elie Halévy, *The Growth of Philosophic Radicalism*, trans. Mary Morris (Boston: The Beacon Press, 1966), p. 11.

[12] Ibid., pp. 126-140.

science of morality can be developed based on a moral calculus. That is good which leads to the greatest good of the greatest number.

The problem, of course, is to explain why people should be willing to look beyond their own happiness to take into account that of others, even to sacrifice their happiness for that of others. This was accounted for in different ways. Adam Smith in his economic theory held for a spontaneous identity of interests—the "invisible hand." As such, matters took care of themselves and there was no need for government involvement. Jeremy Bentham, however, was not so sanguine. "The general object which all laws have, or ought to have, in common, is to augment the total happiness of the community; and therefore, in the first place to exclude, as far as may be, every thing that tends to subtract from that happiness; in other words, to exclude mischief."[13] And the chief means to this end is to mete out punishment (which is itself evil) for doing mischief. In that way, people are educated and prompted to avoid what is evil for the greatest number.

As a theory of moral decision-making used to respond to quandary situations, utilitarianism has developed and changed in the course of its history. What the good is, for example, has been understood in different ways.[14] Nonetheless, the basic principles of the theory remain. These carry with them a number of the presuppositions as well as the problems of individualism.

Utilitarianism is built on the belief that the basic unit we are dealing with is the individual acting out of self-interest; it understands society as an aggregate of individuals; and it defines reason in scientific terms, making use of a calculating rationality to determine what is morally correct—all of which accords with individualism.

In addition, utilitarianism, despite appearances to the con-

---

[13]Jeremy Bentham, *An Introduction to the Principles of Morals and Legislation in a Bentham Reader*, ed. Mary Peter Mack (New York: Pegasus, 1969), p. 120.

[14]Within utilitarianism, various theories of the good have been advanced: a hedonistic utilitarianism sees the good as pleasure; a eudaimonistic utilitarianism equates it with happiness; an ideal utilitarianism identifies it with intrinsically valuable human goods such as friendship, beauty, learning.

trary, leaves the individual out of the moral situation. Pleasures and pains are, of course, highly personal realities. But, while the securing of pleasures satisfies self-interest, it is not clear that the attainment of happiness makes any substantial difference in the individual who achieves this. Neither the self nor the interests change because of it. Furthermore, even though pleasures and pains are highly personal, enough homogeneity must exist to weigh the pleasures of some against the pains of others. As such, while the individual is the one deciding, the distinctiveness of that individual does not enter into the equation. This supports rather than challenges the loss of self in individualism.

Finally, utilitarianism runs the danger of overlooking the dignity of the individual. If the central concern is the greatest good of the greatest number, what happens to those who are not included among the majority? Are they simply sacrificed for the good of the majority?

It is precisely in light of this last point that *deontology* was developed. Basing himself on the contract theory which the utilitarians dismissed, Kant sought to uphold the individual's importance as underlined by the theory of natural rights, and to do so in a way that was in line with the rationality of the science of his day (Newtonian).[15] He maintained that the core of morality is not the pursuit of good results; rather, it is the intention to act in accord with one's duty. This duty requires that we behave in a reasonable way; that is, that our moral decisions are logically consistent and universally applicable.

Thus, for example, I hold myself morally obligated to tell the truth because I believe this is something everyone should do. This moral demand is not based on the consequences of what would happen if all should lie—that is the utilitarian approach. Rather, it is grounded in the recognition that I can only get away with lying because all people expect the truth and so are willing to accept what I say as true. For, if it is generally accepted that everyone lies, it becomes impossible for me successfully to deceive someone. To tell a lie, then,

---

[15]Sullivan, p. 84.

and thereby to accept this as a pattern of behavior everyone can follow, is to involve myself in a logical inconsistency: if all lie, lying becomes impossible. Our most fundamental duty is to respect every person as a rational being. This requires that we treat each individual as an end and not a means.

As a principle for moral decision-making in quandary situations, Kant's theory certainly addresses the problem of the place of the individual raised by utilitarianism. But it still comes out of the individualism of the Enlightenment and carries with it a number of its problems. First, as Sullivan points out, Kant's theory does not replace "the utilitarian conception of action as a calculus of consequences whose notion of good is the subjectively pleasant and useful. Thus there could literally be no *reasonable* disagreement over taste or preferences, that is, about mores."[16] Kant leaves this in place and simply adds his morality of obligation to it.

Second, Kant's theory is based on the rationality of modern science. Granted it does not result in a mathematics of morality as is the case in utilitarianism. But it does rule emotions out of court, emphasizing the obligation of acting in accord with reason. And it leads to an abstract morality; for it requires that we do what anyone in similar circumstances would do, thus leaving no place for the particulars of time, place, and person.

Third, while Kant rescues the individual endangered by utilitarianism, he loses society. Individuals are to respect the dignity of other individuals; but they are given no sense of society as something more than an aggregate of individuals. In addition, Kant's theory can cause individuals to concentrate on protecting their own rights. As a result, it can easily lead to an individualistic morality, especially in a culture marked by individualism. In his book on business ethics, for example, Richard DeGeorge raises the question whether or not people have a moral obligation to help those suffering from famine. His response, based on Kant's principles, is as follows:

[16]Ibid., p. 87 Emphasis in original.

> As a general principle no one is obliged to sacrifice himself for others. To do so may be morally praiseworthy, but it is not morally required because, as a moral agent, each person is an end in himself, as worthy of respect as any other person. We can also argue that each person has a greater obligation to feed those for whom he is responsible than to feed those for whom he is not so responsible, because of this special relationship.
>
> We can push this a step further. In general, everyone is obliged to help others in serious need, if he can do so at little cost to himself.[17]

In a society marked by individualism and consumerism, the cost to self could well be computed on whether helping someone starving interferes with the purchase of the newest in stereo speakers or the latest in compact disk players.

Fourth, even though Kant's theory upholds the individual in one way—by emphasizing the importance of the dignity of the person—in another way it loses the individual. As in utilitarianism, the distinctiveness of the person as an individual, as a self, makes no difference whatsoever. The individual is to act in a manner that can become a universal law for all. Thus, while the individual is making a decision, he or she acts as Everyperson, not as a particular person defined by particular ways of interacting with the environment.

Finally, while Kant's theory is by no means authoritarian, it can be understood that way, particularly when interpreted in an individualist culture. According to Kant, people meet their duty not by following the dictates of someone in charge, but by acting in a way that is internally consistent and universally applicable. However, the language of duty connected with his theory, especially since it eschews any reference to consequences, can easily be heard as or co-opted by an authoritarian approach to morality.

In light, then, of this book's perspective tracing the diffi-

---

[17]Richard T. DeGeorge, *Business Ethics* (New York: Macmillan Publishing Co., Inc., 1982), p. 265.

culties we face in this country back to its roots in individualism, both utilitarianism and deontology are problematic.
Both are rooted in the Enlightenment and neither offers a
way to address individualism creatively. But this does not
mean they should be discarded totally. Each points to an
essential element of the moral experience and of the moral
enterprise. Maguire sums this up well.

> Consequences and results, though not all, are part of the
> reality that we judge when we make moral judgment. Not
> to assess them and be sensitive to them is ethically irre-
> sponsible...
> What the deontologist is on to is that there can be im-
> portant appreciations in the present moment that cannot
> be sacrificed to all the felicitous consequences imagin-
> able....[18]

The difficulty, of course, is to retain these essential
elements while at the same time overcoming the shortcomings
of individualism. Some Roman Catholic theologians have
been exploring an alternative to utilitarianism and deontology; and, although it is not without its own difficulties, their
proposal has definite possibilities.

This system which, as I noted earlier, goes by different
names, I shall call "mixed consequentialism." Its proponents
want to take into account consequences without falling into
the type of consequentialism associated with utilitarianism.
Central to this is a change in terminology. Traditionally,
Roman Catholic thought has identified certain actions as
"intrinsically evil" and allows them to be performed only

---

[18]Maguire, *The Moral Choice*, pp. 158-159. Ogletree makes the same point using
a phenomenological approach. "Consequentialist theories direct attention to the
values which provide the final justification for our action choices; deontological
theories bring to light the regulative principles which establish the basic ground
rules of action." Ogletree also discusses a virtue, or what he terms a "perfectionist,"
ethic: "Perfectionist theories of the moral life highlight the personhood of the moral
actor." All three, he claims, are needed and must be synthesized. Thomas W.
Ogletree, *The Use of the Bible in Christian Ethics* (Philadelphia: Fortress Press,
1983), pp. 23, 28.

when conditions conform to the demands of the principle of double effect.[19] The theologians supporting mixed consequentialism speak instead of "premoral" or "ontic" or "nonmoral" good and evil. Thus, abortion and contraception and war are premoral evils; truth-telling and saving a person's life through medical care and helping an elderly person carry a heavy package are premoral goods. In a concrete situation, the relation of these premoral goods and evils to one another have to be discerned, and then a decision made determining how best to realize the good. O'Connell describes the process in this way:

> How do we discover the right thing to do? We discover it by balancing the various "goods" and "bads" that are part of the situation and by trying to achieve the greatest proportion of goods to bads. What constitutes right action? It is that action which contains the proportionally greatest maximization of good and minimization of evil.[20]

One of the problems with this theory is that it sounds so much like utilitarianism. While the proponents of this theory speak of premoral good and evil rather than pleasure and pain, they still seem to depend ultimately on some sort of moral calculus.

But, as Lisa Sowle Cahill points out, the theologians proposing this theory are more *teleologists* than utilitarians.[21] Teleologists such as Aristotle and Aquinas saw the fulfillment of the person as the goal or telos of morality; and their theory was based on a substantive understanding of the nature of the person. In other words, they were concerned about the consequences of an action. But the consequences

---

[19]The principle of double effect is used to adjudicate situations in which an action has two or more effects, at least one of which is good and one bad. The action may be performed if (1) the action itself is morally good, or at least morally neutral; (2) the good effect is intended; (3) the good effect is not achieved through the bad effect; and (4) the good achieved is proportional to the evil allowed.

[20]O'Connell, p. 153.

[21]Lisa Sowle Cahill, "Teleology, Utilitarianism, and Christian Ethic," *Theological Studies* 42 (December 1981): 601-629.

to which they referred were not the individualistically assessed pleasures and pains of a self who remained fundamentally unaffected by his or her own actions. Rather, Aristotle and Aquinas considered the qualitative impact actions have on the self or character of the person acting and on the self or character of those whose lives were touched by the action.

I agree with what the theologians arguing for a "mixed consequentialism" are trying to do. But in my judgment, the teleological dimension of their theory will come across clearer and will be better served if it is discussed in terms of a virtue ethic such as I set forth in chapter four. What this might look like I present here in outline form.

(1) The terms "premoral" and "nonmoral" and "ontic" when used to describe good and evil are helpful in one sense but problematic in another. First the good news. These terms refer to actions considered apart from their involvement in the complexity of a particular situation. Abortion, for example, is called "premoral" evil. The designation "premoral" keeps us aware that morality is primarily concerned with actions taken in concrete situations by particular people; and that moral judgments about these actions have to take into account the particular people and the particular circumstances involved.

In other words, this terminology helps protect us from seeing morality as a discussion of abstract actions. If killing or failing to respond truthfully or premarital intercourse (to take some evils as examples) are called immoral actions regardless of the persons and the specific circumstances involved, the action is an abstraction. Discussed in the abstract, the act is removed from, and emphasized at the expense of, the agent; and so, the self, who is the source of the action, and the particular historical/cultural context, within which the action occurs, become insignificant. This plays into the hand of individualism.

The bad news is that the terms "premoral," "nonmoral," and "ontic" (particularly the former two) can leave the impression that the aspects of a situation under consideration are all morally neutral. Killing and failing to respond truthfully and premarital intercourse, then, seem to have moral import only after they have been included in a moral decision. That means we basically live in a morally neutral world—which also fits in easily with individualism.

How is this problem of language to be solved? I personally can see no way to do so. But I do think it important—and here is where a virtue ethic can be of help—that these pre-moral evils and goods not be treated as abstractions or as atomistic elements. They are judged to be positive or negative because of the effect they have on the character of the person and on the type of interaction that occurs between the individual and his or her environment. Thus, in making a moral evaluation of various forms of behavior, the question is: What type of self results? What type of society results? The criterion we use for evaluating the answers to these questions is based on our understanding in faith of what God is doing in our midst.

These questions and this criterion are also the basis for making moral decisions. Such decisions are always made in concrete situations involving particular people with particular perspectives and commitments. Reaching moral decisions is not primarily a matter of balancing various values or of acting in a universalizable and logically consistent manner, but of pursuing conscientiously what enhances the self and brings greater flourishing to the environment. At base the question is: what type of person should I be, and what type of world should exist, and how can I best act in this situation to achieve that? In other words, the issue of moral decision-making is always the moral life.

(2) Introducing consequences into our moral judgment does not mean that we cannot hold certain types of behavior (such as rape or torture or slavery) unacceptable regardless of whatever other good outcomes may occur. Teleology is not the same as utilitarianism. Utilitarianism deals with abstract moral values that are weighed out apart from any substantive view of what person, society, and interaction should be. It is concerned with the relative mix of pleasure and pain, not the type of person or society or interaction that results. As such, it always leaves open the possibility that anything may at some time find a legitimating circumstance. Slavery, for example, may not be a particularly appealing

institution; but in certain given circumstances, it may be the best we can do.

Teleology considers action in light of a goal—a vision of person, society, and interaction. Because of its effect on these, a particular action (for example, slavery) can be held unacceptable regardless of other good results. Some of the results of slavery may be positive under certain circumstances, but slavery affects self, society, and interaction in ways that cannot be countenanced.

And so, in reaching moral decisions, we do not have a totally open realm of possibilities. Some areas necessarily are closed off. But this limitation is not the result of the directives of some authority or an exercise of logic. It follows from the basis on which we make our decisions: some types of behavior, even though these may issue in some good results, are of a character that distorts our vision of what the self and the world should be like.

(3) At the same time, this judgment that certain types of behavior are unacceptable regardless of certain positive results cannot be made in the abstract. It is the subject of dialogue within society (civil and ecclesial) in a specific historical and cultural context. And, part of decision-making is a willingness to participate in, and submit our decisions to, that dialogue. The question is: What is necessary *here and now* to protect and promote the self as a distinctive but nonetheless participatory member of society? What is necessary *here and now* to protect and promote the types of interaction between self and environment essential to the human person and to the world?

This is not to say that everything is always up in the air, or that at some future time everything we now hold unacceptable regardless of its further consequences will be found acceptable. It merely recognizes the historical and cultural nature of humanity; and this allows us to explain why morality has in fact changed in the past—within both civil and ecclesial society; why certain types of behavior—torture, for example—could be allowed at one time and now be seen as unacceptable under all circumstances.

(4) Difficulty arises when the environment is changing and as a result the moral wisdom a community has inherited no

longer responds adequately to new situations. Moral principles and moral demands that seemed so clear only a short time ago now create confusion and raise questions. How are we to know how to act in such circumstances?

Here it is not a matter of moving from a deontology to a utilitarianism. In a teleological approach, the central concern is the goal. And that goal is a vision of the self flourishing within a society that is a substantive whole, and interacting with the environment in a way that protects and promotes life. This is the criterion for all moral decisions and all moral stances. Consequences always have to be taken into account, even in determining what types of behavior are unacceptable regardless of further results.

These consequences, however, are judged in relation to a vision of self, of society, of interaction; they are not looked at as somehow distinct from this vision. And decisions are not reached through a process based on a mathematical model in which discrete units of good and bad are weighed out in a moral calculus.

The model of the artist is more appropriate. In determining the angle from which to paint a landscape, the artist does not resort to weighing and calculating. It is more a matter of balancing and ordering to achieve an integrated whole. So too with the moral decision-maker: the task is to find the right angle from which to interpret the situation. (For the Christian, that angle is determined by our understanding in faith of what God is doing in our midst.) Then the various elements and dimensions are balanced and ordered to bring integrity to the self, justice to society, and a quality to the interaction that leads to greater flourishing.

When that has been determined, then we know what our duty is. It is a product of reason charged with emotion. It is unique to the individual, based on the distinctive way in which he or she participates within society. And, as such, it has a social dimension and is not purely a private affair.

In sum, moral decision-making, indeed the whole moral life, is essentially a social justice matter. Not that the individual is overlooked or subordinated to society. By no means. The individual is understood not as apart from society but as a distinctive way of participating in it. Consequently, everything we do as individuals has social implications. And we cannot presume and expect that those implications will automatically be constructive. Likewise, everything that happens to society affects the lives of its individual members and no invisible hand is present to assure that it will be positive.

Individualism has bequeathed to us a deep respect for the individual we must not lose. But to honor that inheritance, we have to recover the essential connection and interaction of the individual with the world, both physical and social; and we have to develop a vision of what that self, that world, that interaction is—that is, what it should be.

The growing concern for social justice in the U.S. and in the Roman Catholic community certainly is a step in the right direction. But, while it is important to challenge official social structures and change them where necessary, the difficulties caused by individualism run deeper than that. These problems reach into our everyday life, into our customs, our habits, our self-perceptions, our ways of identifying and responding to moral situations. A fundamental reorientation is needed here.

Because of the strong current in its tradition emphasizing the social texture of all life and because of its pervasive use of symbols which can touch the roots of who we are and how we perceive and interact with our world, the Roman Catholic Church has much to offer here—indeed, it is, I believe, a primary resource in addressing the negative consequences of individualism. But first the church must take on the task of self-criticism, identifying the ways in which it implicitly and unconsciously supports the individualism it explicitly challenges, and then alter them so that it can present an alternative vision.

# Subject Index